*Exploring the Boundaries
of Caribbean Creole Languages*

Exploring the Boundaries of Caribbean Creole Languages

Edited by

Hazel Simmons-McDonald

and

Ian Robertson

University of the West Indies Press
Jamaica • Barbados • Trinidad and Tobago

University of the West Indies Press
1A Aqueduct Flats   Mona
Kingston 7   Jamaica
www.uwipress.com

© 2006 by Hazel Simmons-McDonald and Ian Robertson
All rights reserved. Published 2006

10 09 08 07 06   5 4 3 2 1

CATALOGUING IN PUBLICATION DATA

Exploring the boundaries of Caribbean creole languages / edited by Hazel Simmons-McDonald and Ian Robertson.
p. cm.
Includes bibliographical references.

ISBN: 976-640-186-1 (cloth)
ISBN: 976-640-187-X (paper)

1. Christie, Pauline G. 2. Creole dialects – Caribbean, English-speaking. 3. Language and education – Caribbean, English-speaking. 4. Sociolinguistics – Caribbean, English-speaking. I. Christie, Pauline G. II. Simmons-McDonald, Hazel. III. Robertson, Ian.

PM7834.C37E86 2006   427.9729

Cover art by Paul Gibbs.
Jacket and cover design by Robert Harris.
Book design by Robert Harris.
Set in Adobe Garamond 11/14.5 x 24

Printed in the United States of America.

The editors gratefully acknowledge the support given to this project by the University of the West Indies.

DEDICATED TO AND

IN HONOUR OF

DR PAULINE CHRISTIE

This page intentionally left blank

Contents

Tributes

The Contribution of Pauline Christie to the
Study of Linguistics in the Caribbean / **ix**
Robert Le Page

"Memory of Mona" / **xii**
Frederic G. Cassidy

Introduction / **xiii**
Ian Robertson and *Hazel Simmons-McDonald*

Section 1   Definition and Description

1   Challenging the Definition of Creole / 3
Ian Robertson

2   Tense and Aspect in Belize Creole / 21
Donald Winford

3   Phonological Signatures of Tobagonian Speech in
Trinidad and Tobago / 50
Winford James

4   On the Status of Diphthongs in Jamaican:
Mr Vegas Pronounces / 72
Hubert Devonish

Section 2   Language and Education

5   The Use of the Vernacular in West Indian Education / 99
Dennis Craig

6   Vernacular Instruction and Bi-Literacy Development:
French Creole Speakers / 118
Hazel Simmons-McDonald

7   Issues of Face-Saving in the Pre-School Classroom / 147
Valerie Youssef

Section 3   Language and Caribbean Society

8   Creole Representation in Literary Discourse:
Issues of Linguistic and Discourse Analysis / 173
Barbara Lalla

9   Is the Pain in Your Belly-Bottom? Extending the Boundaries
of Jamaican Creole to Non-Native Users / 188
Kathryn Shields-Brodber

10   Asou Down-There: Code-Mixing in a Bilingual
Community / 211
Martha Isaac

11   Globalization and the Language of Rastafari / 230
Velma Pollard

Contributors / 242

TRIBUTES

THE CONTRIBUTION OF PAULINE CHRISTIE TO THE STUDY OF LINGUISTICS IN THE CARIBBEAN
ROBERT LE PAGE

DURING ALL THE YEARS that we have co-operated in the study of Caribbean Creole languages, I have regretted that I did not get to know Pauline Christie ten years earlier: during the ten years, in fact, when I was teaching at what was then the University College of the West Indies (1950–1960) in Jamaica and she was teaching French just a few miles down the road at St Andrew High School. (In those days, the very idea that one should pay any attention to "bad talk", or "broken talk", or "patois" was abhorrent to the Jamaican Ministry of Education; I was regularly reviled by a columnist in one of the Jamaican newspapers for my efforts.)

Pauline had done her first degree, in French, at Edinburgh University (1951–1954) and followed it with a Postgraduate Certificate of Education in London in 1955. She returned to Jamaica to teach and in due course to become head of the Department of Latin and French at St Andrew High School (1955–1966). She spent a sabbatical year as an assistante at the Lycée de Grasse in France (1962–1963). I first met her after I came back to England from the University of Malaya in 1964 to establish the Department of Language at the new University of York. Here, unlike at the University

College of the West Indies, which had been tied at first to the London University degree syllabus, we could establish the first department in Britain centrally concerned with the study of language, with sociolinguistics, psycholinguistics and Creole languages, alongside a more conventional syllabus for European, African and Asian languages. I revisited Jamaica, where I met Pauline at a conference, and lured her to York for postgraduate work on a Commonwealth scholarship.

She came in 1966, working on a projected study of the teaching of French in Jamaica and taking the basic training in linguistics, which we gave to all our students. However, she slotted so well into our larger (and hugely ambitious) research plan for a description – linguistic, psycholinguistic and sociolinguistic – of the vernacular of each of the former British colonies in the Caribbean that we persuaded the new Ministry of Overseas Development in London to extend her scholarship to allow her to do a DPhil. Her subject was the Creole French of Dominica. She spent some months there on her fieldwork, successfully submitted her thesis and took her doctorate in 1969. She then returned to Jamaica and began a lectureship in French at the university.

By now, the study of Creole languages was expanding healthily, and Pauline became a founder-member of three societies which promoted it. One of these had a rather long-winded title: The International Group for the Study of Language Standardization and the Vernacularization of Literacy (soon to be reduced to IGLSVL). At two successive conferences in the 1960s, I found myself giving papers which covered ground in the British colonies overlapping with that of Andrée Tabouret-Keller in the French colonies – she was at that time head of the Psychology Department of Université Louis Pasteur, in Strasbourg, and a specialist on bilingualism and its implications for education. Together with Pauline, we invited colleagues with similar interests to a series of workshops. IGLSVL gave form to these – held in 1986, 1988 and 1990 in York and held in 1992 in Sèvres. At each of these we gave brief research reports and then had a discussion. Everything said was recorded and transcribed. For the first three, we published a complete transcription in mimeograph from York, but from the Sèvres meeting we published, in 1997, the book *Vernacular Literacy* (Oxford University Press). Pauline's contribution to all of this activity has been considerable.

Even more considerable was her contribution to an earlier book, *Acts of Identity* (Cambridge University Press, 1985). This was based on extensive and intensive fieldwork and recording in Belize, St Lucia and London, studying the emergence of varieties of Creole and the social identities to which they gave expression. Pauline was the chief fieldworker and analyst for Belize; she spent several months recording informants in Cayo District and many more transcribing and analysing the data with her usual conscientious devotion. She continued in this way through the second stage, in St Lucia, where, of course, her command of French was invaluable.

The other societies in which she has been involved are the Society for Pidgin and Creole Linguistics and the Society for Caribbean Linguistics. She was at the meeting at the St Augustine campus of the University of the West Indies in 1972 when the former was proposed and formed. In spite of a very heavy administrative load, she has managed over the years to give papers at their meetings and to publish. But she made the mistake of becoming the dean of the faculty in Jamaica and doing it so well that there was no competition to replace her. When the time came for her to retire she was pressed into further service at the beginning of 1999 to take over (for six months) and sort out the administration of what, I understand, has become an adjunct of the University of the West Indies – the United Theological College.

I hope that she will feel that this volume gives some recognition to the debts we all owe her in Creole language studies and in the cause of education in the Caribbean. Certainly, my own debt has been considerable.

The editors were saddened to learn of the death of Professor Robert Le Page on 12 January 2006.

MEMORY OF MONA
Frederic G. Cassidy

A VERY SHORT WHILE before his death, Frederic Cassidy sent the following poem. He wished to have it included in this collection, which was being planned at the time. He wrote: "While working on a project in Jamaica I used to wake everyday to the sound of birdsong. I must have told Pauline about the song of this particular bird. The memory of his singing always evokes powerful memories of my days at Mona. I would like to submit this poem (if you think it is appropriate) to the collection for Pauline."

Memory of Mona

We are in the same world
   but he is young, I old –

For overnight, I put his cot in my former corner
   where as a visiting scholar, I would wake
   ages ago
   to the aubade of a Jamaican Nightingale . . .

"tri-Ling!" it would sing, "tri-Ling,"
   and flirt its tail, "tri-Ling . . . tri-Ling,"
   and look me in the eye from its branch,
   enjoying its song, enjoying my attention . . .

It was a personal relation – "tri-Ling!"
   And so I would start another day.
   And the bird would sing,
    "tri-Ling!"

Now, today, ages later,
   This young man, visiting scholar,
   Has much to learn, to learn . . .
   May he too sing!

May he rise in my former corner
   To my nightingale's song . . . "tri-Ling . . ."
   the sun soaring and new scholars off to school,
   to learn the echoes of the mind . . .
   glad of the morning's song,
   the nightingale's remembrance
   of the old singing,
   forever, on new mornings,
   his old song –
    "tri-Ling!"

INTRODUCTION

Ian Robertson and
Hazel Simmons-McDonald

This work is an acknowledgement, by her colleagues, of Dr Pauline Christie's contribution to linguistic studies in the Caribbean. Her contributions to the discipline reflect, from the earliest description of Dominican French-lexicon Creole to her most recent *Language in Jamaica* (Kingston: Arawak, 2003), an interest that is broad, well-informed and insightful. This collection attempts to indicate the esteem accorded to her work by colleagues and to celebrate the breadth of her contribution to the study of Caribbean language.

The chapters in the collection fall easily into three areas significant to the person whose work they seek to honour: definition and description, language and education, and language in Caribbean society. Robertson's chapter focuses on definition, bringing to the fore issues raised by, and perhaps enlightened by, the study of one Caribbean Creole which could lay some unique claims even among the unique set that constitutes Caribbean Creole languages. Creole languages continue to defy definition, to the point where their very existence as a category of languages may be questioned. Time is even running out on this issue as other areas of Caribbean scholarship have mounted credible challenge to linguists' appropriation of the term *Creole* for their own narrow concerns.

Winford's chapter, "Tense and Aspect in Belizean Creole", is important as a linguistic analysis of the workings of the tense and aspect systems of yet another Caribbean Creole. Tense aspect is an area of continuing concern for Creole studies and the more ample the range of systems described, the more fundamental will be the understanding of the nature of Creole languages. The chapter returns to the study of one of the languages of Belize, a complex linguistic society in which Christie herself had worked earlier.

James's analysis of the phonological signatures of Tobagonian throws light on another area of concern to the Caribbean linguist. Tobagonian is one English-lexicon Creole that has suffered for the lack of linguistic attention. In addressing the phonology, James deals with the concern for knowledge of a much wider range of languages in discourse on Creole and with the concerns for the oft-ignored area of phonology in Creole Studies. Again, the work parallels the pioneering description of Dominican French-lexicon Creole that Christie did more than thirty years ago.

James's chapter is well-complemented by Devonish's reanalysis of the diphthongs of Jamaican Creole. Devonish challenges the description offered by two foundation members of the study of Caribbean language and Creole linguistics. Their work, unconstrained by the rigours of Chomsky's request for explanatory adequacy, was in clear need of reanalysis and re-evaluation. This chapter indicates how a different description may be arrived at in the current contexts. It also attempts to elucidate the matter of competence in a Creole environment.

The section on education reflects another area central to Christie, who has been known to question the adequacy of linguistic positions for the cause of language education in the Caribbean. Craig's chapter on the use of the vernacular in West Indian education revisits an area of considerable controversy. With the clarity of a very experienced educator, Craig presents the central issues for West Indian schooling. This matter will not go away and must be addressed with the insight and informedness that Craig presents.

Craig's chapter is balanced well by the practical, research-based approach to the relevance of vernacular literacy for education found in the chapter by Simmons-McDonald. The latter takes the discussion out of the realm of debate and into a research project in St Lucia. Simmons-McDonald's chapter reports on a part of a wider study, the significance of which will be very far reaching. Caribbean linguists need this chapter to urge them to a greater appreciation of the need to move beyond theory and to the practical grounding of their contributions to Caribbean education in general and Caribbean language education in particular, through research within the formal education system itself.

The third chapter in this section is Youssef's exploration of face-saving strategies, their source and their acquisition in early Caribbean education. One issue is the need to determine the source of coping strategies adopted by students who find themselves in classrooms that can be quite hostile to their own linguistic preferences.

The third section deals with sociological concerns. Lalla brings together two important but seldom-discussed areas in Creole linguistics. Through the exploration and analysis of the use of Creole in Caribbean literary discourse, with reference to carefully selected works by creative writers, she addresses the representation of Creole in literary texts. Shields-Brodber chooses another perspective to examine the use of language in the interaction between patient and doctor on Jamaican talk shows. Her chapter examines the compromises that need to be negotiated between the speaker of Standard English and the speaker of Jamaican. Those compromises can readily be a matter of life and death and raise the importance of the role of language in ensuring that proper patient care is extended to the speaker of Jamaican.

Isaac's chapter returns to a concern expressed by Christie herself and others: determining dialect boundaries, especially in linguistic situations where Creoles from two distinct lexical bases vie for social space and supremacy. Her chapter presents the possibility for challenging the erroneous perceptions that these situations are simple bilingual ones, a perception derived from Bloomfield and still holding significant force today.

Pollard examines the expansion of Rastafarianism, which was originally a Jamaican religious practice but has now increased in significance across the world. She does this through a comparison of lexical items found in two dictionaries. This allows her to comment on word formation devices and the extent to which they reflect Rastafarian thinking.

The book is therefore structured to promote the exploration of specific themes in Caribbean language as well as to provide three clear perspectives on Caribbean language.

Section 1
Definition and Description

This page intentionally left blank

Chapter 1

Challenging the Definition of Creole
Ian Robertson

Appropriate characterization of languages labelled "Creole" has been a matter of considerable insufficiency and continuing controversy. According to Winford (1997), "There has been a long history of controversy over the definitions of pidgins and creoles and the specific criteria that distinguish them from other languages and each other."

Controversy on this issue will not be easily resolved. One essential factor in the resolution of any controversy is adequacy of data. The case presented in this chapter, that of Berbice Dutch, brings significant enough new information to the discussion to require yet another look at the adequacy with which these languages are classified and described. This is particularly true since at the time of the earlier discussions of these matters, Berbice Dutch was not known to exist.

Berbice Dutch represents one of only two instances, perhaps the first, in which the Dutch language formed the dominant lexical base of a Creole developed in a Dutch colony. Ironically, the second, Skepie Dutch, developed in the Essequibo colony immediately west of Berbice. Prior to the discovery of Berbice Dutch, the absence of a Dutch lexicon Creole language in a Dutch colony remained one of the lacunae in the linguistic heritage of European colonialism in the Caribbean.

The late discovery of Berbice Dutch is not in itself unique since there are other Creole languages of the Caribbean which have not been the subject of close linguistic scrutiny. What is noteworthy about Berbice Dutch is that a significant creolist, Derek Bickerton, expressed considerable doubt that it ever existed.

The only other documented Dutch-lexicon Creole, Negerhollands of the Danish West Indian islands, boasts the earliest published Creole grammar (Magens 1770). Eighteenth-, nineteenth- and twentieth-century discussion of Creole had the benefit of awareness of this Negerhollands, but clearly not of Berbice Dutch. Since Berbice Dutch was one (and probably the first) instance in which a Dutch-lexicon Creole was known to have developed in a Dutch colony, its discovery provides another opportunity to improve our understandings of Creole languages. The characteristics of Berbice Dutch could not have been factored into the early attempts to define Creoles, to determine each language's genesis, typology or structure. Discussions of Creole languages, especially those which sought to define the phenomenon from either a social or linguistic perspective, or from any combination of the two, could have benefited from consideration of some of the Berbice Dutch characteristics, a significant few of which are unique among the languages of this type in the Caribbean. This Creole language brings a number of features to the discussion of Creole languages. The more significant of these could have considerable bearing on the way in which Creole languages are defined.

SIGNIFICANCE OF LAST SPEAKERS

At the time of its discovery, Berbice Dutch was spoken by people of mixed Amerindian/African stock, popularly referred to in Guyana as *Bovianders*. They inhabit the middle reaches of the Berbice River and its most significant tributary, the Canje Creek. Unlike the Creoles of the remainder of the Caribbean or of the Guyana coast, Berbice Dutch was an upriver development – the earliest Dutch plantations were located in the lower middle reaches of the river and its two major tributaries, the Canje and the Wiruni. At the time of the arrival of the Dutch, these areas were inhabited by groups of indigenous peoples.

Throughout the plantation period, the Dutch depended on the indigenous peoples for food and for protection. The role of the languages of the Amerindians in the development of the Creole languages of the Caribbean has never been seriously addressed. Indeed, the study of the languages of the region has never seriously addressed the linguistic dimensions of early European contact with indigenous peoples. Pidgin/Creole studies, in particular the former, should have a strong interest in such an obvious opportunity for studying the communication strategies or the emergence and fates of contact languages in the early phases of European colonial expansion.

In failing to investigate the role of indigenous peoples in the development and retention of Creole languages in the region, linguists have merely been following in the wake of those naïve historians who continue to hold to the theory of mutual hostility between Amerindians and the African descendants of former plantation slaves and runaway slaves in the mainland territories. Those historians argue that the use of Amerindians to police the bush and track down runaway Africans slaves and their maroon communities led to mutual hostility between the Amerindians and the descendants of the slaves in general.

Though it may well be that the indigenous languages have had no vital input into the Creole languages – indeed the case for Berbice Dutch makes this clear – it is important that this early contact be properly investigated rather than be taken as given. There is some historical reason to pursue the matter of the communication practices in the earlier phases of European contact with the indigenous peoples of the Caribbean. Kirke (1898, 173) notes that "runaway slaves were sometimes not captured but formed settlements in the forest and were known as maroons. These men took Indian wives and their descendants were gradually absorbed into Indian stock." Kirke's point is supported by C. Barrington Brown's earlier (1876, 5) comments that "the inhabitants of this place are chiefly a mixed race, the descendants of the progeny of Indians, Negroes [sic] and the early Dutch settlers".

If this was as significant an occurrence as the quotations seem to suggest, then there could not have been significant mutual hostility since people do not normally have children by those to whom they are hostile. The fact that this language was retained into the last quarter of the twentieth century by persons of mixed Amerindian and African ancestry, rather than by persons of African stock, is readily explained by acknowledging the existence of reasonably normal relationships between the two groups. Such retention would have been more likely in those who were less influenced by exposure to the effects of English. Since the descendants of the slaves tended to move downriver to the coast and acquire English-based education much earlier than their indigenous counterparts, the upriver groups were more likely to retain the language through succeeding generations.

Substratum Input

Berbice Dutch is unique among Creole languages of the Caribbean in its clear and direct links to one West African language cluster: Eastern Ijo. Berbice Dutch, from internal linguistic evidence as well as from sociohistorical evidence, was most probably an early Creole. At the very least it is a conservative one. The language has maintained the characteristic phonetic characteristic tendency of West African languages to retain a "cv" canonical structure, a feature associated with the earlier or more conservative Creole languages of the Caribbean region. Historical support is evident in the fact that the period of early expansion of the Berbice colony coincides with the period in which the Dutch were in control of the Niger Delta trade at places such as Calabar, in the heart of Ijo territory. Examination of its core vocabulary and aspects of its phonology and grammar (Smith, Robertson and Williamson 1987; Robertson 1988) supports the thesis that Eastern Ijo is the only substratum source of this language.

The clear identification of a substrate language has important implications for the assumption that a defining feature of Creole languages is heterogeneous substrate input. The argument is that the main impetus for creolization came from the difficulties encountered by West Africans of different linguistic backgrounds who were forced to interact in the harsh conditions of plantation slavery. The difficulty in identifying the specific West African linguistic inputs into Caribbean Creole languages has often been explained by the heterogeneity criterion since language, as a phenomenon, could not readily participate in the cafeteria-type selection of features which a heterogeneous input suggests.

In circumstances where significant numbers of slaves already shared a common language, as would have been the case of Berbice Dutch, heterogeneity of input has not been carefully enough examined to be identified as motivating the slaves' acquisition or development of a new language. The heterogeneity criterion is reasonable except for the fact that it does not take into consideration two factors, one linguistic and one sociological.

To begin with, the linguistic exposure of the slave, prior to the experience of slavery, would have been one of heterogeneity. Even today, it would be difficult to survive in West African societies with only one language. Creole linguistics has never really considered the linguistic predisposition of Africans to be multilingual, a predisposition in accordance with the requirements of their native societies. The new linguistic context encountered in the Caribbean would have been met by a people already predisposed to treat with new languages by acquiring them. This predisposition would remove the absolute need to rely on linguistic heterogeneity as the sole or even the primary motivation for developing alternate communication systems.

At any rate, the claim for heterogeneity of substrate input can only be sustained if the conditions that could have caused such heterogeneity were both timely and adequate. The mixing of slaves is an historical fact. However, the degree of mixing necessary for the development of a Creole would have to be established. The mixing would also have had to be timely since it would have had to take place before the Creoles were formed if it were to be critical to their formation. The evidence regarding the mixing of slaves indicates that they were mixed either deliberately, mainly to avoid rebellion, or else by the sequence of actual acquisition from different points on the West African coast. In the case of the former, the slaves would probably have had to demonstrate a willingness to revolt before such conscious mixing was done. Depending on the time of emergence of the particular Creole language, the mixing might not have had much impact on language development. In the earlier period, mixing by place of origin was less likely than it would have been as resources became more depleted or there was more competition for them. The slave trials after the 1763 revolt in Berbice reveal that, at that time, individual plantations along the Berbice River displayed variously both ethnic specialization and ethnic mixing.

Berbice was a private plantation, begun in 1627, and a viable colony during the period when the Dutch controlled the slaving in the Niger Delta at Calabar, the location of the Ijo. One of few surviving documents of the time indicates that a shipload of some five hundred slaves from Calabar was expected in Berbice (Jones 1988). Given the suggestion earlier that Berbice Dutch was probably an early Creole, the document indicates a possible source for the dominance of Ijos in the colony at the time of the development of the Creole. The establishment of a single input language into this Creole suggests that mixing of slaves was subsequent to the formation of the language and could have been only a sufficient and not a necessary condition for creolization. At the minimum, in order to determine whether there is linguistic evidence to support a similar claim for homogeneous rather than heterogeneous substrate inputs, Berbice Dutch should invite the reconsideration of other instances of creolization in the Caribbean.

There seems to be support from other places as well. Le Page (1960, 118) notes, for instance, that Twi seems to have had a greater lexical input into the Jamaican Creole than any other West African language or language group. Daleman (cited by Bickerton 1981, 49) points to a dominant Kikongo lexical input into Saramaccan, and Smith (1987) suggests that substratum input into Sranan Tongo could not have been very heterogeneous. The role of heterogeneity as a necessary condition for creolization appears to have been overstated.

IMPACT OF SOCIALLY DOMINANT LANGUAGES

The Dutch ceded the colony of Berbice to the British at the end of the eighteenth century. For a while the British tolerated an English/Dutch bilingualism. Within the first fifteen years, however, the British issued a decree that all legal matters had to be issued in English or be accompanied by an English translation. In spite of this, Berbice Dutch survived two hundred years of increasingly hostile English dominance.

In its last phase, Berbice Dutch presented considerable evidence that contradicts the standard position, first posited by Bloomfield (1933) and adopted by many without question, that once the lexically related superstrate language is replaced by another in these Creole speaking communities, *a simple bilingual situation develops*. Berbice Dutch presents an unusual case in the Caribbean, in which European languages closely related enough to provide cognate forms serve as successive dominant languages

The close genetic relatedness of lexical input languages raises the real possibility of a much higher availability of cognate forms. Where there are related forms and structures, a higher level of transfer is possible. This would suggest an almost imperceptible transition from one base to the other in the areas of greater lexical similarity. The matter may not be simple code-switching or code-mixing, as normally assumed, but more of the seamless formal whole described by Bickerton (1975) as the less well-accepted notion of a post-Creole dialect continuum but involving a prior gradual shift from one lexical base to another. The ability of the speaker to distinguish between the two donor possibilities would become compromised to the point where, for that speaker, the system may well be seen as one rather than as any sort of hybrid.

REASSESSMENT OF CRITERIA

These features of Berbice Dutch should have urged Creole linguists to revisit a number of criteria. Because significant counter-evidence has been ignored or downplayed, as has been the case with heterogeneity of input, some criteria have attained a false level of assuredness. Perhaps the most significant reasons for this are the tendency to be preoccupied with theory, the tendency to have the theory drive the analyses rather than adapt to them, and the tendency to use one tiny subsection of the language (usually the TMA system) to make far-reaching decisions about the language. These tendencies often obscure the value of careful analysis and evaluation of sufficient data. This limitation has led to an unfortunate situation where the complex nature of theory, or the complexity of its consequent explanations, has caused creolists to believe that Creole linguistics has advanced considerably more than it actually has. Basic questions of the nature of Creole languages and their development remain unanswered except for the partisan positions of this or that theorist. Assumptions about sociological correlates have been made into axioms rather than subjected to rigorous evaluation.

One good example of such false assuredness is the fact that Holm (n.d.) argues:

> The unusually important role that a single African Language (E Ijo) played in its [Berbice Dutch's] genesis raises the question of whether Berbice Dutch is even the same kind of language as the other Atlantic Creoles, or whether it belongs to a

category of mixed language for which we do not yet have a name and whose genesis we do not fully understand.

But Winford's (1997) comments about the controversy over definitions and criteria, noted at the beginning, suggest a sense of false security.

LINGUISTIC FEATURES

Although the last forty years of studies in Creole linguistics have witnessed considerable discussion on the nature and processes of creolization, an adequate linguistic characterization of Creole languages continues to elude linguists. Indeed the discipline appears to be no closer to consensus than it was in the mid-1960s when Robert Hall (1966) accepted a Creole as a "nativised Pidgin". Time is rapidly running out because other disciplines (for example, Shepherd and Richards 2002) have begun to question the right of linguistics to the sole or defining use of the term.

Bickerton's (1981) attempt to identify the features of Creole languages, controversial though it may be, remains one of few cogent attempts to deal with nativization as a central defining characteristic in creolization. However, even Bickerton is quite arbitrary in determining what the vital sociological correlates are. He uses Creole to refer to languages which

1. arose out of a prior pidgin *which had not existed for more than a generation*;
2. arose in a population where not more than 20 per cent were speakers of the dominant language and *where the remaining 80 per cent was composed of diverse language groups.*

The first criterion has the questionable merit of excluding Tok Pisin, a problem recognized by Bickerton himself. The second would, if the arguments presented above as well as those in Smith, Robertson and Williamson (1987) were right, rule out Berbice Dutch.

The second criterion is itself normally based on the assumption that slavery forced the need for intra-group communication of slaves and that this need was central to the development of Creole languages. The need for intra-group communication was also thought to be important in explaining the rather low survival of West African input into the lexicon of Creoles.

The assumption of heterogeneity, as noted earlier, like so many others in Pidgin and Creole studies, has never really been tested. Though it is at least part of the sociological correlates of creolization, some creolists, for example, Muhlhausler (1986, 115) seem to accept that some Creoles emerged in conditions where the substratum influence was much less heterogeneous than is generally accepted to be the case. Complex heterogeneity is a feature of all Caribbean societies. As noted earlier, this may be a sufficient but not a necessary condition for creolization.

Bickerton's attempt (1981) was not the first to seek to identify the linguistic features by which Creoles might be defined. It is, however, an important attempt, especially since Bickerton himself (1986) argues that a valid linguistic theory must have the power to account for or to explain linguistic phenomena that distinguish a particular language from others. The features listed by Bickerton (who clearly indicates that the features are common, but not always all present, in any one Creole) form the basis of a linguistic argument for the Creole status of Berbice Dutch.

This chapter seeks to match the features of Berbice Dutch to the features identified by Bickerton. It draws the logical conclusion that, despite some unique features, Berbice Dutch must be classified as a Creole. The unique features should indeed be seen as further evidence of the processes involved in creolization. Bickerton lists the following features:

1. movement rules involving front focusing
2. the peculiar distribution of articles
   a. definite article for pre-supposed specific NP
   b. indefinite article for asserted specific NP
   c. zero for non-specific NP
3. the use of preposed tense-modal-aspect particles to signal anteriority, irrealis and non-punctuality, in that order. Further modifications are made possible through varying combinations of those particles
4. a distinction between realized and unrealized complement and the systematic marking of their distinction
5. relativization and subject copying
6. non-definite subject as well as non-definite VP constituents must be negated as well as the verb
7. the use of the same item to signal the existential and the possessive

8. copula usage
   a. locative is introduced by specific locative copula (though this use is extended by existential in GCE)
   b. split in the case of nominal compliment
      i. use of distinct verb in less superstrate-influenced Creoles
      ii. zero manifestation of copula with adjectives
      iii. no surface manifestation of copula with adjectives
9. adjectives as a sub-category of stative verbs (at least in terms of some analyses)
10. use of identical order of constituents for statements and alternative questions
11. use of passive equivalents

Bickerton does not claim that these features are diagnostic of Creoles, but he does use them to argue for the Creole status of Hawaiian Creole English.

Berbice Dutch Evidence

The examples listed below indicate that Berbice Dutch displays an even larger proportion of these features than does Hawaiian Creole English and, indeed, even larger than a significant number of Caribbean Creole languages.

Movement Rules

Bickerton's selection of this criterion was based on the fact that it is only one of a range of focusing devices used in the world's languages. Creoles have generally selected fronting to focus items of structure. The following examples highlight the practice in Berbice Dutch:

1. *da twee soot yuu niinte*
   is two type you know
2. *een mantuku a ha mete drii jerma*
   one man child she has and three woman
3. *staatii a wa jenda alma titii*
   town he past locative all time

4. *alma diida eke doz paam eke seelfu*
   all that I (hab) tell me self
5. *da krishii a krishii*
   is cry he cry

The examples indicate that movement applies to a wide range of constituents: subject verb, locative adverb. In addition, there is also the use of preposed *da* to the focused constituent.

THE ARTICLE

The article in Berbice Dutch follows the conditions specified for NPs in Creole languages. This is particularly significant since the claim made for Hawaiian is that "virtually all Creoles have a system identical to that of HCE" (Bickerton 1981, 56). The third sentence in Example 6 represents the generic use.

6. *dii potman bii a suukuu fii muu ka*
   the oldman say he want to go (neg)

   een doomnii wa kom hiirii een kruukruu doomnii
   a pastor (past) come here a black pastor

   man lombo keke waatii
   man bad like what

TENSE-MOOD-ASPECT MARKERS

There are two significant differences in the tense-modal-aspect system of Berbice Dutch. The Creoles of the Caribbean usually mark these features on the predicate, through a combination of pre-verbal particles the grammatical categorization of which has been the subject of slightly different description from linguist to linguist. Berbice Dutch uses a mixture of pre-verbal particles and suffixes for the same set of features. In addition, Berbice Dutch signals a difference between perfective suffix *-te* and preposed past particle *wa*. The possible combinations of the particles follow the rules established by Bickerton (1975).

7. *eke muu+a muu luuruu dii tokop*
   I go (imp) go look/see the child+plu

   eke suuku +a fii muu bot eke maama doz tiir eke kane
   I want (hab) to go but me mother does send me neg

8. *juu ma nit wat em bii krushee*
   you (irr) knit what they say crochet

   dii man mo +te watii shiikii
   the man go (perf) who sick

   juu ma buu alma gutu wat ju niinte
   you (irr) drink all thing what you know

The Berbice Dutch tense-aspect system is perhaps unique among Caribbean Creole languages in its use of suffixes *-te* and *-a(re)* to signal perfective and imperfective/non-punctual aspects respectively. The system is slightly more complex than those set out by creolists for most other Creole languages of the region. However, it is instructive that the combinations of markers which are possible in this Creole are identical to those of the other Creoles of the region. This is easily demonstrated in Examples 9 and 10:

9. *ek wa moo+te tootoo aafta dii niu jaarii*
   I pst go (perf) until after the new year

10. *ek wa ma fal +te*
    I (past) (irr) fall + (perf)

The data set out in Examples 1 to 10 support the contention that this language makes use of all but one of the features identified by Bickerton. Other grammatical criteria used by other linguists are unlikely to reveal anything different. Bickerton himself acknowledges that there is no Creole language in which all these features may be found.

NEGATION

Negation is another area in which Berbice Dutch is slightly different from other Creoles of the region. As with the other Creoles, non-definite subjects as well as non-definite VP constituents must be negated as indicated by Bickerton. However, there is also an obligatory postposed negator -*ka*.

11. *een gut-ka maan eke fende een gutu-ka*
    one thing (neg) man I find (comp) one thing (neg)

    een noko pii eke noko ka
    They (neg) give me neg/yet not

Berbice Dutch represents the existential and the possessive with the same lexical item, but again Berbice Dutch has an additional marker that is identical to the locative copula

12. da twee soot yuu niinte een ha(bu) een
    is two sorts you know they have one (there is one)

    eke ha(bu) drii toko
    I have three child

13. *jende tuun been*
    she (loc) field in

    took-p jende
    child + (plu) there (exist)

COPULA

The copula in Berbice Dutch behaves like the copula in all Caribbean Creoles. It is obligatory with the NP predicator but not normally used with the non-past adjective complement. There is also an obligatory locative copula, which is distinct in form from that used with adjectival or nominal complements. In addition, Example 14 indicates that the adjective may be treated as a predicator like the verb is and may therefore pattern with pre-verbal particles. The suffix -*te* is also attached to adjectives such as *blente* – "blind" – to give *blente+te* – "become blind".

14. *a moi*
    it good

15. *dida da eke bukuu*
    that is me book

16. *oorii wa siikii*
    He (past) ill

Questions

The word order of alternate questions in Berbice Dutch is the same as that for statements. This is in keeping with the practice in other Caribbean Creoles. In the cases of content questions, the appropriate interrogative word is inserted before the sentence and the same basic word order is retained. They all rely on a rising final intonation contour to signal the interrogative.

17. *yuu trau + te*
    you marry (perf) (question)

18. *waatii juu ma mia*
    what you will do

If, then, Berbice Dutch displays such a high percentage of what may be regarded as the defining grammatical features of Creole languages, it must be classified as such. Regardless of the few areas of significant difference or unique patterning, it is no further from the structural features suggested than is any other language considered to be a Creole, and indeed it is closer than many.

Significance of Berbice Dutch

The main linguistic features noted so far as unique to Berbice Dutch are its high lexical input from one substrate language cluster, use of suffixes and system of negation. The use of several pronominal forms *a, o, oorii* for the third person singular is unusual in Caribbean Creoles. The forms all derive from Eastern Ijo (Robertson 1988). As is typical for Creole languages of the Caribbean, these forms show no sensitivity to gender.

19. *a jende warii been*
    he/she/it (loc) house in

Early creolists (Le Page 1960) have argued that suffixes are the most likely casualties in pidginization since they represent modifications of meaning which are not essential in a Pidgin. More recently (Muhlhausler 1986), it has been argued that the extent to which suffixes would have survived would have been a factor of the level of heterogeneous substratum input into the development of a particular Creole. This would readily explain the retention of suffixes from Eastern Ijo in Berbice Dutch since the input was not heterogeneous.

The suffixes, which are all of Eastern Ijo origin, are distributed between the noun system – pluralizer/plural nominalizer *-aapuu,* singular nominalizer *-je* – and the verb system – *aa(re)* imperfective and *-te* perfective. The suffixes are all of Eastern Ijo origin. In the case of noun suffixes, the Eastern Ijo gender/class distinctions have disappeared. The system of pluralizing in the English-lexicon Creoles of the Caribbean uses the third person plural personal pronoun, which is postposed to the noun. It has even been suggested that the form may be considered a suffix in Jamaican.

The retention of the nominalizer is unusual among Creoles of the Caribbean. It should be noted that though its use is not infrequent it is not obligatory in Berbice Dutch nominalization. The verbal suffix *-a(re)* marks a distinction that is marked in all Creoles of the region. Bickerton regards it as non-punctual. The only peculiarity, therefore, is its suffixal status. The most frequent manifestation of the form is *-a*. Robertson (1984) noted that a preverbal particle *"a"* appears in the speech of some Berbice Dutch speakers. This might be a reflection of the Guyanese English-lexicon Creole particle. Had the relatively few instances of the full form *-aare* not survived, there would have been no conclusive evidence of its substrate source.

Among Creole languages of the Caribbean, the retention of nominalizers as exemplified by *-apuu* and *-je,* is unique to Berbice Dutch. Their presence is not obligatory, and it is therefore probably a feature that would have been lost eventually.

The second verbal suffix *-te* marks the perfective. Its functions overlap with the preverbal particle *wa* which marks the past. In this area, Berbice Dutch differs from other Creoles of the region (except Papiamento) in that it has one more tense-aspect marker than the others. Of the verbal suffixes, the perfective might well have been reinforced by the *-te* allomorph of Dutch past so that its retention indicates a level of reinforcement of the substrate form by a variant from the superstrate. What this implies is that, as would normally be expected, transfer is part of the process. This is one obvious outcome of second-language acquisition in untutored situations.

20. *ek biunte juu wa traute*
    I thought you past marry+perfective

The suffix *-aare,* on the other hand, gives some indication of the effect of phonological processes on creolization. The full form is seldom used in twentieth-century Berbice Dutch, the second syllable having been unstressed into silence. There is some evidence that a preverbal particle *a* is creeping into the language, and one could speculate that this could easily have led to the eventual disappearance of the already rare suffix *-aare.* Had the few instances of the full form not survived, the source of the suffix might have been as much a matter of conjecture as the sources for other forms and lexical items in other Creoles are. The important point here is that this particular transitional feature suggests that the limited instances of readily documented West African inputs may well have resulted from this or similar phonological processes.

The Berbice Dutch system of negation is also unique among Caribbean Creoles. It is based on the obligatory use of the Eastern Ijo negative form *-ka.* The form is usually postposed to the entire structure. It is normally sentence final, a characteristic of its distribution in Ijo. All other negators are optional. Whereas, according to Bickerton (1981, 69) all non-definite subjects and VP forms must be turned to negative in other Creoles, in Berbice Dutch this is optional. It is the use of *-ka* that is obligatory though the other forms may be negated as well.

The use of several pronominal forms for the third person singular is significant, especially since all may be traced to various forms extant in Eastern Ijo. What is important, however, is that distinctions of gender and emphasis are lost in the transition to Berbice Dutch. One form, *"a",* never functions as a possessive. There are some residual uses of stress to mark emphasis, but these are generally few.

The use of postpositions in Berbice Dutch is not only unique but appears to be in direct contravention of the typological criterion that SVO languages do not admit postpositions. Once again, the feature is explained as a direct transfer from Eastern Ijo, itself an SOV language with which the feature is entirely compatible.

CONCLUSION

Virtually every new description of a Creole language has the potential to present new challenges to theory, forcing creolists to re-examine and sometimes abandon positions held previously. Berbice Dutch clearly challenges our understandings of these languages and the processes underlying their development. These challenges must be addressed.

Berbice Dutch clearly supports the theory of Creoles being second, rather than first, language developments. The retention of suffixes, for instance, clearly points to transfer, rather than to creation, since it would be ludicrous to suggest that some of these forms were lost in the contraction phase and then reinserted in the expansion phase. The forms were simply never lost. Had they been lost, no child could have reinserted them in the restricted ways in which they now manifest themselves.

Those features that have been identified as unique to Berbice Dutch caution against the argument for minimal substratum influence in the development of Caribbean Creole languages in general. There is a need to re-examine the theory, data and underlying assumptions in the light of the evidence that this language provides.

References

Bickerton, D. 1975. *Dynamics of a Creole System*. Cambridge: Cambridge University Press.

———. 1981. *Roots of Language*. Ann Arbor, Mich.: Karoma Press.

———. 1986. "Creoles and West African Languages: A Case of Mistaken Identity?" In *Substratum versus Universals in Creole Genesis: Papers from the Amsterdam Creole Workshop, April 1985*, ed. P. Muysken and N. Smith, 25–40. Amsterdam: John Benjamins.

Brown, C.B. 1876. *Canoe and Camp in British Guiana*. London: Edward Stanford.

Hall, R., Jr. 1966. *Pidgins and Creoles*. Ithaca: Cornell University Press.

Holm, J. N.d. "Social Factors in Pidginisation and Creolisation". Mimeo.

Jones, A. 1988. "Brandenburg-Prussia and the Atlantic Slave Trade". In *De la Traite à l'esclavage. Actes du Colloque international sur la traite des Noirs*, vol. 1, ed. S. Daget, Actes du Colloque international sur la traite des Noirs, Nantes 1985, 283–98. Nantes: Université de Nantes; Centre de Recherche sur L'histoire du Monde Atlantique.

Kirke, H. 1898. *Twenty-five Years in British Guiana*. London: Marston and Row.

Le Page, R. 1960. *Creole Language Studies I*. Cambridge: Cambridge University Press.

Muhlhausler, P. 1986. *Pidgin and Creole Linguistics*, Language in Society. Oxford: Blackwell.

Robertson, I. 1984. "Some Features of a Post-Creole Transition". Paper presented at the Sixth Biennial Conference of the Society for Caribbean Linguistics, Mona, Jamaica.

———. 1988. "Creole and Uncreole". Paper presented at the Seventh Biennial Conference of the Society for Caribbean Linguistics, Nassau.

Shepherd, V., and G. Richards, eds. 2002. *Questioning Creole: Creolization Discourses in Caribbean Culture*. Kingston: Ian Randle.

Smith, N., I. Robertson and K. Williamson. 1987. "The Ijo Element in Berbice Dutch". *Language and Society*, no. 16: 49–89.

Winford, D. 1997. "Introduction: On the Structure and Status of Pidgins and Creoles". In *The Structures and Status of Pidgins and Creoles*, Creole Language Library, ed. A. Spears and D. Winford, 1–34. Amsterdam: John Benjamins.

Chapter 2

TENSE AND ASPECT IN BELIZE CREOLE
Donald Winford

INTRODUCTION

DISCUSSION OF CREOLE TENSE-ASPECT systems has long revolved around the tripartite set of oppositions proposed by Bickerton (1974, 1981) as definitive of such languages. Bickerton, it will be recalled, suggested that the early stages of all Creoles possessed three verbal categories: an anterior tense, an irrealis mood and a non-punctual aspect. As we are now generally aware, however, this core system is not found in all Creole languages, not even in all that Bickerton first proposed as examples of the Creole prototype. The TMA categories themselves are not identical across Creoles. The meanings associated with each of Bickerton's categories are expressed in different ways across Creoles. Moreover, Creoles generally display more than just the three core categories mentioned above. Hence there are other candidates for consideration as part of the prototypical Creole TMA system, including aspectual notions such as "completive" or "resultative" and modal notions such as "obligation", "ability" and "possibility". Despite all the shortcomings that have been pointed out, Bickerton's analysis was an important and highly insightful first step toward specifying what Creoles actually share – or do not share – in this area of their grammar.

The fact is that there are striking similarities in the overall organization of Creole verb complexes – in the oppositions of meaning, in the mapping of semantic space onto TMA categories, in the basic meanings of the TMA categories themselves and in the range of pragmatic interpretations that each category can convey in discourse. The full extent of such similarities is only just beginning to emerge as a result of research in the last decade or so. It is becoming apparent that comparisons of Creole TMA systems that are based only on the traditional criteria of inventory and positioning of TMA categories are not very revealing. The reasons are as follows:

1. We cannot assume that every Creole divides the semantic space of temporal, modal and aspectual notions in precisely the same ways, or maps each area of space onto grammatical categories and their morphemic expressions in the same way.
2. Hence it is not sufficient to say that two or more Creoles "share" a category such as "anterior" or "irrealis" or "non-punctual" when such putative categories may differ significantly in their range of meanings or uses.
3. There needs to be a clear distinction between the basic meaning (semantics) and use (pragmatics) of TMA categories as a precondition for comparing them across Creoles (or any languages). In other words, we need to address the question of the relationship between the basic meaning of each category and the contribution of context to its interpretation in discourse (Andersen 1990; Jaganauth 1987; Pollard 1989).

This chapter has two broad aims. One is to give an account of the tense-aspect categories of Belize Creole (BC) – a rather conservative Caribbean English Creole (CEC) about which very little has been published to date. The other is to provide a further point of comparison for TMA systems across Caribbean English (and other) Creoles. My approach is based primarily on the frameworks offered by researchers such as Dahl (1985), Comrie (1976, 1985) and Bybee et al. (1994).

The approach I take here is based on the recognition that TMA categories typically display a range of meanings and uses. This has sometimes led to difficulty in determining the *unique* meaning of a TMA category and the *variety of uses* that all categories tend to have (Binnick 1991, 104). To resolve this difficulty, I follow Dahl (1985, 9–10), who distinguishes between the "basic" or "dominant" meaning of a category as distinct from its "secondary" meanings. The dominant meaning of a category is reflected in its prototypical uses, while secondary meanings are associated with context-dependent uses of the category.

In this approach, then, the discourse context plays a crucial role in deciding the interpretation of TMA categories. Both the actual linguistic context of an utterance and the wider discourse context are relevant. In Caribbean English (and other) Creoles, for instance, unmarked verbs may be interpreted as referring to past as well as present situations, depending both on the aktionsart of the verb and on the time reference established in the discourse. Similarly, the completive perfect category, expressed by *don,* may refer to past-before-past, as well as present or future situations, depending on the temporal frame established in the context: it may also be interpreted as both a perfect of result and a kind of resultative, depending on the predicate type involved. This is just a rough overview of a rather complex framework for talking about TMA categories. Further details can be found in Dahl (1985) and Winford (2000).

THE TMA CATEGORIES OF BELIZE CREOLE

The inventory of TMA morphemes in BC is in many respects similar to that found in other varieties of CEC. In this chapter, I focus on the subsystems of tense and aspect, and discuss each of the tense-aspect categories in turn. The system of modality will not be discussed any further, except where it may be relevant to questions concerning tense and aspect.

TENSE IN BELIZE CREOLE

Like all other varieties of Caribbean English Creole, Belizean Creole has only two categories whose dominant meaning and use is to express time reference. These are relative past and future, as shown in Table 2.1. I will discuss each in turn.

Table 2.1   Tense Categories in Belize Creole

Form	Category	Example
mi	Relative Past	*i mi gat plees op ya we mi an hi mi liv.* "He had a place up here where he and I lived."
wã	Future	*a wã giv yu wan jook wid J. an M.* "I'll give you a joke about J. and M."

RELATIVE PAST TENSE

The relative past is expressed in Belizean Creole by auxiliary *mi*, derived from *min*, an alternant of the more common CEC past marker *bin* or *ben*. The analysis suggested for *ben* in Jamaican Creole (JC) (Pollard 1989) and *bin* in Guyanese Creole (GC) (Jaganauth 1988) applies equally to Belizean *mi*. The function of the relative past is to locate a situation as past, either with respect to the moment of speech (S), or with respect to some other past situation. An explanation like this accounts for Bickerton's (1975, 36) observation that the meaning of anterior *bin* in GC shifts from "simple past" to "remote past" to "past-before-past". As Jaganauth (1988) explains, "If we bear in mind that it is the reference point which moves", then there is no need to view the various uses of *bin* as distinct.

This analysis applies equally well to the past tense category of Belizean *mi*. Its prototypical use is to distance some situation (event or state) from the reference point under focus in the discourse, or the "tense locus" (Chung and Timberlake 1985), which may coincide with S, or with some other point in the past. The following examples illustrate:

1. *bot i mi liv op ya wan taim, no?*
   "But he lived up here once, no?"
   yes man, i mi gat i plees op ya we mi an hi mi liv, man.
   "Yes, man, he had his place up here, where he and I lived, man."

2. *ai noo mista E frã rancho deez.*
   "I've known Mista E since [our] Rancho days."
   fra wee bak den, no?
   "From way back then, no?"

jes, wen i mi gat i fos gyal, C den taim i mi de da rancho.
"Yes, when he had his first girl, C. In those days he was at Rancho."
i fos gyal da no L?
"His first girl wasn't L?"
no man. afta C ded den i tek L, bikaaz i mi liv rait de da rancho de tuu.
"No man. After C died then he took L, because she lived right there at Rancho too."
ai mi see L da mi i fos leedii.
"I had thought that L was his first lady."
no, i mi gat wan gyal neem C, den hin an i mi paat. an den frã de den hin marid tu L.
"No, he had a girl called C, then he and she parted. And then after that he got married to L."

These extracts reveal several aspects of the subtlety with which the BC past is used. We might note first its use with stative verbs like *gat,* which tend to have present time reference unless specifically marked as past by *mi* or by some other means in the discourse context. Thus utterances like *i mi gat i plees op ya, i mi gat i fos gyal* and *den taim i mi de da rancho* convey the sense that the subject in question no longer has either the place or his first spouse and is no longer at Rancho. Contrast the ø-marked stative *noo* in the first line of Example 2, which conveys the sense that the speaker still knows E.

The choice of *mi* rather than ø-marking with non-statives is also instructive. The default reading of an ø-marked non-stative is past temporal reference, with the added implication that the past event is still somehow linked to, or relevant to S. (See Jaganauth 1988; Pollard 1989; and the discussion below.) All the instances of ø-marked non-statives in these extracts seem to convey this sense of current relevance. As Pollard (1989, 63) explains, unmarked verbs typically present "foreground information", while anterior usually presents "background information" in discourse. Thus, in Example 2, in response to C's question *i fos gyal da no L?*, A replies *no man, afta C ded den i tek L.* The use of ø-marked *tek* is required to mark the relevance of this act to the question posed in the present. By contrast, the use of *mi* in *bikaaz i mi liv rait de da rancho de tuu* conveys the sense that L had been living in the same village prior to becoming Mr E's spouse. A similar contrast between *mi* and ø-marking is found in A's response to C's last comment. The utterance *den hin an i mi paat* locates the loss of Mr E's first spouse prior to his marriage to L, the current relevance of which is established by ø-marked *marid* (which is incidentally a base form, not inflected). These facts demonstrate that *mi* can be used with both statives and non-statives to convey the sense of "past-before-past", contrary to Bickerton's claim that "anterior" conveys this sense only with non-statives. Similarly, contra Bickerton, *mi* and other past markers in CEC can be used with both statives and non-statives to convey the sense of an absolute past, with the added implicature that the past event or state is distanced from S, or no longer relevant at S. Examples are as follows:

3. *i mi gat gud memri, unoo. i luuz i memri nou, bot i juuztu gat gud wan.*
   "He had a good memory too, you know. He's lost his memory now, but he used to have a good one."

4. *a rimemba yu mi kil tuu big bruut arong ya so.*
   "I remember you killed two big brutes around here."
   ratla. dat da ratl sneek, tiicha. a mi giv di ratl tu di mjusiam. de tuu big tuu, big. dis wan mi gat totiin ratl pan i teel. a mi show yu, tiicha.
   "Rattler. That was rattle snakes, teacher. I gave the rattle to the museum there too. Big too, big. This one had thirteen rattles on its tail. I showed [it to] you, teacher."
   yes, a rimemba yu mi shoo mi, wen a mi paas di dee an yu sed da mi rait onda wan a di trii yu mi miit ã, no?
   "Yes, I remember you showed me when I passed by that day and you said it was right under one of the trees you had come upon it, no?"

The crucial sense conveyed by relative past *mi*, then, is that of some past event or state seen as prior to the tense locus (either S or some other point in the past) or as distanced from it in some way. As noted earlier, the semantics and use of relative past in Belizean and other varieties of CEC are in many respects similar to those described for other past categories in certain other languages. Of special relevance here is that West African languages such as Akan seem to use a past tense category in very much the same way as CEC uses its past. Dahl (1985, 148) refers to the use of what he calls a "framepast" in Akan, which appears to have the function of providing a "backdrop" for other events, both present and past, that is quite similar to that proposed here for the CEC relative past.

The relative past is also used in BC and all other varieties of CEC to express counterfactuality in conditional clauses, as in the following:

5. *a tel ā boi if a mi hav transpoteshan a wuda go go luk fu ā, inoo, dat da no woriiz.*
   "I told her, boy, if I had transportation I would have gone to look for her, you know, that's not a problem."

This secondary use of relative past has parallels in English and other languages. The meanings and uses associated with past *mi* are shown in Table 2.2.

Table 2.2   Summary of Meanings of Relative Past

> Basic Meaning: Relative past temporal reference.
>
> Primary use: To locate situation in past (before S or another point in the past).
>
> Discourse function: To distance situation from the reference point. To provide background for situation in focus.
>
> Predicate types: All.
>
> Secondary use: To express counterfactuality in conditionals.

FUTURE TENSE

As noted earlier, future time reference is typically conveyed in BC by *wā*, which appears to derive from wāā, "want", while *gwain* is often used to express the sense of a more immediate future.[1] For the moment, I focus on the former auxiliary, which I refer to simply as the marker of future. *Gwain* is referred to as a prospective marker. The range of meanings associated with the future is rather restricted. Its primary use is to convey "later time reference" as in:

6. *J see i wā kum luk fu yu wan a diiz deez.*
   "J says she'll come to look for you one of these days."
   i tel ā a wā duu eniting fi satisfai yu.
   "He told her, 'I'll do anything to satisfy you.'"

7. *If yu go fu se yu wāā bai fuud, i wā kos yu wan lat, i wā kos yu plentii.*
   "If you go and say you want to buy food, he'll curse you a lot, he'll curse you plenty."

if wi no get somting fi kantrool di wii-wii gud wi no wã manij.
"If we don't get something to control the wee-wees [insects] properly, we won't manage."

It must of course be acknowledged that the Belizean future, like future tenses in many languages, often has modal overtones. Dahl (1985, 102) explains:

> Normally, when we talk about the future, we are either talking about someone's plans, intentions or obligations, or we are making a prediction or extrapolation from the present state of the world. As a direct consequence, a sentence that refers to the future will almost always differ modally from a sentence with non-future time reference.

The Belizean future does in fact seem to convey modal overtones such as "intention" and "prediction," as can be seen in Examples 6 and 7 respectively. But neither intention nor prediction is the essential semantic element of the future. In other words, it is true only of a subset of uses of the future that they express some intention on the part of the speaker, or some prediction of a later event. These modal overtones are more like implicatures drawn from the context. The constant element that underlies all these uses is simply "later time reference", and, following Dahl's guidelines, that is what I take to be the dominant meaning of the Belizean future.

Like other Caribbean English Creoles, Belizean Creole makes a distinction between the general future and a prospective (more immediate) future. The latter is expressed by *gwain (to)* in Belizean, as in:

8. *i see if yu no pee mi fu ã, a gwain tu shuut yu nou.*
    "He said if you don't pay me for it, I'm going to shoot you now."

However, occurrences of *gwain (tu)* were quite rare in my data. In fact, *wã* was more commonly used to express the sense of immediate intention, as in:

9. *a wã giv yu wan jook wid J an M.*
    "I'll give you a joke involving J and M."
    a wã ruut op wan rait nou an shoo yu.
    "I'll root up one right now and show you."

It would appear from my data that *wã* is a general all-purpose future marker in BC, covering both prospective and remote meanings, while *gwain (tu)* is more marginal.

Finally, we may note that there are certain secondary uses of future *wã* that also have parallels in other varieties of CEC. For instance, *wã* may be used to refer to future in the past, as in the following, where the speaker is describing an encounter he had with a snake.

10. *a staat tu luk, luk, a no sii a ataal, tiicha. a se gyal a no sii a ataal. a see a wã kum bak, a no gwain fooda. a se a wã kum bak, an a gwain rong.*
"I started to look, look, I didn't see it at all, teacher. I said girl, I don't see it at all. I said I would come back, I wasn't going further. I said I'd come back, and go round."

This suggests that *wã* is a kind of relative future marker, as Jaganauth (1987) and Winford (1993a) have suggested for the future in GC.

Moreover, *wã* often expresses predictability or characteristic behaviour in both present and past contexts. The following examples illustrate the former use.

11. *if yu gwain eniwee we paat ratlsneek de, yu no hafu wori bikaa i no wã bait yu laik tomigaaf, i wã waan yu, if yu no iivn sii ã.*
"If you're going any place where there's a rattlesnake, you don't have to worry because it won't bite you like a tommygaaf, it will warn you, even if you don't see it."
yu wã fain dat dẽ no wã kum ya da dee, tiicha, bot dẽ kum da nait.
"You'll find that they won't come here by day, teacher, but they come at night."

There are similar uses in past contexts, as in the following examples. In the first, the speaker is reminiscing about the low cost of going to a dance in the old days; in the second, another speaker describes part of the procedure for logging mahogany, which he had learned as a young man.

12. *an homoch somtaim yu pee wen dẽ mek wan lii pee dans? fifti sens fu go in, wid foo drink. yu wã get foo drink.*
"And how much would you sometimes pay when they arranged a little pay dance? Fifty cents to go in, with four drinks. You'd get four drinks."
yes, aha, yes, wi gat wan skwad a man we di chap di treel, aha, fi tel yu we di mahagani di gaan, no? den yu wã falo dat.
"Yes, aha, yes, we had a squad of men that were clearing the trail, aha, to tell you where the mahogany lay, no? Then you'd follow that."

See Table 2.3 for the meanings and uses associated with future *wã* in BC.

Table 2.3 Summary of Meanings of Future

Basic meaning:	Relative future time reference (R = S or some point in past)
Primary uses:	Later time reference. Intention. Prediction.
Secondary uses:	Future in the past. Predictability or characteristic behaviour (present or past).

These meanings and uses seem to match those described for Guyanese Creole by Jaganauth (1987) and Winford (1993a) exactly. This is in itself significant, given the geographical distance between these Creoles and the fact that they do not use the same marker of futurity. When we add to this the close similarities in the meanings and uses of the past, it would appear that the tense system as a whole may be more or less identical in all varieties of CEC.

ASPECT IN BELIZEAN CREOLE

Table 2.4 summarizes the aspectual categories in Belizean Creole.

Table 2.4 Aspectual Categories in Belizean Creole

Form	Category		Examples
Ø	Unmarked (perfective)	Stative:	*yu gat wan gud hag de man.* "You have a good hog there man."
		Non-stative:	*i get it kot aredi, aha, i kot ā aredi.* "He got it cut already, aha, he cut it already."
di	Progressive	Non-stative only:	*a tel ā a di get ool nou.* "I told her I'm getting old now."

Table 2.4   Aspectual Categories in Belizean Creole *(cont'd)*

Form	Category		Examples
don	Completive/ Perfect	Stative:	*a don gat evriting redi, inoo, mis B.* "I already have everything ready, you know, Miss B."
		Non-stative:	*dis wuman don dischaaj yu haas, yu noo.* "This woman has let go your horse, you know."
juustu/doz	Habitual past	All predicates:	*di ool man neva juustu iit bikaaz i doz trobl wid presha.* "The old man never used to eat because he used to suffer with [high blood] pressure."

Now I will consider each category in turn and discuss its semantic range and uses.

THE UNMARKED VERB

In all varieties of CEC, the unmarked verb displays perhaps the widest range of uses and interpretations of any TMA category. In Belizean Creole, its range covers past as well as present temporal reference, including present and past habitual or generic situations, present states, past events, along with use in subordinate clauses whose time reference is dependent on that of the matrix verb. In all these respects, Belizean is identical to Jamaican and other western varieties of CEC such as Providence Island Creole. In eastern Caribbean Creoles, present habitual meaning is conveyed by a distinct aspectual category (imperfective *a* in conservative rural Guyanese, present habitual *doz* in intermediate Creoles like Bajan, urban Guyanese and Trinidadian), rather than by the unmarked verb. The unmarked verb is neutral with respect to both temporal and aspectual reference, and is crucially dependent for its interpretation on two things: the nature of the predicate involved, and, more important, the role of temporal adverbs and the wider discourse context in establishing a temporal frame for the situation referred to.

The primary uses of the unmarked verb in Belizean and CEC generally are to express simple past events (with non-statives) and present states. This does not mean, however, that unmarked non-statives and statives will always be interpreted as having past and present time reference respectively, as Bickerton (1975) erroneously claimed for GC. As we shall see, depending on the context, both types of predicate may have present or past reference when unmarked. In fact, the use of the unmarked verb to express simple past with non-statives is its most common use in my Belizean data, due perhaps to the fact that non-statives are far more common than statives, since so much of the conversation is devoted to narratives and past experience generally. The following extract provides many examples of this use of the unmarked verb:

13. *so di man tel mi see dat, mmm, i gaan da i faam wã maanin suun, bout faiv toti, i se an wail kumin bak frã de, about siks di maanin wen i luk pan i wach, i se an i gaan go kot planteen fu kyeri hoom fu iit ar put ā fu raip. enihou, i se, kumin dong di benksaid i se i get wã slip. i se an i fait di faaldong fu mek i neva tombl dong. i se an i staat tu fait di faaldong frā siks til tuu oklak an i se i neva riich grong. i se an wen i rikova di faaldong i woz tuu an all di planteen we mi griin raip pan i bak. yu kuda mi iit den.*

"So the man told me that, mmm, he went to the farm early one morning, about five thirty, he says and while coming back from there, about six in the morning, when he looked at his watch, he says and he went to cut plantain to carry home to eat or put to get ripe. Anyhow, he says, coming down the bank he says he slipped. He says and he fought against falling down so that he wouldn't tumble down. He says and he started to fight against falling down from six until two o'clock and he says he never hit the ground. He says and when he recovered from the fall it was two o'clock and all the plantains that had been green were ripe on his back. You could have eaten them."

The fact that unmarked non-statives normally have past time reference is primarily a matter of pragmatics, based first on our understanding of the inherent semantics of such verbs, which primarily express processes and other dynamic events, and the discourse context, whether implied or overtly stated. It is worth emphasizing that the effect of the discourse context is always present, whether it is overtly stated or not. If the verb in question is dynamic, then it will be interpreted as past in the absence of any other clue, since this is the common-sense reading of an unanalysed process or event. Stative verbs, on the other hand, are inherently durative, and the default reading of an unmarked stative in the absence of any other clue will be that it has present time reference. In both cases, the listener will assume that the moment of speaking is the point of reference for the state or dynamic situation described. A good illustration of this is seen in the following, where the time reference changes between stative *noo* and non-stative *hib* and *sii*, while the discourse context remains the same.

14. *da bakut liif da fi chroo wee pikni.*
    "That bakut leaf is for throwing babies away [terminating pregnancy]."

    yu hib wan wee wid ā aredi, no? hou di hel yu noo dat?
    "You've thrown one away with it already, huh? How the hell do you know that?"

    no, a sii wan gyal duu ā.
    "No, I saw a girl do it."

In general, then, it is not strictly true to say that an unmarked stative will by itself have present time reference, since this is always dependent on the point of reference established in the discourse. The following illustrates this.

15. *ai no noo bout dat. ai noo i mi gat L.*
    "I don't know about that. I know he had L."

    so i se, chiif, i see, ai laik gwaana, yu noo.
    "So he says, 'chief,' he says, 'I like iguana, you know.'"

    yu gat wan gud hag de, man.
    "You have a good hog there, man."

In these cases, the discourse context establishes the moment of speech as the reference point, and thus the unmarked stative is interpreted as present. To illustrate the point that it is not primarily the stativity of the verb, but rather the discourse context that affects interpretation, we can note that unmarked statives can in fact have past time reference, once the discourse establishes the point of reference as past:

16. *aha, bot unu wuda gat wan skwad a man we di mek di treel fu unu.*
"Aha, but you would have had a squad of men making the trail for you."
yes, aha, yes. wi gat wan skwad a man. yu gat said-man we go op iina di paas an hi nootis fu suu homoch gaan ya.
"Yes, aha, yes. We had a squad of men. You had a side-man who would go up into the pass and he would investigate to see how much [mahogany] was there."

17. *Bot de mi veks wid ā bikaa de noo da G mi rang wid mii.*
"But they were angry with him, because they knew it was G that was at fault with me."

These examples, like those for non-statives, demonstrate that it is not the unmarked verb by itself that conveys time reference, but rather the interaction of inherent verbal aspect and discourse context as well.

Similar considerations explain why unmarked verbs may convey other kinds of temporal and aspectual meaning in Belize Creole. For instance, they convey the sense of habitual or generic situations in both present and past contexts. Examples of the former use are

18. *yes man, dat no groo arong dis said doo. balsam baak no groo ya, i grow da haya rij.*
"Yes man, that doesn't grow around here though. Balsam bark doesn't grow here, it grows on higher ground."

    dat da di provizhan baak. yu bail dat an yu drink dat.
    "That's the provision bark. You boil that and you drink it."

    bikaaz da so P hin duu den. hi no shuut sneek. hin get tuu krochstik, a miin kot wan kroch stik laik dis, hi gwain rait ya an i duu so "jing" an hool ā dong.
    "Because that's how P handles them. He doesn't shoot snakes. He gets two forked sticks, I mean [he] cuts a forked stick like this, he goes right here and he does like this 'jing' and holds it down."

19. *so som a yu seem grong fuud an ting yu gi dem, no?*
"So you give them some of the same ground food and stuff, no?"
yes, ai juuz mi keen, aha, keen, pomkin, skwashiz, aha. dē iit di puteeta slip gud tuu, aha, veri gud.
"Yes, I use my cane, aha, cane, pumpkin, squashes, aha. They eat the potato peel well too, aha, very well."

Similarly, we find examples of past habitual reference like the following:

20. *Wen deelait di kom, yu noo wa dē duu, laik di wan frā dis said, dē go da waatasaid an de shub aaf aal di doorii.*
"When day was breaking, do you know what they'd do? like, the ones from this side [of the river] they'd go to the waterside and push off all the boats."

i neva juuztu tel anansi stori. we i duu nou, meebi hontin, kot i planteeshan, i padl i doori aal laik fra BL tuu big faalz go kyeri griinz op de fu sel.
"He never used to tell anansi stories. What he'd do now, maybe hunting, cut his planting area, he'd paddle his dhory all the way from BL [Bermudian Landing] to Big Falls to carry produce up there to sell."

yu gat said man we go op iina di paas an hi nootis fu sii homoch gaan ya, an wen yu shub op pan wā saatin distans iina di rood, yu wā luk fu sii hi.
"You'd have a side-man who would go up into the pass and he'd investigate to see how much [mahogany] was there, and when you pushed up a certain distance up the road, you'd look to catch sight of him."

Notice that in these cases, the unmarked verb alternates with other verbs marked for habituality by auxiliaries such as *juutu* or *wā*, which help to establish its interpretation in this discourse context.

The various examples cited above provide ample evidence that the unmarked verb by itself is quite neutral with respect to temporal reference and that its interpretation is due primarily to the type of predicate involved and the pragmatics of the discourse context. The unmarked verb might be regarded as a general all-purpose default choice in cases where the context establishes its meaning without ambiguity.

Table 2.5 summarizes the meaning and uses of the unmarked verb in Belize Creole.

Table 2.5 Summary of Meanings of the Unmarked Verb

Unmarked.	Basic meaning:	Unanalysed event or state; situation viewed as single whole
	Primary uses:	Simple past events
		Present states
		Present habitual/generic events
	Secondary uses:	Past states
		Past habitual situations
		Predicate types: All

Progressive

The semantic notions subsumed under "imperfective", which include "habitual" and "progressive", are mapped onto three distinct categories in BC. Present habituality is one of the primary uses of the unmarked verb as just discussed. Past habituality is usually rendered by *juuztu,* alternating in speakers' usage with *doz,* while progressive meaning is conveyed by *di* (apparently derived from older *de,* which is also the progressive marker in some varieties of Jamaican Creole).

Progressive *di* in Belizean is a purely aspectual category, quite neutral with respect to time reference, which once again is supplied by the discourse context. In cases like the following, the point of reference is S, and *di* marks processes or events in progress at S.

21. *da yu blod, yu blod no di saakjuleet.*
    "It's your blood. Your blood isn't circulating."

    bikaaz a tel mi waif, a tel ã a di get ool nou.
    "Because I told my wife, I told her I'm getting old now."

    da meni yeez yu di wok dis ting nou an yu gat di rait kemistri nou.
    "It's many years you've been practising this thing now and you have the right chemistry now."

    yes man, a hier CJ dem di giv da plees hel rait nou.
    "Yes man, I hear that CJ and his friends are giving that place hell right now."

But it is equally common to find *di* used in cases where the time reference is established as past.

22. *aha bot unu wuda gat wan skwad a man we di mek di treel fu unu.*
    "Aha, but you would have had a squad of men who were clearing the trail for you."

    i luk laik di pus mi wãã kech ã an di man disaid fu giv alaam wid i teel an i di sheek da ratl.
    "It seems that the cat wanted to catch it and the guy [a snake] decided to sound an alarm with his tail and was shaking the rattle."

    so nou i di ring op nou, i di ring op di nait bout wan oklok.
    "So now he's telephoning now, he's telephoning that night about one o'clock."

wel ai get mi gon an ai statid tu waak, waak, waak, an a di luk, a di nootis.
"Well I got my gun and I started to walk, walk, walk, and I'm looking, I'm investigating."

It would appear then that the primary uses of *di* include the expression of both present and past occurrences in progress. This suggests that *di* simply has "relative present time meaning". In other words, it expresses the simultaneity of an ongoing activity relative to some other event or time, either present or past.[2] This is most clearly seen in cases like the following, involving embedded clauses containing *di*, or serialization or coordination to convey simultaneous events in the past:

23. *an i see wen i luk i kech glims a wan blak ting di paas.*
"And he said when he looked he caught glimpe of a black thing passing."

an wen yu shub ā wid di bulduuza bleed somtaim yu sii tuu pail op ondaniit de man, we di kom out.
"And when you pushed it with the bulldozer blade sometimes you'd see two piled up underneath there man, coming out."

dē de rong di teebl di iit, di drink tii, an ool PT hin di de di taak an i di giv jook. an i don put pepa iina i dina, bot wen i wiil rong an i di taak, BJ tek di pepa waata an put ā iina i tii.
"They were round the table eating, drinking tea, and old PT was there talking and telling jokes. And he'd already put pepper in his dinner, but when he turned around and was talking, BJ took the pepper water and put it in his tea."

In such cases, the time neutrality of *di* allows it to be used in embedded clauses, where it picks up its time reference from the matrix verb or the context as a whole.[3] Similar evidence has been adduced by, for instance, Mufwene (1984) to support the view that certain Creoles have a "relative tense system". But I have argued elsewhere that the verbs in the embedded clauses in such cases display dependent time reference, similar to what occurs in other cases of embedding in CEC, for instance in complements to perception verbs, desideratives and so on (Winford 1993a). This is in keeping with the view expressed earlier that the dominant meaning of *di* is relative present time meaning, or simultaneity.

We should note that past progressive events can also be marked by the combination of past *mi* and *di*. But these cases are distinct. Use of *mi* is called for when the event in progress is seen as anterior to the situation in focus, or as background to it.

24. *y, a mi di gi ā di jook jes nou.*
"Yeah, I was telling him the joke just now."

di dokta kom an i see kyeri ā, bikaa i mi di distaab di ada peeshan den, i mi di kik op an taak aal nait.
"The doctor came and said to carry him away, because he was disturbing the other patients, he was kicking up and talking all night."

In these cases, the use of *mi* conforms to its usual discourse function of distancing situations from some time, either present or past.

In some cases, use of *di* seems to convey the sense of habituality.

25. *evritaim hin and L. di kwaril, man.*
"He and L are always quarrelling, man."
yu moosli de hoom nou, yu haadli di fuul arong.
"You're mostly at home nou, you hardly fool around."
bikaa yu noo da nait sneek aalweez di swim kraas di riva.
"Because you know that nait snakes are always swimming across the river."
somtaim a de rait hoom ya an a di luk street da lemonal, a di luk street da govana kriik.
"Sometimes I'm right at home here and I'm looking straight at Lemonal, I'm looking straight at Governor's Creek."

This kind of use represents a very common extension of progressive to convey repeated or continuous instantiations of an occurrence. It is therefore a secondary use of progressive in BC, in the sense discussed earlier. Note also that much of the sense of habituality is conveyed by adverbials like *evritaim*, *haadli*, *aalweez* and *somtaim*. It would therefore be erroneous to claim that habituality is one of the dominant senses or prototypical uses of *di*.

We can sum up the uses of progressive in BC in Table 2.6.

Table 2.6   Summary of Meanings of Progressive *di* in BC

Progressive *di*:	Basic meaning:	Ongoing activity
	Primary use:	Events in progress at R (R = S or some other time)
	Secondary use:	Repeated or habitual events
	Predicate types:	Non-statives

HABITUAL PAST

The usual marker of past habituality in BC is *juuztu*, as illustrated in the following:

26. *so wit dat, aal di taim nou wi juuztu go da lemonal an den lemonal kum oova dis said . . . an wi juuztu de rait de hapi wid wan anada. mod, wi no freed fa. oo, wi rool op wi frak teel pan di lii rood so. hamadili rood wi kaal de. bot wi juuztu hav reeli gud taim da dobl hed an lemonal.*
"So with that, all the time now we used to go to Lemonal and then [people from] Lemonal would come over to this side . . . and we used to be right there, happy with one another. Mud, we weren't afraid of. Ooh, we'd roll up our frock tails on the road like this. Hamadilly Road we called there. But we used to have really good times at Double Head and Lemonal."

dende taim wi juuztu hav dem bwai we juuztu hav dem big paatii, an mista Y juuztu gat i big bootdee da yongbenk.
"In those times we used to have those boys who used to have those big parties, and Mr Y used to have his big birthday [celebration] at Youngbank."

In some cases, *juuztu* alternates with *doz*.

27. *de mi gat wā man da landin we de mi juuztu kaal ool DA ai juuztu heng out wid ā inoo. i juuztu ritaadid, bot i doz go an kom, i neva juuztu trobl nobadi.*
"There was a man at Landing whom they used to call Old DA. I used to hang out with him, you know. He used to be retarded, but he'd go and come, he never used to bother anyone."

This use of *doz* is relatively rare, and is always restricted to past habitual meaning in BC – which contrasts with its use to express both past and present habitual meaning in eastern CEC varieties like rural Guyanese and with its restriction to present habitual meaning in intermediate Creoles like Barbadian and Trinidadian, as well as urban GC. The differences in the meanings of *doz* across these Creoles is a strong caveat against attempts (such as Schneider 1990) to compare Creoles simply on the basis of inventory of forms, to the exclusion of the range of uses to which the forms are put. Another interesting fact is that use of *doz* has not been attested for JC, despite the close affinity between this Creole and BC. It is likely that *doz* was introduced into Belizean by immigrants from the eastern Caribbean, but its restriction to past habitual is a peculiarity of this Creole alone.

We can sum up the uses of *juuztu/doz* in BC as follows:

Table 2.7   Summary of Meanings of Habitual Past *juuztu/doz* in BC

Habitual Past.	Basic meaning: Habitual past
Primary uses:	Past habitual occurrences or states
Predicate types:	All

COMPLETIVE PERFECT *don*

The status of auxiliary *don* within the TMA systems of CEC has been controversial ever since Bickerton (1975) claimed that it was a mere "performance" feature that did not combine freely with other TMA auxiliaries in GC, and excluded it both from the GC system and his "prototypical" Creole system. It has become clear from recent work on GC (Gibson 1986, 1992; Jaganauth 1987; Winford 1993a) and JC (Winford 1993a) that *don* is an integral part of CEC tense-aspect systems, though the range of uses of this auxiliary is not the same in all varieties.

The semantics and uses of *don* are among the more difficult problems in describing tense-aspect categories in CEC. "Completive" is the label traditionally used to describe the grammatical category expressed by this auxiliary. But other labels such as "resultative-perfective" (Stolz 1987) and "perfect" (Youssef 1990) have been suggested for similar categories in other Creoles. The problem is compounded by the limited data available on the uses of *don* and by the absence of any clear definition of the category it purportedly represents.

I argue that Belizean *don* represents a subtype of the cross-linguistic category "perfect", which I refer to as "completive perfect". The following sentences illustrate the use of *don* with non-statives – a use which is common to all varieties of CEC:

28.   *aaz wi don lisn tu ā, ai kuk taak jos laik hou i taak.*
      "As soon as we've listened to him, I can talk exactly as he talks."

dem men dẽ wikid man, de don get help and de no wãã pee.
"Those guys are wicked man, they've already got help and they don't want to pay."

i se kom mis B, mek a gi yu wã raid iina dis ting. a tel ã noo, a don sidong iina dis, man, wan neks taim.
"He said come Miss B, let me give you a ride in this thing. I told him no, I've already sat down in this, man, some other time."

In these examples, *don* marks some event as having been completed at S, hence the label "completive" that is generally preferred among creolists.[4] There is indeed a strong sense of "completion" in the above uses of *don*. This is one of the prototypical uses of this auxiliary in all varieties of CEC. "Completion" itself is subject to varying interpretations. One of these is termination of an event or process, that is, the sense of "finishing." Indeed, when used with non-statives, as in the first example, *don* can often be translated as "finish" or "stop." This also applies in some cases involving tense marking or negation, like the following:

29. a see mai god, H, da wen yu wã don drink?
    "I said My God, H, when will you stop drinking?"

    di man no don fiks yu kyar yet.
    "The man hasn't finished repairing your car as yet."

In most cases, however, the emphasis seems to be more on the result of the event that has been completed, not on its termination as such. In the second and third sentences in Example 28, for instance, *don* is best translated as "already," rather than as "finish". In general, it appears that neither "termination" nor "completion" by itself accounts for the full meaning of *don*. In all the examples given so far, the past event is portrayed as having led to a result at S which has implications of consequence for the present situation. The notions of completion and having a result at speech time (or any relevant reference point) are of course closely related, and they seem to be inextricably bound up in the semantics of *don*. This use clearly has a close resemblance to one of the uses associated with the category "perfect" cross-linguistically – the so-called perfect of result. This fact seems to have led researchers such as Youssef (1990) to label *don* (in Trinidadian Creole [TC]) a marker of the category "perfect".

Since TC *don* appears to function in identically in TC, BC and GC (not to mention other Creoles like Barbadian), any label we apply to it in one Creole should also be applicable to the others. If *don* can be labelled a "perfect" at all, it is a very different kind of perfect from the SE perfect. Like its counterparts in Swedish, Spanish, and so on, the SE perfect portrays a past situation as linked to S and has several distinct "uses" or pragmatic interpretations, including the perfect of result (or stative perfect), the perfect of experience (or experiential), the perfect of persistent situation (or continuative) and the perfect of recent past (or "hot news" perfect). Each of these areas of semantic space could in principle be grammaticalized as distinct categories in different languages, thus making more difficult the task of identifying the common properties of such categories cross-linguistically, as Anderson (1982) demonstrates. For instance, Hiberno English has grammaticalized the perfect of result and the perfect of recent past but subsumed the continuative and experiential readings under present and past tense, respectively (Harris 1984). Of all these areas of semantic space, only one – that associated with the perfect of result – seems to show any significant similarity with the use of *don* in CEC.

Contrary to what Youssef claims, neither TC nor any variety of CEC employs *don* to convey the sense of an "experiential", "continuative", or "recent past" perfect. For instance, *don* is incompatible with adverbials like *eva, neva* and so on, which are typically associated with experiential meaning. The following TC examples (based on my own intuitions) illustrate this:

30. *yu eva (*don) sii da piktja?*
    "Have you ever seen that movie?"

    wi neva (*don) go dong bai da riva.
    "We've never gone down by that river."

In fact, Winford (1993b) demonstrates through a quantitative sociolinguistic analysis that such experiential past meanings are usually conveyed by the unmarked verb, along with appropriate adverbials. The same is true of the recent past meaning, while the sense of a continuative is conveyed by unmarked statives or by the progressive. The same appears to be true in Belizean Creole as well.

It would seem then that *don* corresponds most closely in its semantics and use to some sort of perfect of result. However, as Dahl warns us, "it turns out that categories that appear to exhibit only one of the typical uses of PERFECT are often subtly different from PERFECT in their semantics" (1985, 133). The differences are more than just subtle ones and appear in two aspects of the use of *don* – its time reference and its compatibility with stative predicates. We can examine each of these in turn.

Like other CEC aspectual markers, *don* is essentially neutral in time reference. In the examples considered so far, *don* conveys the sense of a present perfect, but the time reference itself is due entirely to the discourse context, which establishes S as the point of reference. As, Example 31 shows, *don* may also convey the sense of a pluperfect as well as a future perfect (see Example 32), without the aid of tense markers.

31. *so aftawaadz wen hin don iit hin kum pan di step an i sidong.*
"So afterwards when he had finished eating, he came onto the steps and he sat down."

an wen a luk, tiich, di boga don kum out fra kraaswee di soovee and nou i di kum out iina di oopnin.
"And when I looked, teacher, the bugger had already come out from across the canal and he was coming out in the opening."

an ool FT him di de di taak an i di giv jook, an i don put pepa iina i dina, bot wen i wiil rong an i di taak, BJ tek di pepa waata an put ā iina i tii.
"And old FT was there talking and telling jokes, and he had already put pepper in his dinner, but when he turned round and was talking, BJ took the pepper sauce and put it in his tea."

an wen L don bail aal i medsn pan isabela bank dat da mi di dokta fu di hool lemonal, di hool panya kriik, di hool plees.
"And when L had boiled all the medicine in Isabella Bank, that was the doctor for the whole of Lemonal, the whole of Panya Creek, the whole area."

32. *if yu get wan kot an yu greeta wan lii piis laik notmeg an yu put ā rait pan di wuun an tai it, tumaro i don drai op.*
"If you get a cut and you grate a little piece just like nutmeg and you put it on the wound and tie it, by the next day it will have already dried up."

These examples, which are possible in other varieties of CEC, as well as in intermediate Creoles like TC, show that *don* is not the exact equivalent of the

SE perfect, contra Youssef's suggestion. Unlike the latter, which normally has to rely on tense support to convey "pluperfect" or "future perfect" meaning, *don* simply picks up its time reference from the discourse context. There are cases where *don* is also marked for past or future by the appropriate auxiliaries when these meanings would not otherwise be clear from the discourse, as in the first sentence in Example 29 above, or the following:

33. *i see wel boi wen yu step iin de, mi main mi cheenj. Ai mi don disaid fi lef dis ya plees bikaaz a di trespaas.*
"He said well boy when you stepped in there, my mind had changed. I'd already decided to leave this place because I was trespassing."

In these cases, *don* behaves quite similarly to progressive *di* and its equivalents in other varieties of CEC.

Perhaps the most striking peculiarity of Belizean *don* is that it can be used with stative verbs as well as with copulas and progressives. This is also true of certain other varieties of CEC, such as Trinidadian and urban Guyanese, but interestingly, it is not found in JC, a close relative of BC. The following examples from Belizean illustrate. Sentences from Example 34 are from my recorded data; those in Example 35 are elicited.

34. *mi don fifti aredii, mi no wāā lef miself so.*
"I'm already fifty, I don't want to neglect myself like that."

   wel, i see, a don gat evriting redi inoo, mis B.
   "Well, he says, I already have everything ready you know, Miss B."

35. *di pikni don noo di ansa.*
"The child already knows the answer."

   Jan da don wā rich man.
   "John's already a rich man."
   di mango don raip.
   "The mango's already ripe."

   di gyal dē don de da yaad.
   "The girls are already in the yard."

In these cases, *don* conveys a state or situation which is already in existence, or which has been entered into sometime in the recent past. The interpretation of *don* here is subtly different from the sense it conveys with non-stative verbs, discussed earlier.

What all of these examples suggest is that *don* conveys meanings such as "termination" or "completion", "result with current relevance", "implied consequence", and the like. These meanings may vary according to predicate type or discourse context, as we have seen. But there is always the clear implicature that the event or state marked by *don* has implications for the situation at hand. These consequential overtones are an integral part of the semantics of *don* and seem to represent a kind of conventionalization of implicatures in the sense of Dahl (1985, 11).[5] In other words, the associations of "result" and "consequence" that *don* has are quite likely due to its regular or obligatory choice in contexts where this condition of use is satisfied. The dominant sense of *don* in all these cases is that of *already*. I therefore conclude that the label best suited for the category expressed by *don* is "completive perfect". There may be different nuances of meaning arising from its use with different predicate types or in different discourse contexts (a familiar characteristic of all the tense-aspect categories surveyed so far), but in all cases the common element is some result that has consequences.

Table 2.8 sums up the various meanings and uses of completive perfect *don*.

Table 2.8   Summary of Meanings of Completive Perfect *don*

Basic meaning:	"Already"; result or consequence arising from an event or existing state
Primary uses:	Past event leading to current result (perfect of result); state already in existence (resultative)
Secondary uses:	Past situations linked to past R; completion of events in the future
Discourse function:	Backgrounding for consequential or emphatic overtones
Predicate types:	All

We might note finally that the possibilities for combinations involving *don* and other TMA auxiliaries are far wider in Belizean than in JC. As the following elicited examples from Belizean show, these combinations may be quite complex.

36. *Jan don di iit.*
"John's already eating."

Jan mi don iit.
"John had already eaten."

Jan wā don iit bai i taim wi kom bak.
"John will have eaten by the time we come back."

Jan don mi di iit wen wi get de.
"John was already eating when we got there."

if yu kom ten aklak, we wā don di plant rais aredi.
"If you come at ten o'clock, we will already be planting rice."

Jan mosi don di iit.
"John must be already eating."

Jan don mi wā di iit if i mi kom in taim.
"John would have already been eating if he had come in time."

A similar variety of combinations is found in GC as well (Winford 1993a). Such data do not support Bickerton's claim that *don* is marginal to CEC grammar and not central to the TMA prototype which he associates with the earliest grammar of "radical" Creoles. Interestingly also, Belizean differs from both GC and JC in not having VP-final *don,* as in the following example (acceptable in GC and JC).

37. *Jan iit di mango don.*
"John has finished eating the mango."

It is not clear why this use of VP-final *don* was never adopted by Belizean, given its close historical relation with JC in particular.

Acknowledgements

I have the greatest pleasure in contributing this chapter to the collection in honour of my long-time friend Pauline Christie, who first introduced me to Belize Creole when I was a graduate student at the University of York in the early 1970s. I am very grateful to her for all her help, support and friendship over the years.

The research on which this chapter is based was conducted with the assistance of NSF grant no. SBR-930635, for which I wish to express my gratitude. I am deeply indebted to Allan Herrera, my principal Belizean fieldworker, without whose help these data could not have been collected. Thanks also to two anonymous reviewers who made useful comments on an earlier draft of this chapter.

Notes

1. In general, future *wã* seems to have a short nasalized vowel, while *wã̄ã̄* ("want") has a long nasalized vowel. But this is impressionistic and needs to be confirmed by a phonetic analysis. It is often difficult to distinguish between the two.
2. This is the meaning that Dahl (1985, 25) assigned to the present participle of English, which is used in the progressive construction, but is usually supplied with time reference by tensed auxiliary *be*.
3. Andersen (1990, 73) has noted a similar use of imperfective *ta* in embedded clauses in Papiamentu and concluded that its time reference must be inferred from the total context.
4. Perhaps the earliest use of the term "completive" in reference to *don* is found in Bickerton (1975, 42), where he refers to the difference between GC "*bin*-completive" and "*don*-completive". He notes that the latter "may require to be translated by English simple present, simple past, perfect or perfect + finish + V-ing", but he doesn't suggest any label for the category itself. Later, however, he suggests that the sense of "necessary completion" is common to all uses of *don*. As I argue here, while completion is certainly part of the semantics of *don*, it doesn't cover the whole range of meanings or uses associated with it.
5. Dahl (1985, 11) explains thus: "What happens when a conversational implicature is conventionalized may be described as follows: if some condition happens to be fulfilled frequently when a certain category is used, a stronger association may develop between the condition and the category in such a way that the condition comes to be understood as an integral part of the meaning of the category." The case of *don* seems to be a good example of this type of grammaticalization.

References

Andersen, R. 1990. "Papiamentu Tense-Aspect, with Special Attention to Discourse". In *Pidgin and Creole Tense-Mood-Aspect systems*, ed. J. Singler, 59–96. Amsterdam: John Benjamins.

Anderson, L. 1982. "The 'Perfect' as a Universal and as a Language-Specific Category". In *Tense-Aspect: Between Semantics and Pragmatics*, ed. P. Hopper, 227–64. Amsterdam: John Benjamins.

Bickerton, D. 1974. "Creolization, Linguistic Universals, Natural Semantax and the Brain". *University of Hawaii Working Papers in Linguistics* 6, no. 3, 125–41.

———. 1975. *Dynamics of a Creole System*. Cambridge: Cambridge University Press.

———. 1981. *Roots of Language*. Ann Arbor, Mich.: Karoma.

Binnick, R. 1991. *Time and the Verb: A Guide to Tense and Aspect*. Oxford: Oxford University Press.

Bybee, J., R. Perkins and W. Pagliuca. 1994. *The Evolution of Grammar: Tense, Aspect, and Modality in the Languages of the World*. Chicago: University of Chicago Press.

Chung, S., and A. Timberlake. 1985. "Tense, Mood and Aspect". In *Language Typology and Syntactic Description*, vol. 3, ed. Timothy Shopen, 202–58. Cambridge: Cambridge University Press.

Comrie, B. 1976. *Aspect: An Introduction to the Study of Verbal Aspect and Related Problems*. Cambridge: Cambridge University Press.

———. 1985. *Tense*. Cambridge: Cambridge University Press.

Dahl, Ö. 1985. *Tense and Aspect Systems*. Oxford: Blackwell.

Gibson, K. 1986. "The Ordering of Auxiliary Notions in Guyanese Creole". *Language* 62: 571–86.

———. 1992. "Tense and Aspect in Guyanese Creole, with Reference to Jamaican and Carriacouan". *International Journal of American Linguistics* 58, no. 1: 49–95.

Harris, J. 1984. "Syntactic Variation and Dialect Divergence". *Journal of Linguistics* 20: 303–27.

Jaganauth, D. 1987. "Predicate Structures in Guyanese Creole". MA thesis, University of the West Indies.

———. 1988. "Relative Time Reference in Guyanese Creole: Some Problems for Sentence-Level Analysis". Paper presented at the Seventh Biennial Conference of the Society for Caribbean Linguistics, Nassau.

Mufwene, S. 1984. "Observations on Time Reference in Jamaican and Guyanese Creoles". *English World-Wide* 4, no. 2: 199–229.

Pollard, V. 1989. "The Particle en in Jamaican Creole: A Discourse-Related Account". *English World-Wide* 10, no. 1: 55–68.

Schneider, E. 1990. "The Cline of Creoleness in English-Oriented Creoles and Semi-Creoles of the Caribbean. *English World-Wide* 11: 79–113.

Stolz, T. 1987. "The Development of the AUX-Category in Pidgins and Creoles: The Case of the Resultative-Perfective and its Relation to Anteriority". In *Historical Development of Auxiliaries,* ed. M. Harris and P. Ramat, 291–315. Berlin: Mouton de Gruyter.

Winford, D. 1993a. *Predication in Caribbean English Creoles.* Amsterdam: John Benjamins.

———. 1993b. "Variability in the Use of Perfect *have* in Trinidadian English". *Language Variation and Change* 5: 141–87.

———. 2000. "Tense and Aspect in Sranan and the Creole Prototype". In *Language Change and Language Contact in Pidgins and Creoles,* ed. J. McWhorther, 383–442. Amsterdam: John Benjamins.

Youssef, V. 1990. "The Early Development of Perfect Aspect: Adverbial, Verbal and Contextual Specification". *Journal of Child Language* 17: 295–312.

Chapter 3

Phonological Signatures of Tobagonian Speech in Trinidad and Tobago

WINFORD JAMES

Introduction

THIS CHAPTER SETS out to identify phonological elements in the language situation in Trinidad and Tobago that are typical of basilectal Tobagonian speech (TOB), but not of the mesolectal Trinidadian vernacular (TRIN), though they may be heard in Trinidad, especially in the speech of migrant Tobagonians. It comes in response to a focus on language awareness approaches in the teaching of Standard English (SE) in Creole-Standard contexts (see, for example, Robertson 1992a, 1992b, 1996; Craig 1999; and Siegel 2002); a long-standing interest among Caribbean linguists in determining the boundaries between co-existing varieties with a common lexicon (see, for example, Bailey 1971; Christie 1983; Devonish 1991); and very little literature on speech differences between Tobagonians and Trinidadians in the same polity. It presents the selected TOB elements or "signatures" as operations on English vocabulary, using pronunciations in standard varieties of English as convenient bases from which to identify them, as well as contrast them with the corresponding TRIN state of affairs. In using standard pronunciations as reference points, it is important to note that the intention is not to suggest that the TOB or TRIN operations/pronunciations derived from them, for the predominant lexifier input in the formative contact situation was undoubtedly substandard varieties (see, for example, Mufwene 2001, 34–36; Winford 2002, ch. 9). Rather, since accounts of the phonology of the latter are not readily available, the intention is to use a source that is.

Ideally, the identification of elements that are typically Tobagonian should be informed by comprehensive sociolinguistic surveys of (the various varieties and sociolects of) both Tobagonian and Trinidadian speech. However, such surveys are still to be done, so one must rely on the partial (socio)linguistic descriptions that are available and fill in gaps by recourse to the memory of informants. For data on TRIN, the chapter relies mainly on Solomon (1993) and various Trinidadian informants; for data on TOB, the chapter draws on James (1974), James and Youssef (2002), various Tobagonian informants[1] and audio tapes from the Tobago Language Project of the Department of Liberal Arts of the University of the West Indies.[2] Solomon (1993) is a "reference grammar" of the speech of Trinidad, incorporating findings from Winford's (1972) voluminous dissertation that provides a sociolinguistic description of two Trinidadian communities, one urban and the other rural; it is the most comprehensive description of Trinidadian speech available. Of the published TOB sources, James and Youssef (2002) offers the fullest account, describing, *inter alia*, the sound, verb, and noun systems, with a focus on the basilectal Creole and, to lesser extent, on other morphosyntatic differences from TRIN.

In a small plural polity like Trinidad and Tobago, where the population is composed of the descendants of Africans, Indians, Europeans, Chinese, Portuguese, among others; where there is much movement across social groupings; and, crucially, where there is constant inter-island movement of people, especially heavy migration of Tobagonians to Trinidad for better socio-economic opportunities, there is inevitably a mixing of elements from the different dialects and sociolects. This results in "competition-and-selection" and "restructuring", in the sense of Mufwene (2001, 12–13, 27–28, 157–62), and makes it extremely difficult to draw lines of demarcation. An important chain of questions therefore arises: Given the mingling of different ethnic groups (including Tobagonians), what exactly is TRIN?[3] When did it become TRIN? How does it remain TRIN? Is TRIN separable from TOB? If so, on what grounds? Assuming that in some sense Tobagonians speak differently than Trinidadians, how is that sense to be specified? In ethnolinguistic terms? What precisely are such terms? When Tobagonians migrate to Trinidad, complete with their island speech, does the latter become a part of TRIN, in original or restructured form? If so, when and by what criteria? Does the presumed importation of a new element reconstitute and possibly expand TRIN?

In order to show, ideally, that elements in the polity of Trinidad and Tobago are typical of TOB and not TRIN, there is clearly a need for at least the following: research into the demographic histories of the two islands, especially from union (in 1889) to date; a comprehensive survey of the distribution of elements between them; a quantification of frequency; and a definition of the notion of typicality – none of which exists. Even so, based on familiarity with the studies on TOB/TRIN and long and wide experience of the two varieties, I (as well as others who have a good social experience of the two islands) have developed a fairly good predictive sense of elements that the average Trinidadian who has spent her formative years in Trinidad would use in given communication contexts, as opposed to what the average Tobagonian would use who has spent hers in Tobago.[4] It is this sense that underlies the designation of elements as being typically TOB, and a critical component of it is the fact that the average Trinidadian, having grown up on a diet of mesolectal or intermediate Creole, finds it quite difficult to understand (basilectal) TOB. The designations anticipate the research identified above as being necessary.

Apart from differences that emerged from a comparison of the vowel inventories of TOB and TRIN, twelve elements have been selected as signatures:

1. The rhyme [e(r)] in words ending with optional [r]-coda preceded by a mid front vowel.
2. The rhyme [o(r)] in lexical words ending with optional [r]- coda preceded by a mid back vowel.
3. [a:] instead of [ɔ:] in syllables without an [r]-coda.
4. [a] instead of [ɔ/ɒ] in words whose nucleus is usually spelt "o".
5. The vowels [ɑ:] and [ɔ:] in [ɜ]-words.
6. The monophthong [ɛ] in "say", "make", "take", and "way".

7. The diphthong [ɛɪ] in free variation with [ɑɪ].
8. [ɑɪ], [ɛɪ] in [ɔɪ]-words.
9. Shift from [v] to [b]
10. [s]-deletion in initial [sC]-clusters.
11. Consonant rounding before [ɑɪ], [ɑ:].
12. Apheticization of more non-monosyllabic words.

This chapter has four sections, including this section. Section 2 provides a brief historical background to TOB and TRIN. Section 3 presents the typical TOB phonological elements and is divided into three parts, which consecutively analyse the signatures in the operation of vowels (1–8 in the list above), the signatures in the operation of consonants (9–11), and more extensive apheticization (12). Section 4 sums up and concludes the discussion.

BRIEF HISTORICAL BACKGROUND TO TOBAGONIAN AND TRINIDADIAN

Tobago and Trinidad are British ex-colonies with different histories.[5] Before they ended up as British colonies, both islands were inhabited by Amerindians and colonized by different European powers, with Tobago changing hands far more often than Trinidad. Apart from the British, the only Europeans to stay long enough in Tobago to leave a linguistic stamp were the French who, particularly in a twelve-year interregnum (1781–1793) between British and French occupation, left a number of toponyms that remain to this day.[6] Though the Spanish laid claim to Trinidad and Tobago at the end of the fifteenth century, they never established a colony in Tobago, preferring the larger Trinidad where they ruled until 1797. From the 1780s, the Spanish encouraged heavy migration of slaves, free Africans and coloureds from French-colonized islands such as Martinique, Guadeloupe, Haiti, Grenada, St Lucia and from Cayenne.

Effective British colonization of both islands took place relatively late in the sugar enterprise, from 1763 in respect to Tobago, and from 1797, thirty-seven years later, in respect to Trinidad. Both islands therefore got their supply of plantation labour not only from Africa directly, but from already-colonized islands, with Trinidad attracting the vast majority. From the onset of these phases of colonization to emancipation in 1838, the plantation continued to be the centre of slave labour and a context for the encounter of African languages, non-Standard Englishes, Standard English, and English- and French-lexicon Creoles. As long as it was a place where there were conditions such as field slavery versus house slavery, a far greater population of slaves than non-slave whites, intermixing of slaves from different tribes, and far more contact by the field slaves with whites who spoke non-Standard Englishes than with those who spoke Standard English, it favoured the creation and development, by the slaves, of Creole varieties of speech. Field slavery in particular would have favoured basilectalization, that is, the creation and development of speech more informed by patterns in substrate models and universal grammar than by patterns in superstrate models. House slavery would have favoured mesolectalization, that is, the creation and development of speech patterned on superstrate models and also on universal grammar.

In the case of Tobago, where the slaves were generally imported from islands already British-colonized (notably Barbados) as well as directly from Africa, they spoke an English-lexicon Creole and ancestral African languages. In the case of Trinidad, where they came in thousands from both French- and British-colonized islands as well as from Africa, the slaves spoke French Creole, English Creole and ancestral African languages.

From emancipation to date, both islands, while maintaining an economy that essentially follows the plantation model (Best 1968), have developed in different ways into open and highly diffuse societies. Significant aspects of that development include the following:

- Tobago losing its status as a self-governing colony in 1889, when it became a ward in the union of Trinidad and Tobago and was governed from Trinidad;
- receipt by both islands, between 1841 and 1861, of Africans from St Helena and Sierra Leone (where a Pidgin/Creole had developed) who had been "liberated" by the British Navy;
- arrival in Trinidad (but not in Tobago), between 1845 and 1914, of about 145,000 indentured labourers from India, who brought with them Indo-European and Dravidian languages, especially Bhojpuri (a variety closely related to Hindi);
- constant, heavy migration to Trinidad from other British-colonized territories, including Tobago, for better socio-economic opportunity;

- urbanization of certain areas in Trinidad and urban drift as a consequence;
- maintenance of a heavily agrarian economy in both islands, with Trinidad (but not Tobago) shifting to an industrialized, petroleum-based economy at the turn of the twentieth century;
- adoption of English as the official language;
- achievement by Trinidad and Tobago in 1962 of the status of independent nationhood;
- post-independence mass education with Standard English as the language;
- a rise in black consciousness through the Black Power movement of the early 1970s;
- a Tobagonian quest for autonomy from the late 1970s, culminating in partial self-government through watered-down versions of the Tobago House of Assembly in 1980 and 1996;
- encouragement of tourism from North America and Europe; and
- globalization and advances in telecommunications technology.

In the evolution of the islands from the status of slave colonies to that of an independent twin-island state, Tobago has not had Trinidad's heterogeneity of input into its population, has kept losing significant proportions of that population (including significant numbers of its intelligentsia) to Trinidad, has had a more conservative lifestyle focused around agriculture, animal husbandry, fishing, domestic arts and trades, as well as government services, and, after union in 1889, has been the lower-prestige island in social terms. By and large, Trinidadians have not seen it as a society to integrate into, so its resident population has had the space to maintain (basilectal) language forms for strictly Tobagonian socialization, mostly in the (rural) villages, while developing (mesolectal and acrolectal) language forms for communication in Scarborough, the capital, and other urbanizing districts, as well as with a wider public, including Trinidadians.

Trinidad, for its part, has been demographically far more heterogeneous and has had a linguistic situation in which, by sheer force of greater numbers of speakers, an English-lexicon has displaced a French-lexicon, and the English-lexicon Creole has been considerably influenced by Bhojpuri (especially lexically and phonologically) and French Creole (especially grammatically).[7]

For some time now, both islands have come under the influence of North American varieties of English by way of the media, tourism, and relocation and frequent travel to North America.

As a result of the different histories, Trinidad today has a mesolectal English Creole plus a local variety of Standard English, influenced by Creole sound patterns and by lexical items derived from the languages being brought in at different times, while Tobago has these two varieties but also a basilectal Creole. It is this Creole which distinguishes Tobago linguistically from Trinidad and from which the phonological elements to be highlighted as signatures of TOB speech will be drawn.

DISTINCTIVE TOB PHONOLOGICAL ELEMENTS

As indicated in section 2, the speech of Tobago, but not that of Trinidad, contains an English-lexicon basilect as a result of past and present socio-historical factors. It was also pointed out that French Creole and Bhojpuri have been influential in the pronunciation of Trinidadian, but not Tobagonian, vowels. We should expect, therefore, that the vowel system of the TOB basilect would be different from that of the TRIN mesolect.

Signatures in the Operation of Vowels

Solomon analyses the TRIN system taken as a whole as:

Simple Vowels
(Adapted from Solomon 1993, 7, 70–71)

	Long				*Short*		
	F	C	B		F	C	B
H	i	ɜ	u		I		U
M	e		o/õ		ɛ/ɛ̃	ə	ɔ
			ɔː				
L		aː				a	

Diphthongs

    aɪ   ɔːɪ   ɔw

and the earlier, more basilectal French Creole system as (adapted from Solomon 1993, 8, 70–71):

i	u
e	o/õ
ɛ/ɛ̃	ɔ
a	

Diphthongs

ɑɪ   ɔːɪ   ɔw

All the vowels in TRIN as a whole are present in TOB, complete with length distinctions; it is at the level of the basilect that there are differences. By way of comparison, the TOB basilectal system is as follows:

Simple Vowels

Long				Short		
	F	C	B	F	C	B
H	i		u	I/Ĩ		U/Ũ
M	e		o/õ	ɛ/ɛ̃	ə	ɔ/ɔ̃
	ɛː		ɔː			
L		aː/ãː			a/ã	

Diphthongs

sɪ   ɑɪ   ɔw

This analysis varies somewhat from the one in James (1974) in that it treats [e, o] as long and includes the nasalized vowels [Ĩ, ɛ̃, õ], as indicated respectively by the minimal pairs [I] "she/he" versus [Ĩ] "(remote) past marker", [dɛ] "there" versus [dɛ̃] {"they/them"}, [sɔ] "so" versus [sɔ̃] "some"'; and includes the long vowel [ɛː], as in [ɛːz] "ear(s)".

Several differences would have been immediately noticed between this revised system and Solomon's basilectal TRIN system:

12. there are length differences in basilectal TOB, suggesting a less homophonous vocabulary than in basilectal TRIN;

13. all the short vowels and two of the long vowels in basilectal TOB have nasalized versions, whereas in TRIN only [ɛ, o] are nasalized;
14. basilectal TOB has [ɛɪ,], but basilectal TRIN does not; and
15. whereas TRIN has [ɔːɪ], basilectal TOB does not.

Simple tabular matching of the vowel systems of different varieties can reveal facts like the number of vowels and diphthongs in the different inventories, their distribution in the vowel grid, and length distinctions. But they can say very little about the phonotactics, morphological application, or discourse use of the systems in the varieties to which they belong. For our purposes, the important thing about the combinatorial capacity and discourse use of the vowel systems of both TOB and TRIN is their effect on English vocabulary. It must be said immediately that the basilectal TOB system operates on that vocabulary in ways that are noticeably different from the ways in which the TRIN system does. Some of the more striking effects are described in the sub-subsections below.

The Rhyme [e(r)] in Words Ending with Optional [r]-Coda Preceded by Mid Front Vowel

In basilectal pronunciation, the rhyme at the end of English words like the following, which in some metropolitan varieties have an optional *[r]*-coda preceded by a lax mid front diphthong ([Iə] or [ɛə] (Wells 2000), is [e(r)]: "beer", "near", "hear", "pear", "wear", "pair", "fair", "fare", "prepare", "where", "here" and "there".

The vowel is tense, mid front, and monophthongal, and the *[r]*-coda is optional: [be(r), ne(r), he(r), pe(r), we(r), pe(r), fe(r), fe(r), pripe(r), we(r), he(r), de(r)].

The last three words are particularly interesting because, being (deictic) grammatical rather than lexical words, they also have the alternative rhyme [ɛ], which is lax and shorter and is in fact the preferred one. In basilectal TOB generally, grammatical words tend to favour shorter lax vowels for easier system functionality (James and Youssef 2002, 101ff; James 2003) although, after achieving grammatical status, their vowels tend to be used in homophonous words with non-emphasized lexical meaning. *Wɛ* is a WH-question word and relativizer; *dɛ* is a demonstrative suffix, pronoun, and adverb; and *hɛ* is an adverb and benefactive particle meaning something like "take this".

Interestingly, while the longer tense [e] collocates with an *[r]*-coda, the shorter lax [ɛ] does not: *wɛ* versus **wɛr*, *hɛ* versus **hɛr*, *dɛ* versus **dɛr*. Further, the [e(r)] rhyme is used by some (usually older) speakers when special emphasis of message is desired, as in Speaker B's reply in:

Speaker A: [wɛ yu sɛ ɪ dɛ agɛn? ova dɛ?]
"Where did you say it was? Over there?"

Speaker B: [no. ova der!]
"No. Over there!"

In contrast with this basilectal TOB state of affairs, the mesolectal/acrolectal TRIN rhyme, according to Solomon (1993, 3, 15–17), is [ɪə] for some speakers but [ɛə] for others (never both in the same speaker); there is no *[r]*-coda.[8] But Solomon also proposes the rhymes [e] and [ɛ] in "the more basilectal varieties [of TRIN]" (p. 17), with the [ɛ] usually used in "r words" like "ears" [ɛz] and "where" [wɛ], for example. In basilectal TOB, however, "ears" would be pronounced either as [ez] or [ɛːz] and "where" either as (non-emphatic) [wɛ] or (emphatic) [wɛː].

The Rhyme [o(r)] in Lexical Words Ending with Optional [r]-Coda Preceded by Mid Back Vowel

Just as in respect of English words which have an optional *[r]*-coda (in some varieties) preceded by a lax mid front diphthong (Wells 2000), the basilectal rhyme is an optional *[r]*-coda preceded by a tense mid front monophthong, in respect of English words (but only lexical ones) that have an optional *[r]*-coda preceded by a lax mid back diphthong, the basilectal rhyme is the optional *[r]*-coda preceded by a tense mid back vowel. The basilectal pronunciations of the words "before", "door", "four", "more", "pour" and "sore" are [bifo(r), do(r), fo(r), mo(r), po(r), so(r)].

But the words have to be lexical rather than grammatical. All the words, including "more", are lexical ones. In respect of a grammatical word such as "tore", there is no basilectal [to(r)], and the reason is that the word encodes the semantic value of "past" (and, also, did not get reanalysed as a bare verb because, perhaps, it did not have the frequency of, say, irregular "left"), and so is not available for basilectal pronunciation. But in respect of a word like "bore", which can be both a bare lexical verb and the irregular simple past tense form of the verb "bear", only the lexical verb is available for basilectal pronunciation.

It appears, therefore, that in basilectal TOB phonotactics, the phonological feature [+tense] is critical in the correlation between the mid front/back vowels [e/o] and word-final [r]. No such correlation has been reported in the literature on TRIN, nor have I heard it from any of my TRIN informants. The phenomenon seems to be a TOB signature in the Trinidad and Tobago language situation.

[aː] Instead of [ɔː] in Syllables Without [r]-Coda

Words with codas other than [r] preceded by the long lax mid back vowel [ɔː] are produced in TOB with the long lax central vowel [aː]. The pronunciations of words such as "bawl", "born", "God", "gone", "jaw", "Lord", "maul", "mortar", "talk" and "water" are therefore [baːl, baːn, gaːd, gaːn, jaː, laːd, maːl, maːta, taːk, waːta].

In TRIN (and mesolectal TOB), these words will be typically produced with [ɔː], just as in Standard English pronunciations.

[a] Instead of [ɔ/ɒ] in Words Whose Nucleus Is Usually Spelt "o"

The vowel [a] is perhaps the most ubiquitous in TOB (James and Youssef 2003, 74, 79), and one of its effects is that it distinguishes the TOB from the TRIN speaker in the pronunciation of the vowel in monosyllabic words such as "dodge", "fob", "flop", "knock", and "long", and of the first vowel in non-monosyllabic words such as "bother", "common", "confident", "doctor", "follow" and "modern". The (first) vowel is [ɔ/ɒ] in standard varieties, is stressed and is usually spelt with an "o". The TRIN speaker typically pronounces words like these with the vowel [ɔ].

TOB [a] is not only used as described above but is also central to that variety's verb system in the form of copulative and imperfective *a* (James and Youssef 2003, 79, 102–5, 118–19). It is therefore a highly frequent element in Tobagonian speech; it is also highly frequent as both a grammatical and lexical item in most of the other Caribbean Creoles – for example, Jamaican, Guyanese, Grenadian, Vincentian (see Cassidy and Le Page 1980; Winford 1993; Allsopp 1996). Its high saliency ensures that Trinidadians see it as a sound that contrasts with a corresponding, more prestigious one that they use, [ɔ], and some of them have been known to deride and stigmatize its use.[9]

The Vowels [aː], [ɔː] in [ɜ]-Words

In words where some standard metropolitan varieties have the vowel [ɜ] (Wells 2000), basilectal TOB has [aː], and mesolectal TOB/TRIN have [ɔː], as in monosyllabic words such as "learn" and "search", and the stressed syllable of non-monosyllabic words like "MUR.mur" and "con.CERN". In respect of some words, however, there is no basilectal vowel, only mesolectal [ɔː], for example, "dirt", "purge", "perks" and "surname", which will be [dɔːt], [pɔːj], [pɔːks], and [sɔːnem]. The reason for the lack of a basilectal vowel is not clear, but one effect is that homophony with "dart" and "parks" (which have the same vowel as the basilectal one – a vowel that is coincidentally acrolectal in these words) is disallowed. The three vowels are used in the same words in the Trinidad and Tobago language situation, as, for example, in "search", which is [sɜč] acrolectally, [sɔːč] mesolectally, and [saːč] basilectally, but the basilectal vowel pronunciation [aː] is typically Tobagonian and will, in the fashion of [a] in the previous subsection, be stigmatized by Trinidadians.

In some words, particularly names and grammatical words, [ɔː] is shortened to [ɔ], as in "Philbert" [filbɔt], "Albert" [albɔt], "turn" [tɔn], and "first" [fɔs], but the process applies to the general language situation in Trinidad and Tobago and is not peculiar to Tobago. In particular reference to the grammatical application of [ɔ], a few observations would seem to be in order. [fɔs] is a derivative of (earlier) Trinidadian French Creole "afos" (< 17C French "à force") (Allsopp 1996, 12) and, at a particular level of speech, becomes "first", which is the result of "folk etym[ology] and false refinement of . . . a fos" (Allsopp 1996, 232); it is a typically TRIN word that has been adopted by TOB. On the other hand, [tɔn] (from "turn") is a perspectival preposition with a translation such as "according to" (James and Youssef 2002, 166) and is typically a TOB word but one which, unlike the case of [fɔs], has not been adopted by TRIN. Interestingly, unlike [fɔs] > "first", there is apparently no [tɔn] > "turn" (at least, I have not heard it), but it is a potential development.

The Monophthong [ɛ] in "Say", "Make", "Take" and "Way"

Basilectal [ɛ] is used in a trio of high-frequency lexical verbs, "say", "make" and "take" (cf. Francis and Kučera 1982), as well as in the verbal complement "way" that is derived by aphesis from the adverbial particle "away". [sɛ] and [mɛk] join [-wk] in also being grammatical words and are therefore particularly salient in TOB. [sɛ] is a complementizer and report introducer, while [mɛk] is a question word (meaning "why") and reason clause introducer. None of the four basilectal words is typical of TRIN, either lexically or grammatically.

The Diphthong [ɛɪ] in Free Variation with [aɪ]

In words like "by/bye/buy/boy", "bite", "lie", "mind" and "shine", the standard diphthong [aɪ] is used in both TOB and TRIN, but in TOB only, it varies with the less frequent, somewhat stigmatized [ɛɪ]. The diphthong is not one of the three Solomon (1993, 7–8) proposes for TRIN.

[aɪ, ɛɪ] in [ɔɪ]-Words

We come now to the final TOB phonological feature that distinguishes TOB from TRIN – the use of [aɪ, ɛɪ] where mesolectal TOB, TRIN and standard varieties have [ɔɪ]. The TOB diphthongs affect words such as "anoint", "appoint", "boisterous", "boy", "coin", "hoity-toity", "joy", "join", "loiter", "oil", "paranoid", "Roy" and "spoil". There are words that will perhaps sound odd with the pronunciation, such as "coy" and "foible", but only because they are infrequently used in TOB discourse. And there are homophones that, as more and more people speak less-creolized varieties, are being disambiguated by the deployment of [ɔɪ], such as [tɔɪ] "toy" versus [taɪ] "tie", and [graɪn] "grind" versus [grɔɪn] "groin". The deployment of [ɔɪ] also necessarily means that [ɔɪ] and [aɪ] are in free variation in the overall language situation in respect of [ɔɪ]-words (for example, "toy" [tɪ, tɔɪ] (but not "tie", which is already an [aɪ]-word).

As noted before, the Trinidadian aversion to contrastive [a] (part of the diphthong [aɪ]) and the lack of [ɛɪ] in the TRIN vowel inventory mean that the pronunciation of [aɪ, ɛɪ] in words where standard [ɔɪ] is used instead is a TOB signature.

Signatures in the Operation of Consonants

There are at least three differences between basilectal TOB and TRIN in the operation of their consonants on English vocabulary. They relate to restructuring of fricative [v] as plosive [b]; [s]-deletion from initial [sC]-clusters; and rounding, via the approximant [w], of word-initial [b] and [(s)p] before the diphthongal nucleus [aɪ], on the one hand, and of word-initial [g] before [a:] in the restructuring of the phrase "go on", on the other.

Shift from [v] to [b]

In basilectal TOB, [v] becomes [b] in common words like "crave" [kreb], "craven" [krebn], "heave" [hib], "love" [lɔb], "lover" [lɔba], "governor" [gɔbna], "heavy" [(h)ɛbɪ], "liver" [lɪba] and "gravel" [gra:bl].

As the list suggests, it occurs whether the [v] is in coda or onset position (as, for example, in [kreb] and [krebn], respectively). It does not seem to be motivated by any phonological condition. But, in certain contexts, it does have the effect of communicating a negative attitude, as, for example, in (a possible reading of) the following proverbs:

[kreb] aal, luuz aal. (displeasure)
"Crave all, lose all."

Huu konchri [lob], it mek [gobna]. (Gentle mockery? Displeasure?)
"Whomever a country loves, it makes a governor."

In this sentence it expresses discomfort or frustration:

Da doti-ya [ɛbɪ], bō.
"This soil is extremely heavy."

The material aspect of the shift is that fricativity gives way to plosivity or, in other words, spread lips (in the articulation of [v]) are drawn in (for the articulation of [b]). I suspect that, historically, the lips' observable change of position was material to the communication of the negative emotion; speakers may have deliberately switched to the plosive as part of an overt resistance to their subordinate condition.

This kind of phonological signalling does not occur in TRIN, and is dying out in decreolizing Tobago.

[s]-Deletion in Initial [sC]-Clusters

[s]-deletion in TOB is the non-pronunciation of [s] in word-initial consonant clusters composed of [s{k, kw, m, p, t}] in (common) words such as:

skin, skip, skate, skirt
squander, squawk, squeeze
smile, smell, smart, small, smoke
spit, spend, speed, speak, spoon, spoil, spine
stone, stink, still, story, start, stick, style

It makes homophones out of such sounds as [kɪn], [kɪp], [ton], [tɪl], [taɪl], [pɪt], [pn], and [pik], which have both their English meanings in those shapes and the meanings of the words beginning with [s]. But it also produces new words like [pwaɪl] "spoil", [kwanda] "squander", [kwiz] "squeeze", [mɛl] "smell", [mok] "smoke", [kwa:k] "squawk", and [paɪt] "spite".

Synchronically, [s]-deletion seems to be a phonological strategy for emphatically communicating a speaker's negative attitude towards something or somebody (disapproval, displeasure, gentle mockery, discomfort and so on), as the following sentences (can be produced to) suggest:

Di machris [tiŋk] a pii. (displeasure)
"The mattress stinks (very badly) of pee."

Wēt, gyal. [torɪ] de fu taak. (gentle mockery)
"Wait, girl. I have a very interesting (negative) piece of news (about somebody) to tell you."

Wen hi [ta:t] fu fiil pēn so, hi run go a dakta. (gentle mockery)
"When he really started to feel pain, he paid a hurried visit to the doctor."

Di honjred dalaz mi giv am fu laas am di wiik, hi no [pɛn] aal in wan dē? (disapproval)
"The one hundred dollars I gave him to last him for the week, he spent it all in one day, would you believe it?"

Shi [pwaɪl] mi jres, se shi a siimschris. (displeasure)
"She ruined my dress, and she calls herself a seamstress."

Mi [tumɔk] a hat mi. (discomfort)
"My stomach hurts."

The articulation of the restructured [sk, sp, st]-words is straightforward: both consonants in the cluster are voiceless and the speaker has only to pronounce the obstruent remaining as the onset of the words. But the articulation of the [sm]-words is a different matter: for the labial nasal that remains after the deletion, the speaker (apparently compensatorily) expels air through the nose and draws the lips slightly inwards in delay of voice onset.[10] One result is a phonemic distinction between both types of [m]. For example, [maɪl] "mile" would be different from [smaɪl > maɪl] "smile".

[s]-deletion seems to favour initial clusters that contain a voiceless obstruent. In other words, the [s] drops out before another voiceless, low-sonority sound.[11] The process leaves intact permissible standard sequences containing approximants, for example, [sl, sr, sw, sy], which turn out to be more sonorous sounds. In light of this, [s]-deletion from [sm] seems peculiar, especially as words beginning with [sn] keep the sibilant. [s]-deletion does not occur in TRIN, and it is a fading signature of TOB under the pressure of decreolizing forces.

Consonant Rounding Before [aɪ, a:]

The phenomenon of consonant rounding is the copying of the roundness feature of the diphthong [ɔ] onto the word-initial consonants [b, (s)p, g] when [b, (s)p] occur before the nucleus [ɔɪ] in English words and [g] before [ɔ:] in a restructured version of the verb phrase "go on". There are very few words with [b, (s)p] followed by the glide [ɔɪ]. The *Longman Dictionary of Contemporary English* (1978) lists five b-words, six p-words and one sp-word. The rounding in the different categories of words is illustrated below:

"boy" [bʷɔɪ]
"poison" [pʷɔɪzn]
"spoil" [spʷɔɪl]
"go on" [gwɔ:n]

The pronunciations occur in both mesolectal TRIN and TOB. The rounding is clearly regressive and is due to the presence of a rounded long low back vowel or a diphthongal glide that starts off with a rounded mid back vowel and ends with a lax mid front vowel. The long vowel or the whole glide seems responsible, not simply the short or rounded back vowel, because words like *[pʷɔt] "pot" and *[gʷɔ] "go" "future marker", for example, do not occur.

But the interesting thing is that basilectal TOB pronunciations occur, as in the following:

[bʷaɪ]
[pʷaɪzn]
[spʷaɪl]
[gʷa:n]

The fact that the consonants could remain rounded before the glide [aɪ], which contains the contrastive [a] stigmatized by Trinidadians, makes the phenomenon a TOB signature. The phenomenon is phonologically unusual, especially as the rounding does not occur in words like "bile" and "pile", which have only [aɪ] as a nucleus.[12]

The consonant rounding before [aɪ] has an interesting effect as well: the creation of phonemic contrasts between [b, p] and [bʷ, pʷ]. [bʷaɪ] "boy" contrasts with [baɪ] "bye/buy";[13] [bʷaɪl] "boil" contrasts with [baɪl] "bile"; [pʷaɪl] (<[(s)pʷaɪl]) "spoil" contrasts with [paɪl] "pile"; and [gʷa:n] "go on" contrasts with [ga:n] "gone".

Apheticization of More Non-Monosyllabic Words

Aphesis, the optional deletion of initial unstressed non-morphemic vocalic syllables, is a natural process in language evolution (see, for example, Alexander 1988). Alexander shows that it has been used normally in natural English discourse to expand vocabulary. It occurs in TOB and TRIN in, for example, "enough", "allow" and "about", but as it seems to be used much more extensively in TOB, it is treated here as a signature of TOB.

It is used in TOB, but apparently not in TRIN, in, for example, the following high-frequency words: "abandon", "accompany", "accoutrements",[14] "accustomed", "above", "alone", "amount", "apologize", "effrontery", "attach" and "away". So in TOB, you will hear these words pronounced without the initial [a, ə or ɪ], alongside their pronunciations with these sounds.

Why TOB, but not TRIN, should apheticize those words is not very clear. The process has been regular and long-standing enough in English, even though, synchronically, some effects are not fully apparent. For example, as Alexander (1988, 29–31) observes, the *Oxford English Dictionary* dates "aback > back" to 1549, "about > bout" to 1602, "adown > down" to 1548, and "away > way" to 1548. And it lists the following apheticisms, among others, which may not be readily apparent: "abate > bate", "acute > cute", "amend > mend", "apply > ply", "attempt > tempt" and "oppose > pose". Then there is the obvious advantage of speeding up speech through a reduction in the number of syllables, especially from two to one. It may be that the phonological motivation is not merely stresslessness of initial onsetless syllables, but greater preference for initial syllables with onsets, but with the onsetless ones being deleted when they are also stressless. TOB apheticization of the words probably lies in the degree of social stigmatization in the different islands, with Trinidad, as the sociopolitically dominant island, having a much lower tolerance of apheticisms than Tobago, the sociopolitically subordinate island.

SUMMARY AND CONCLUSION

This chapter has shown that there are considerable phonological differences between the basilectal speech of Tobago and the mesolectal vernacular of

Trinidad. It identified and analysed twelve elements as typical of Tobagonian speech in the polity of Trinidad and Tobago. In the mixed varilingual language situation that exists in Trinidad and Tobago (Youssef 1996), they are essentially elements out of a basilectal English-lexicon Creole phonology that sets Tobago linguistically apart from Trinidad. Some, probably all, of them may be heard in Trinidad, given the migration of Tobagonians (and other basilect-speaking West Indians) to that island for better socio-economic opportunities and higher standards of living, but they are not considered to be elements that the average Trinidadian who has spent her formative years in Trinidad would typically use. The designations are made in the absence of either comprehensive sociolinguistic surveys of Trinidad and Tobago or an empirically based notion of typicality, but they could be a stimulus for (dis)confirmatory research.

Apart from testing the validity of the twelve signatures, future research could also seek to answer questions such as: Is Tobagonian speech more nasalized than Trinidadian? Does it manifest more apocope and h-dropping? Is its vocabulary more homophonous? Is the Tobagonian accent different from the Trinidadian accent?

NOTES

1. Including myself.
2. This is a project in which speech data from various villages and districts in Tobago was tape-recorded during the 1990s to be used for various kinds of analysis.
3. Or TOB, for that matter.
4. Solomon (1993, 2) says, on the basis only of the published research, that the differences between TOB and TRIN seem to be "considerable".
5. Historical accounts are provided in James (1997) for Tobago and in Solomon (1993) for Trinidad.
6. For example, L'Anse Fourmi, Parliatuvier, Les Coteaux, Lambeau and Bon Accord.
7. Indeed, so noticeable has been this grammatical influence that, for explanatory purposes, Solomon (1993, 92–93) treats French Creole as if it was the underlying Trinidadian basilect of which the English-lexicon Creole is partially a relexification.
8. Solomon analyses the schwa as "a glide representing syllable-final-r" as in words like "beer" and "bear" (1993, 3).
9. Some Tobagonians who have either moved up in society or been reared in homes that rejected the basilect have also been known to deride the use of "contrastive" [a].
10. The articulation of underived [m] does not involve this delay.
11. The process is reminiscent of the loss of the rightmost member of codas composed of two voiceless consonants, as in "last", "task", "left" > [laːs, taːs, lef]. In the case of [s]-deletion from initial [sC]-clusters, the reverse happens: it is the leftmost member of the cluster, [s], that is dropped. But in each case, only consonants with the same voicing state are involved.
12. It should be noted, however, that [pʷ, bʷ] are permitted word-initial sequences in some African languages (see Bendor-Samuel 1971; Welmers 1973).
13. But it is to be noted that, for some speakers, [bai] also means "boy".
14. Reanalysed as [kʊčʊmɛnts].

References

Alexander, J. 1988. "Aphesis in English". *Word* 39, no. 1: 29–65.
Allsopp, R., ed. 1996. *Dictionary of Caribbean English Usage*. Oxford: Oxford University Press.
Bailey, B. 1971. Jamaican Creole: "Can Dialect Boundaries be Defined?" In *Pidginization and Creolization of Languages*, ed. D. Hymes, 341–48. Cambridge: Cambridge University Press.
Bendor-Samuel, J. 1971. "Ten Nigerian Tone Systems". *Studies in Nigerian Languages* 4. Jos, Nigeria: Institute of Linguistics; Kano, Nigeria: Centre for the Study of Nigerian Languages.
Best, L. 1968. "Outline of a Model of Pure Plantation Economy". *Social and Economic Studies* 17, no. 3 (September): 283–326.
Cassidy, F., and R. Le Page, eds. 1980. *Dictionary of Jamaican English*. Cambridge: Cambridge University Press.
Christie, P. 1983. "In Search of the Boundaries of Caribbean Creoles". In *Studies in Caribbean Language: Papers from the Third Biennial Conference of the SCL, 1980*, ed. L. Carrington in collaboration with D. Craig and R. Todd-Dandare, 13–22. St Augustine, Trinidad: Society for Caribbean Linguistics.
Craig, D. 1999. *Teaching Language and Literacy: Policies and Procedures for Vernacular Situations*. Georgetown, Guyana: Educational and Development Services.
Devonish, H. 1991. "A Reanalysis of the Phonological System of Jamaican Creole". Occasional Paper No. 24. St Augustine, Trinidad: Society for Caribbean Linguistics.
Francis, N., and H. Kučera. 1982. *Frequency Analysis of English Usage: Lexicon and Grammar*. Boston: Houghton Mifflin.
James, W. 1974. "Some Similarities between Jamaican Creole and the Dialect of Tobago". Caribbean Studies thesis, University of the West Indies.
———.1997. "Students' TAM Errors in the Context of the Speech of Tobago". PhD diss., University of the West Indies.
———. 2003. "The Role of Tone and Rhyme Structure in the Organization of Grammatical Morphemes in Tobagonian". In *Phonology and Morphology of Creole Languages*, ed. I. Plag, 165–92. Tübingen: Max Niemeyer Verlag.
James, W., and V. Youssef. 2002. *The Languages of Tobago: Genesis, Structure and Perspectives*. St Augustine, Trinidad: School of Continuing Studies.
Longman's Dictionary of Contemporary English. 1978. Harlow, Essex: Longman.
Mufwene, S. 2001. *The Ecology of Language Evolution*. Cambridge: Cambridge University Press.
Robertson, I. 1992a. "Towards a Meaningful Language Education Policy in Caribbean

States". Paper presented at the Second Biennial Conference of University of the West Indies Faculties of Education, St Augustine, Trinidad.

———. 1992b. "Applying Creole Linguistics". Paper presented at the Eighth Biennial Conference of the Society for Caribbean Linguistics, Cave Hill, Barbados.

———. 1996. "Language Education Policy 1: Towards a Rational Approach for Caribbean States". In *Caribbean Language Issues: Old and New*, ed. P. Christie, 112–19. Kingston: The Press, University of the West Indies.

Siegel, J. 2002. "Bringing Creole into the Classroom: Views from Outside the Caribbean". Paper presented at the Fourteenth Biennial Conference of the Society for Caribbean Linguistics, 14–17 August.

Solomon, D. 1993. *The Speech of Trinidad: A Reference Grammar*. St Augustine, Trinidad: School of Continuing Studies.

Welmers, W. 1973. *African Language Structures*. Berkeley: University of California Press.

Youssef, Valerie. 1996. "Varilingualism: The Competence Underlying Code-Mixing in Trinidad and Tobago". *Journal of Pidgin and Creole Languages* 1, no. 1: 1–22.

Wells, J.C. 2000. *Longman Pronunciation Dictionary*. Essex: Pearson.

Winford, Donald. 1972. "A Sociolinguistic Description of Two Communities in Trinidad". PhD diss., University of York.

———. 1993. *Predication in Caribbean English Creoles*. Creole Language Library 10. Amsterdam: John Benjamins.

———. 2002. *An Introduction to Contact Linguistics*. Oxford: Blackwell.

Chapter 4

ON THE STATUS OF DIPHTHONGS IN JAMAICAN
Mr Vegas Pronounces
HUBERT DEVONISH

EVER SINCE THE BEGINNING of the 1980s, modern Jamaican popular music has been dominated by musical forms loosely labelled dancehall. Critics of dancehall as a genre argue that, by comparison with Jamaican music of the "golden" era of classical reggae, from the late 1960s to the end of the 1970s, dancehall is simpler in its musical form. They also argue that its lyrics, where not outright nonsensical, tend to deal almost exclusively with sexual vulgarity and the glorification of violence. For its critics, dancehall represents little or nothing of value in the Jamaican cultural and musical scene. Rather, its emergence is seen as part of a more generalized descent into societal, cultural and musical decadence: Jamaica would be better off if dancehall had never emerged.

With its synthesized rhythm tracks and a tendency to monotony in the musical sense (that is, the use of a restricted number of tones or musical notes), dancehall is indeed probably simpler than classical reggae. Even if, as well, one concedes on the contentious issue of sexual vulgarity and violence, it is far from proven that dancehall as a genre is totally without value.

In order to be pleasing to its public, an artistic genre has to maintain a balance between what is predictable and what is not. Too much predictability is boring. Too much unpredictability is confusing. Dancehall is a genre which consists of music and lyrics. It is certainly arguable, therefore, that dancehall has become simpler than classical reggae and, as a consequence, more predictable in one area, its musical form. As a result, compensatory changes would have had to be made to the structure of the other area, that of its lyrics, if the genre were to develop and maintain its popularity. Lyrics could be expected to have increased in complexity and levels of unpredictability. Given the long established position of dancehall as the most popular variety of reggae in Jamaica, we can hypothesize that such adjustments have indeed taken place.

If creativity and innovation in dancehall, when compared to classical reggae, have shifted from musical form to lyrical form, analytical tools appropriate to studying lyrical form become essential for scholars of the genre. However, the scientific study of the language forms which make up music lyrics is more obviously the field of the linguist than that of the literary or musical critic. This is particularly true when studying the phonetics and phonology of the lyrics rather than the imagery and metaphor. Much of the creativity in dancehall, therefore, may have fled beyond the domains accessible to the technical competence of those who traditionally study and write about popular Jamaican music. It may now dwell in areas only accessible to the linguist. This chapter is a linguist's contribution to the study of precisely one such case. At the same time, however, the chapter tries to demonstrate why linguists, for their own narrow disciplinary purposes, can and should pursue such cases of creativity, and how the insights gained could be used to develop an understanding of the form and structure of the phonological system of Jamaican (Creole).

WHERE CAN WE FIND THE RULES OF A LANGUAGE?

When linguists study the structure of a language, they want to identify the rules which govern that language. Their aim is to discover what permits speakers to produce an infinite number of well-formed sentences and yet allows these speakers to immediately recognize ill-formed ones. In every speech community, these rules involve knowledge possessed even by the unschooled and the illiterate. Often, speakers will claim to be able to state rules which they imagine operate in their language. However, when one attempts to form sentences using such rules, utterances are produced that would be rejected by the very person who proposed the rule. The problem of what constitutes genuine rules operating in the heads of speakers, as distinct from bogus ones which speakers may declare that they use, exists in all language situations. This is true whether one is dealing with standardized languages like English or non-standard vernacular languages such as Jamaican (Creole).

A classic example, one oft repeated for Jamaican, is a rule which states that the form *dem* is the plural marker in Jamaican and that it is the equivalent of the English *-s*. Let us look at an example of this claim being made. Smith (2001, A5), having declared herself an authority on her native language, Jamaican, goes on to state: "The syntax does not necessarily lend itself to equivalence ... In a possible lesson singular and plural nouns:– Boys, books and beds would be 'bwoy dem', 'book dem' and 'bed dem' " (Smith 2001, A5).

The problem is that the Jamaican equivalents of the English sentences "I do not like boys", "I do not like books" and "I do not like beds" are *mi no lov bwaai, mi no lov buk* and *mi no lov bed,* respectively. The Jamaican equivalent of the English forms "boys", "books" and "beds" is the unmarked form of the noun as in *bwaai, buk* and *bed.* The sentences **mi no lov bwaai dem, *mi no lov buk dem* and **mi no lov bed dem,* would be judged to be unacceptable sentences by speakers of Jamaican. This is because the form *dem* is only used as a plural marker of definite noun phrases. Examples of definite noun phrases would include those which involve the use of the definite article, *di,* as in *mi no lov di bwaai dem, mi no lov di buk dem* and *mi no lov di bed dem,* "I do not like the boys/the books/the beds."

Since the opinions of native speakers about the rules of their language can be so unreliable, linguists do need to try to observe language behaviour, recording and studying what is actually said. In describing a language, linguists set themselves the goal of identifying what speakers know at the instinctive and intuitive level that allows them to produce an infinite number of well-formed utterances.

The study of the phonology of a language variety usually starts with recording and analysing sounds as they present themselves in actual speech. However, the resulting inventory of phones and phonemes does not, on its own, tell us a great deal about the intuitive system which speakers use to produce the sounds of meaningful utterances in their specific language. Neither can this be identified by asking speakers for their opinions or by merely describing the structure of a body of utterances produced in the language. At the same time, it is not possible to open the head of a speaker and see the rules that have been internalized by the speaker.

The only option available to the linguist is to follow a procedure of description and analysis which is so rigorous that its results might be presumed to represent rules that exist in the head of the speaker. In order to develop a model of these intuitive rules, linguists propose that their grammatical descriptions should achieve three levels of adequacy. The linguist's grammatical description should be "observationally adequate". It should, therefore, account for the particular data on which it is based. It should also be "descriptively adequate". This requires that the rules proposed as applying to a small set of data in the language are special cases of more general rules applying to a wider body of data in the language. Linguists presume that children, in acquiring their native languages, will opt for rules with the widest degree of generality (Newmeyer 1986, 73).

There is additionally, however, the problem of selecting from a range of descriptively adequate grammars. If one took a non-linguistic example, the rising and setting of the sun may, potentially, be explained in more than one way. It could be that the sun orbits the earth. It may, on the other hand, be the earth's rotation around its axis that produces the rising and setting of the sun. There has to be a basis for selecting between these two possible explanations. The process of selection, therefore, has to be based on a set of clear principles. Linguists seek to identify such principles and employ them in the writing of what they call "explanatorily adequate" grammars. A grammatical description which is explanatorily adequate would, linguists hope, be a model of the intuitive processes which take place in the heads of members of a speech community as they hear and speak their language (Newmeyer 1986, 73).

INSIDE HEADS: ENTERING THROUGH LANGUAGE GAMES AND POETRY

One aspect of the intuitive language knowledge possessed by speakers involves what they know of the phonology of their language, in this case

Jamaican. Speakers of a language very often give evidence of their intuitive knowledge of their language when they deliberately restructure language for certain special uses. In many speech communities, language play, in the form of gibberish and other manipulations of regular language, is employed in order to disguise what is being said. The use of language play as external evidence for proposed phonological descriptions is a well-established feature of modern phonology. Thus, Chomsky and Halle (1968), in their groundbreaking work, *The Sound Patterns of English*, used Pig Latin to justify the necessity of rule orderings in their theoretical proposals. In fact, Bagemihl (1996, 701) refers to an evaluation of the relative merits of different types of evidence in phonological descriptions which concludes that language play is one of the most reliable forms of evidence.

Phonological evidence can also be derived from another form of language play, poetry. In poetry, language is structured in an artificial manner in order to produce aesthetically pleasing utterances. Language use in poetry conforms to artificial constraints on otherwise natural language use. Rigid rules involving metre and rhyme are some of these constraints. The application of these rules gives us additional information about what speakers intuitively know about the structure of their language. Thus, Fabb (1997, 132) is able to show how the rules for rhyming in modern Chinese support proposals which linguists make concerning the sound system of that language. Linguists would, for example, argue that there is a rule in that language which deletes the schwa vowel [ə] when it follows another vowel. Thus, a word with an underlying sequence of sounds /nuəŋ/ is actually pronounced /nuŋ/ with the [ə] vowel removed by the rule which deletes it when it is preceded by another vowel. As it turns out, in Chinese poetry, the words /fəŋ/, and /nuŋ/ rhyme with each other even though, as is evident, the vowel involved in each case is different. The linguist takes this as evidence that inside the heads of speakers of Chinese, the underlying forms of these words are /fəŋ/ and /nuəŋ/ respectively, both of which end in /əŋ/ underlyingly. What is being rhymed, therefore, are the underlying structures rather than those which are actually pronounced. Thus, even though the /ə/ vowel is not present in the surface realization of the second word, it is there in the knowledge of the speakers and is used as a basis for the rhyme. This is taken by linguists as an indication that, within speakers' heads, there is knowledge that there is an underlying /ə/ following /u/ in /nuŋ/

Inside "Heads High"

This chapter examines data provided by the lyrics of a popular dancehall piece, "Heads High" (*Edz Ai*) by Mr Vegas. Within this piece, there is a feature associated with language play the world over – the reversal of the sequences of sound in normal speech (Bagemihl, 1996, 710).

This reversal is combined with a poetic device employed in the lyrics, that of a rhyme scheme. The focus of this chapter is on, in the main, the rhyming words at the ends of lines, large numbers of which have their vowel sounds reversed. We will examine the phonological principles behind the playful or ludic reversal in the order of sounds in these rhyming words. The principles discovered here, I will demonstrate, can be used as external evidence which would help solve a problem existing in current analyses of the Jamaican Creole phonological system.

"Heads High" is typical of one type of dancehall piece, that of praise songs to women (Devonish 1996, 227). This piece, performed by a man and addressed to women, exhorts women to be proud, to not submit themselves to disrespect from men, and to keep their "heads high". The underlying metaphor, however, is that of women saying no to oral sex, refusing to bend down low in order to perform what is portrayed as a demeaning act. This is embodied in a regularly repeated formula within the song.

Edz ai, kil dem wid yu nou
Jos mek a bwai nuo yu naa blou
"Heads high, kill them with your 'no'"
Just make that boy know that you don't blow (that is, perform oral sex)"

These lines are fairly explicit and are treating a taboo subject, oral sex. The song would run the risk, if presented in an undisguised form, of being banned from play on the radio, a major source of exposure for the art form. However, the rhyming words at the end of the lines in the chorus, as in the examples above, /nou/ and /blou/, are disguised by having their vowels altered. The normal pronunciation of these words is /nuo/ "no" and /bluo/ "blow", with the diphthong being /uo/. However, the sequence of vowels in the diphthong is switched around in the song, with Mr Vegas producing /ou/ rather than /uo/ in these words. They end up being pronounced to rhyme with /kou/ "cow", rather than as would normally be the case, to rhyme with

/tuo/ "toe". This gives us /nou/ and /blou/, neither of which is normal for the Jamaican words meaning respectively "no" and "blow".

The reversal of vowel sounds in the final word of each of the above lines serves to partially obscure the content of the song. However, the reversal is systematic and is a generalization of a very limited variation in normal Jamaican speech between /uo/ and /ou/ in a small number of words, all of which end in /l/. The words in question are /uol/ "old", /buol/ "bowl" and /kuol/ "cold", which have, respectively, alternative forms, /oul/, /boul/ and /koul/. Any native speaker of Jamaican who realizes that sound play is taking place can easily decode it. The effectiveness of the disguise lies not in the fact that the vowels in the diphthongs are switched around but in the need for the audience to realize that sound play is at work. The rhyming words to which vowel reversal is applied end up as a sequence of apparently nonsense rhyming words, an aesthetically pleasing sound sequence quite capable of being appreciated for itself, without any reference to meaning. The necessity of disguise is here turned into artistic virtue.

The piece provides a unique opportunity for the linguist "to get inside the head" of Mr Vegas, the performer, and by extension inside the heads of the speakers of Jamaican, among whom the piece was extremely popular. It furnishes a means for arriving at explanatory adequacy.

THE PROBLEM: CHOOSING BETWEEN ALTERNATIVE ANALYSES

The Cassidy–Le Page Solution

Jamaican, according to Cassidy and Le Page (1980, xxxix), hereafter has five simple or short vowels. Two are front vowels. The first of these, [ɪ], is a vowel sound similar to but not identical to that in the pronunciation of the vowel in the word "it" in most varieties of English. The next, the mid front vowel, [ɛ], approximates the vowel in the word "egg" in most varieties of English. The front vowel phonemes are presented below along with their phonetic realizations as follows:

Front Vowels

/i/ [i]
/e/ [ɛ]

The third front vowel phoneme /a/ has two allophones, [a] and [ɐ]. The former has the front of the tongue slightly raised, whereas the latter involves a slightly raised centre of the tongue. I adopt the cover phonemic symbol /a/, to represent the phoneme which has the two allophones [a] and [ɐ].

/a/ [a], [ɐ]

There are two back vowel phonemes, the high back /u/ and the mid back /o/. These approximate Caribbean English pronunciations of vowels in "would" and "cut", respectively.

Back Vowels

/u/ [u]
/o/ [o]

The chart below is a stylized version of the mouth. The two front vowel phonemes /i/ and /ɛ/ are presented on the vowel chart below as are the back vowels /u/ and /o/ and the low front or central vowel /a/.

Figure 4.1   Vowel Chart

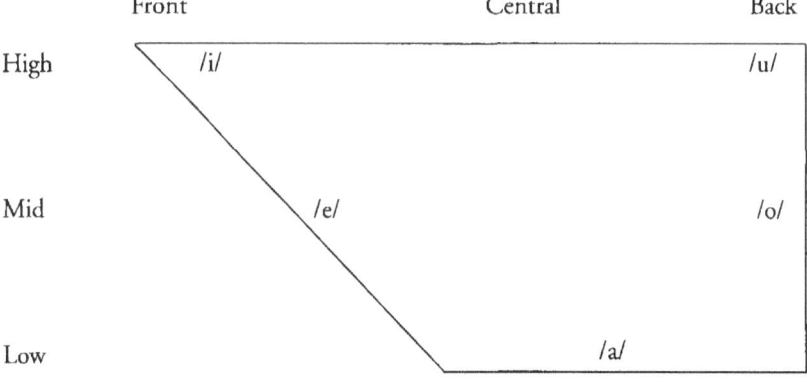

Jamaican has four diphthongs. Of these, there are two which end in a high vowel, respectively /i/ and /u/. These diphthongs are represented by Cassidy and Le Page (1980, xxxix) as /ai/ and /ou/. The former would approximate the vowel in the pronunciation of words "mice" and "light" in most varieties of English, and the latter the pronunciation of the vowel in words such as "out" and "now". The pronunciation of these diphthongs involves the movement of the tongue from a position lower in the mouth to one that is higher.

The Low-to-High Diphthongs

/ai/   [ɐi]
/ou/   [ou], [ɐu]

The representation of the first diphthong phoneme as /ai/ suggests that it is a combination of the monophthongs /a/ and /i/. Given that the monophthong /a/ is often pronounced with the low central allophone [ɐ], the actual phonetic realization of /ai/ as [ɐɪ] is consistent with the notion that this diphthong is underlyingly a combination of the two monophthong phonemes.

We see a much more complicated picture with /ou/. We have two alternative allophones for this diphthongal phoneme. The first pronunciation, that of [ou], is consistent with the idea that it is a combination of /o/ and /u/. The second one, however, is not. If we look back at the simple vowels, /o/ is never pronounced as [ɐ]. It is /a/ which is pronounced as [ɐ]. This means that the second pronunciation, that is, that of [ɐu], is consistent with the diphthong being a combination of /a/ and /u/. However, it would be uneconomical for us to present the [ou] allophone as the product of an underlying diphthong phoneme /ou/, and [ɐu] of /au/, since the phones [ou] and [ɐu] function as non-contrastive allophonic variants. These two diphthongs must be considered to be allophones of the same phone. However, suggesting as Cassidy and Le Page (1980, xxxix) do, that the diphthong is /ou/, or making the alternative proposal, that it is /au/, is not significant in any immediate sense. It is the same diphthong, whether we think of it as /ou/ or as /au/. Applying our principles of adequacy to the Cassidy and Le Page proposal for the /ou/ diphthong, we would have to say that it is observationally adequate since it accounts for the facts.

The Cassidy and Le Page analysis, however, falls short in the area of descriptive adequacy, which requires that any proposal can be generalized to related sets of data. Any attempt to extend the Cassidy and Le Page analysis of the /ou/ diphthong to that for the other diphthong ending in a high vowel, /ai/, runs into a problem. If there is going to be a generalization, it would involve establishing a parallel between what happens with the diphthong /ou/, which ends with the high back vowel and the diphthong /ai/, which ends with the high front vowel. Since /o/, the mid back vowel is the first vowel in diphthong which ends in the high back vowel, /ou/, a generalization would lead us to expect that the first vowel in the other diphthong would be the mid front vowel /e/, producing */ei/. However, the Cassidy and Le Page proposal is that /a/ is the first vowel in this diphthong, removing any parallelism between their proposal for /ou/ and that for /ai/. In the event that an alternative proposal can link the two diphthongs into a single analysis, such a proposal would be more descriptively adequate than that provided by Cassidy and Le Page.

Jamaican has two other diphthongs, those *beginning* with a high vowel. Cassidy and Le Page (1980, xxxix) describe these as involving a combination of the high vowel, either /i/ or /u/ with the mid vowel to which it corresponds in terms of backness or frontness, that is, /e/ and /o/ respectively. This produces the diphthongs represented by Cassidy and Le Page (1980, xxxix) as /ie/ and /uo/. These vowels appear in Jamaican words such as /kien/ "cane" and /guot/ "goat".

The suggestion, according to Cassidy and Le Page (1980, xxxix), is that the /ie/ and /uo/ diphthongs involve a combination of high and mid vowels of corresponding backness or frontness. Let us see how this matches against the facts of their phonetic realizations.

The High-to-Low Diphthongs

/ie/ [iɛ], [iɐ]
/uo/ [uo], [uɐ]

These phonetic facts produce a bit of a puzzle. The use of [ɐ] as the second phone in the second allophone of each of the above diphthong phonemes raises a question. The proposal for /ie/ and /uo/ as phonemic representations of these two diphthongs is observationally adequate insofar as such representations relate the [iɛ] and [uo] allophones respectively. This is so since, in the case of the monophthongs, [ɛ] is an allophone of /e/, and [o] of /o/. Descriptive adequacy in this situation, however, requires that whatever proposal is made for the [iɛ] and [uo] allophones should be generalizable to cover the [iɐ] and [uɐ] allophones as well. Unfortunately, when we examine the monophthongs, [ɐ] is not listed by Cassidy and Le Page (1980, xxxix) as an allophone of the either the /e/ or /o/ phonemes. It is, in fact, restricted to functioning as an allophone of the phoneme /a/. The distribution of phones within the monophthongs does not, therefore, justify a proposal that [ɐ] functions as an allophone of /e/ or /o/ in the diphthongs. This presents a problem for the descriptive adequacy of the Cassidy and Le Page proposal that the two diphthongs in question should be represented phonemically as /ie/ and /uo/.

THE ALTERNATIVE SOLUTION

If we follow the Cassidy and Le Page analysis of the diphthongs represented as /ai/ and /ou/, we would have to treat [ɐ] as an allophone of /o/, but only in the case of the diphthong /ou/. The Cassidy and Le Page approach permits a much less general statement about the behaviour of the phones than is otherwise possible. I would propose /au/ as preferable to /ou/. With the /a/ as the first unit in this diphthong, it is possible to make a general statement that [ɐ] is an allophone of /a/, not only in its function as a monophthong but in the diphthongs /ai/ *and* /au/. The Cassidy and Le Page proposal, is therefore, arguably less descriptively adequate.

In the Cassidy and Le Page proposal for the vowels represented as /ie/ and /uo/, the phonetic target of the second vowel would be the mid vowels [ɛ] and [o] respectively. The fact that phonetically, these two diphthongs are often realized as [iɐ] and [uɐ] with the second vowel in the diphthong being the lower vowel, [ɐ], has to be explained by the suggestion that the tongue overshoots the target vowel. We would have to be arguing for dissimilation, proposing that there is pressure for even greater differentiation between the vowels in the diphthong than the underlying form requires.

The alternative proposal involves /ia/ and /ua/ as the phonemic forms of these diphthongs. The target of the second vowel in each diphthong would be phonetically [ɐ]. It is being suggested that there is often, however, a phonetic falling short, resulting in the phonetic mid vowel allophones, [ɛ] and [o], rather than the target low phonetic vowel, [ɐ], being produced. This could be explained by the process of assimilation, with the phonetic realization of the target phoneme, /a/, a low vowel, coming under the influence of the high vowel which precedes it. This is what produces an articulation higher in the mouth involving mid vowels [ɛ] and [o].

It is known in phonology that processes of assimilation are far more general than those of dissimilation. Faced with a choice between an assimilatory rule and a dissimilatory one, the former is considered to be more natural. This again leads to the conclusion that the Cassidy and Le Page proposal is less descriptively adequate than the alternative being proposed here. This descriptive adequacy is further emphasized by the fact that the alternative proposes the use of just three vowels, /u/, /a/ and /i/, to generate four diphthongs. Any diphthong in this system is simply a reversal of the phoneme order of another diphthong, that is, /ai/ and /ia/, /au/ and /ua/. The Cassidy and Le Page proposal requires five vowels, /i/, /e/, /a/, /o/ and /u/ to generate these four diphthongs and they cannot be all generated by simply reversing the order of the vowels in the component diphthongs.

Based on the above, the two sets of proposals for the diphthongs of Jamaican are:

Proposed Alternative	Cassidy–Le Page
/ai/	/ai/
/ie/	/ia/
/ou/	/au/
/uo/	/ua/

MR VEGAS PRONOUNCES: ANALYSIS OF *Edz Ai* OR "HEADS HIGH"

Even though I have argued above that my alternative analysis is superior to that of Cassidy and Le Page at the level of descriptive adequacy, there is a higher level of adequacy that needs to be satisfied in linguistic descriptions.

That is the level of explanatory adequacy. This can be achieved by evaluating competing descriptions by using evidence generated when the language is put under stress as a result of being used in unusual situations. Poetry, word play and, in this case a combination of these, present such an occasion, one which can serve to open, albeit slightly, a window into the head of a speaker. The data, in the form of song lyrics, will be employed to evaluate the relative explanatory adequacy of the two competing proposals.

Edz Ai or "Heads High" is a dancehall piece in which an eight line chorus is repeated six times in the course of its performance. There are four verses, three of twelve lines and the other of just four lines. Two of the three verses of twelve lines are identical.

The chorus has rhyming endings, all of the form /ou/ or /au/, that is, the vowel sound in the English word "out". This produces eight rhyming endings. These are as listed below, alongside the ending as it would be pronounced in normal speech. An English gloss is also provided.

Pronunciation in Song		Normal Pronunciation		English Gloss
Cassidy–Le Page	Alternative	Cassidy–Le Page	Alternative	
nou	nau	nuo	nua	"no"
blou	blau	bluo	blua	"blow"
nou	nau	nuo	nua	"no"
you ~ shou	yau ~ shau	yuu ~ shuo	yuu ~ shua	"you", "show"
nou	nau	nuo	nua	"no"
blou	blau	bluo	blua	"blow"
nou	nau	nuo	nua	"no"
sou	sau	suo	sua	"so"

Note that all of the rhymes in the chorus, with the exception of /you/ or /yau/, show an inversion of the normal /uo/ or /ua/ pronunciation of items to produce /ou/ or /au/ versions instead. The exception, /you/ or /yau/, is used only once in the six occurrences of the chorus and is derived from a /yuu/ normal pronunciation. This may be based on either or both of the following. There may be a play on a spelling-based pronunciation of the English equivalent, "you", which suggests an /ou/ or /au/ pronunciation similar to the vowel in the English word "thou". Otherwise, the exception may be influenced by the Jamaican vocative form /you/ or /yau/, "You there!"

For the casual listener, unaware of the sound play taking place, this systematic phonological play helps disguise the topic of the song, oral sex. The sound play, involving the switching of /uo/ or /ua/ in words to /ou/ or /au/, is extended in some measure to a verse which occurs twice in the song and which presents the following rhyme scheme for six of its twelve lines.

Pronunciation in Song	Normal Pronunciation	English Gloss
vou/vau	vou/vau	"vow"
you/yau	you/yau	"you there!"
chou/chou/chau-chau	chuo-chu(o)/chua-chu(a)	"cho-cho"
brou/brau	brou/brau	"brow"
nou/nau	nuo/nua	"know"
blou/blau	blou(z)/blau(z)	"blouse" (expletive)

Here, four of the six items have a /ou/ or /au/ pronunciation in normal speech, which is maintained in the song. However, in the case of /chuo-chu(o)/ or /chua-chu(a)/ and /nuo/ or /nua/, we see the same vowel inversion we saw in the chorus.

Twelve lines in the verses have rhymes with syllables ending in /iip/, /iik/, /iit/ and another twelve ending variously in /iim/, /iin/ and /in/. However, what is significant is the ninth verse, the short one with four lines. These involve rhymes with the diphthong /ai/. These are presented below.

Ending	Normal Pronunciation	English Gloss
badai	badi	"body"
rai-rai	rie-rie/ria-ria	"loose woman"
bai	bie/bia	"bay"
diijai	diijie/diijia	"deejay"

Of these four items, three involve the conversion of /ia/ pronunciations into /ai/ ones. Arguably, for purposes of forcing the fourth item, /badi/, into the rhyme scheme, the performer treated it as if it were /badai/. What is significant about this four-line verse is that the switch around for /ua/ words, particularly in the chorus, is also being applied here to /ia/ words.

I would suggest that it is not by accident that the performer has opted to disguise /ia/ word endings in the same way as /ua/ endings, producing /ai/ and /au/, respectively. Rather, he recognizes that /ia/ is constructed essentially in the same way as /au/, that is, beginning with the low central vowel /a/ and rising to a high vowel. As a result, he ends up feeling he can apply the same disguise, reversal of the vowel sequence, to the /ia/ words that he has applied to the /ua/ words. The deliberate nature of the disguise is reinforced by another observation. The relationship between /ai/ and /au/ is critical to the construction of the entire piece. In every alternate line of the eight-line chorus, with the chorus itself occurring six times in the song, the vowel /ai/ in the middle of the line is given prominence and contrasted with the /au/ which ends the line. The line, which begins the song and appears twenty-four times in a song of eighty-eight lines, is /Edz ai, kil dem wid yu n*au*/ – "Heads high, kill them with your 'no'."

The conclusion is clear. Treating these vowels as /ai/ and /au/ captures the relationship that Mr Vegas and his audience perceive far more accurately than Cassidy and Le Page's treatment as /ai/ and /ou/. In addition, switching the vowel sequences around, to produce as proposed in the alternative analysis, /ia/ and /ua/, is far more in keeping with what Mr Vegas seems to know about his language than the Cassidy and Le Page representation, /ie/ and /uo/.

MISS LOU TOO: PHONOLOGICAL AND POETIC PRECEDENT

Mr Vegas, in devising the core element of his sound play, the switching of /ua/ pronunciations to /au/ ones, is much more extensive and radical in his approach than anything tried before. However, as is true for much that passes as entirely new, there is some precedent.

In the regular pronunciation of Jamaican, before /l/, there are /ua/ words, notably /kual/ "cold" and /ual/ "old", which have alternative /au/ pronunciations, /kaul/ and /aul/, which rhyme with /faul/ "fowl". In fact, the /kaul/ and /aul/ alternants have the meaning "very cold" and "very old", distinguishing their meanings from those of their /ua/ equivalents. Switching from /ua/ to /au/ to signal emphatic meaning, albeit in an environment that does not involve /l/, may be what was intended by Mr Vegas's replacement of /nua/

"no" by /nau/ in *Edz Ai*. The core message of the song was after all, an injunction to his female audience to say "No!"

In the regular pronunciation of Jamaican, the /ua/ ~ /au/ variation is both limited to occurring the environment before /l/ and restricted to certain words. Thus, /ual/ "hold" cannot appear as */aul/. Similarly, a word like /ruol/ "roll" has no acceptable alternant */raul/. Yet, Louise Bennett (1966, 126), decades before the appearance of Mr Vegas, in a poem entitled "Mrs Govanah", does take phonological licence, Mr Vegas–style. This occurs, however, in the much more restricted phonological environment before /l/, to have "rowl" /raul/, that is, "roll" rhyme with "fowl" /faul/:

> *Den ah look an see how all de nayga*
> *Y'eye dem was a rowl* (/raul/)
> *Ah wonder ef de Maja was*
> *A-sell new kine o' fowl* (/faul/)

CONCLUSION

I have presented an alternative to the Cassidy and Le Page (1980) treatment of Jamaican diphthongs, involving them as consisting of /ia/, /ua/, /ai/ and /au/. This approach, unlike that of Cassidy and Le Page, argues for the same relationship between /ia/ and /ai/ as exists between /ua/ and /au/. Mr Vegas, in his performance of *Edz Ai*, himself opts to treat the two sets of relationships as parallel. This suggests that this parallel relationship does exist in his intuitive understanding of the phonology of his language. For the linguist, he has provided external evidence that the alternative proposal is more explanatorily adequate than that of Cassidy and Le Page. The evidence from Mr Vegas points to the alternative analysis being more faithful to the intuitive linguistic knowledge of native speakers of Jamaican who make up his primary audience.

More important, however, our phonological analysis of the rhyming words in the song tells us why, from the perspective of the audiences, the song has been so wildly popular. Far from these audiences being a mindless mass, consuming monotonous and meaningless pap, they demonstrate a keen and sophisticated appreciation of a structured and sophisticated manipulation of the sound patterns of their language. The problem lies with the critics of dancehall who are very often trying to cope with aesthetics well beyond the analytical capacity of the intellectual tools in their possession. Not surprisingly, they condemn what they cannot understand.

Appendix

"Heads High" (*Edz Aî*)

By Mr Vegas
(C. Smith/H. Browne)
Produced by Danny Brownie and D. Juvenile for Main Street Records.
Greensleeves Records 1998

Transcribed by Hubert Devonish, using the Cassidy (1961) writing system reproduced and elaborated in Cassidy and Le Page (1980). Rough English glosses are provided.

1.

Na na na, na na na, na na na, na na na, nou
Kil dem wid yu nou
Na na na, na na na, na na na, na na na, nou
Kil dem wid di, kil dem wid di, kil dem wid di . . .
Edz ai, kil dem wid yu nou
Jos mek a bwai nuo yu naa blou
Edz ai, kil dem wid yu nou
No bwai ent gat no siikrit fi you-ou-ou
Edz ai, kil dem wid yu nou
Jos mek a bwai nuo yu naa blou
Edz ai, kil dem wid yu nou
Tel dem se Viegas se sou
[Na, na, etc., no,
Kill them with your "no"

Na, na, etc., no,
Kill them with the . . . kill them with the . . . kill them with the . . .
Heads high, kill them with your "no"
Just make that boy know you don't blow
Heads high, kill them with your "no"
No boy holds any secrets for you
Heads high, kill them with your "no"
Just make that boy know you don't blow
Heads high, kill them with your "no"
Tell them that Vegas says so.

2.

Mi waan yu skin yu tiit
An mek mi siit
Mek mi shuor fram yu baan se yu neva dwiit
Yu a no friik
Wan man yu kiip
An yu neva get dong ple se yu dwiit
Yu mek a vou
Yu no ansa to you
An a wan man a sampl yu chou-chou
Nit op yu brou,
mek a gai nou
se im fi muuv im blou-ou

I want you to show your teeth
And make them see it
Make me sure that from the day you were born, you have never done it
You are no freak
One man you keep
And you have never gotten down to even pretend that you would do it
You have made a vow
You don't answer to "Yow!" [a disrespectful greeting]
And only one man samples your "cho-cho" [referring to the vagina]
Knit your brow
Make that guy know
That he must move his bl . . .

3.

an sing agen
hedz ai, kil dem wid yu nou,
Jos mek a bwai nuo yu naa blou
hedz ai, kil dem wid yu nou
mek a bwai nuo yu a nuo papi shou-ou
edz ai, kil dem wid yu nou
jes mek a bwai nuo yu naa blou
edz ai, kil dem wid yu nou
Tel dem Viegas se sou

And sing again
Heads high, kill them with your "no"

Just make that boy know you don't blow
Heads high, kill them with your "no"
Make that boy know you aren't a "poppy-show" [a joker]
Heads high, kill them with your "no"
Just make that boy know you don't blow
Heads high, kill them with your "no"
Tell them that Vegas says so.

4.

Mi waan heer yu skriim
If yu mout kliin
No man neva ruop yu hiin
Fi no aiskriim
Yu no smel griin
Laik Charliin
Yu huol a fresh, yu av a helti haijiin
Som asyuumin wail yu kiip bluumin
Laik a priti likl lili in a di mawnin
Yu nat brawlin
Fresh az dem dawliin
Wen yu raizin dem kiip fawlin

I want to year you scream
If your mouth is clean
No man ever roped you in
For any ice cream.
You don't smell "green"
Like Charlene
You bathe regularly, you have a healthy hygiene
Some are assuming while you keep blooming
Like a pretty little lily in the morning
You are not vulgar
Fresh as those darlings
When you are rising, they keep on falling.

5.

So sing agen
Edz ai, kil dem wid yu nou,
Jos mek a bwai nuo yu naa blou

Edz ai, kil dem wid yu nou
No bwai kyaan tek a yu fi papi shou-ou-ou
Edz ai, kil dem wid yu nou,
Jos mek a bwai nuo yu naa blou
Edz ai, kil dem wid yu nou,
Dem no ha no sikrit fi you

So sing again
Heads high, kill them with your "no"
Just make that boy know you don't blow
Heads high, kill them with your "no"
No boy can take you for a "poppy show"
Heads high, kill them with your "no"
Just make that boy know you don't blow
Heads high, kill them with your "no"
They don't hold any secrets for you.

6.

An sing agen
Edz ai kil dem wid yu nou
Jos mek a bwai nuo yu naa blou
Edz ai kil dem wid yu nou
No bwai kyaan tek a yu fi papi shou-ou-ou
Edz ai, kil dem wid yu nou
Jos mek a bwai nuo yu naa blou
Edz ai, kil dem wid yu nou
Tel dem Viegas se sou

And sing again
Heads high, kill them with your "no"
Just make that boy know you don't blow
Heads high, kill them with your "no"
No boy can take you for a "poppy show"
Heads high, kill them with your "no"
Just make that boy know you don't blow
Heads high, kill them with your "no"
Tell them that Vegas says so.

7.

Mi waan yu skriim, brok out, wain op yu badai
Han in a di ier kaa yu a no rai rai
Wan ship aloon kyan dak pan yu bai
Pan no bwai maik yu naa diijai

I want you to scream, break out, shake up your body
Hands in the air because you are not a "ray-ray" [a loose woman]
One ship alone can dock on your bay
On no boy's mike will you deejay.

8.

An sing agen
Edz ai kil dem wid yu nou
Jos mek a bof nuo yu naa blou
Edz ai kil dem wid yu nou
No bwai kyaan tek a yu fi papi shou-ou-ou
Edz ai, kil dem wid yu nou
Jos mek a bof nuo yu naa blou
Edz ai, kil dem wid yu nou
Tel dem Viegas se sou

And sing again
Heads high, kill them with your "no"
Just make the man know you won't blow
Heads high, kill them with your "no"
No boy can take you for a "poppy show"
Heads high, kill them with your "no"
Just make the man know you don't blow
Heads high, kill them with your "no"
Tell them that Vegas says so.

9.

Mi waan yu skin yu tiit
An mek mi siit
Mek mi shuor fram yu baan se yu neva dwiit
Yu a no friik

A wan man yu kiip
An yu neva get dong ple se yu dwiit
Yu mek yu vou
Yu no ansa to you
An a wan man a sampl yu chou-chou
Nit op yu ai brou,
mek a boi nou
se im fi muuv im blou-ou

I want you to show your teeth
And make them see it
Make me sure that from the day you were born, you never did it
You aren't a freak
It is one man that you keep
And you never get down to even pretend that you would do it
You make a vow
You don't answer to "Yow!"
And it is just one man who samples your "cho-cho"
Knit your brow
Make the boy know
That he should move his bl . . .

10.

Edz ai, kil dem wid yu nou
Jos mek a bwai nuo yu naa blou
Edz ai, kil dem wid yu nou
Mek a bwai nuo yu a no papi shou
Edz ai, kil dem wid yu nou
Jos mek a bwai nuo yu naa blou
Edz ai, kil dem wid yu nou . . .

Heads high, kill them with your "no"
Just make the boy know you don't blow
Heads high, kill them with your "no"
Make the boy know you aren't a "poppy show"
Heads high, kill them with your "no"
Just make the boy know you don't blow
Heads high, kill them with your "no". . .

REFERENCES

Bagemihl, B. 1996. "Language Games and Related Areas. In *The Handbook of Phonological Theory*, ed. J. Goldsmith, 697–712. Oxford: Blackwell.

Bennett, Louise. 1966. *Jamaica Labrish*. Kingston: Sangster's Book Stores.

Cassidy, F., and R. Le Page. 1980. *Dictionary of Jamaican English*. Cambridge: Cambridge University Press.

Chomsky, N., and M. Halle. 1968. *The Sound Pattern of English*. New York: Harper and Row.

Devonish, H. 1996. "Kom Groun Jamiekan Daans Haal Liriks: Memba Se a Plie Wi a 'Plie' ". *English World-Wide* 17, no. 2: 213–38.

Fabb, N. 1997. *Linguistics and Literature: Language in the Verbal Arts of the World*. Oxford: Blackwell.

Newmeyer. F. 1986. *Linguistic Theory in America*. Orlando: Academic Press.

Smith, B. 2001. "Patois Has Its Place, but Let's Teach English". *Daily Gleaner* (Jamaica). 12 October, A5.

This page intentionally left blank

Section 2

Language and Education

This page intentionally left blank

Chapter 5

THE USE OF THE VERNACULAR IN WEST INDIAN EDUCATION
Dennis Craig

In WEST INDIAN COUNTRIES, the vernacular can be regarded as excluding the Standard Local Variety of English (SE) that is part of Internationally Acceptable English (IAE) and as being a continuum of language which can include basilect English-lexicon Creole (EC, as in Belize, Guyana, Jamaica), or French-lexicon Creole (FC, as in Dominica, St Lucia), and a Mesolect (M) which, in form, is somewhere between EC and SE in all countries. In countries where FC has traditionally been dominant (Dominica, St Lucia), the lexis of M can be expected to show influences of FC.

Since the 1960s, when most of these countries became politically independent of Britain, significant changes have been taking place in the functional roles of language varieties in West Indian countries; however, it has gone unnoticed that these changes justify a re-examination of the issues relevant to the use of the vernacular in West Indian education. This chapter is a step towards such a re-examination.

When the issues first came to the fore, the search for a national cultural identity was, in each case, only at its beginning. A review of the situation, in Craig (1976, 100), bears repeating:

> Growth in knowledge about . . . the West-Indian Creole-English situation coincided with the growth of new nations in the Third World and the international

recognition of the need for these new nations to have educational systems that would be fully relevant in each case to the specific national identity, environment, and goals; part of this recognition implied the need for each child to receive at least his earliest education in the language that was most natural to him: his mother tongue. In the light of this recognition, the fiction, maintained for over a century, that Standard English was the mother tongue of West Indian Creole-speaking or Creole-influenced children could no longer be maintained. One of the first concrete reactions to this recognition was the proposal that the Creole or mesolectal language of children, in officially English-speaking West Indian territories should be used as the language of primary, even if for no other, education. An early example of such a suggestion is to be seen in the UNESCO (1953) monograph on the use of vernacular languages in education, where it was suggested that some of the officially English-speaking territories in the West Indies were among the areas of the world where Creole languages might well be used in Education. Up to the present however, more than two decades after this suggestion, none of these territories has attempted to implement it.

The latter perspective focuses on education. It is possible (though not essential, as will be subsequently noted) that developments in education become contextualized within a wider framework of national policy. For example, Devonish (1986, 112) is concerned with this wider framework:

The major goal of official language policy reform in the Commonwealth Caribbean should be to provide access. All institutional areas of knowledge, information and general culture should be available to every individual in the society, regardless of language background. The general way in which this is phrased is quite deliberate. Speakers of language varieties other than English-lexicon Creole also suffer deprivation of their language rights in the countries of their birth. The plight of minorities who speak American Indian languages in Guyana and Belize, including Garifuna (the language of the "Black Caribs" of Belize), are particularly worthy of mention. There are, as well, East Indian speakers of Bhojpuri in Trinidad and Guyana, and French Creole speaking minorities in Trinidad and Grenada who ought not to be forgotten. Nevertheless, the focus will be on the roles and functions of English-lexicon Creoles, the majority language in all these countries with the exception of St Lucia and Dominica.

Over the years, West Indian countries have tended to reject both the wider framework and its educational application. The reasons for that rejection are instructive. Devonish (1986, 114) comments as follows:

There is a standard objection to the use of Creole as an official language in these countries. It is often argued that the prevailing language situation has ". . . the advantage to the community of possessing a national language which is at the same time international in its acceptability." (Craig 1978–80, 105). If, by "the community" is meant the English speaking élites who control these Caribbean societies, then the statement has validity. However, for the large mass of the primarily Creole speaking populations, the prevailing situation has no such advantage. In fact, the prevailing situation has two huge disadvantages for Creole speakers. It excludes them from access to both the official language of internal communication and the language of external communication.

The latter comment however, does not take into account Creole speakers' known attitudes to their language and to the acquisition of English in the situation prevailing at the time. It also ignores the extent of language variability, its effect on attitudes in that situation and the unwillingness of Caribbean governments (dependent on democratic support) to initiate policies, however well-meaning, that could offend either their élites, or their masses, or both. In this regard, Craig (1976, 101) comments as follows on attitudes that prevailed:

> The chief reason why the Creole or Creole-influenced language of West Indian children has not been used in education lies in deep-seated community attitudes to Creole. The old official attitude of ignoring its existence or advocating its eradication has already been mentioned. In the community at large, Creole language has generally been identified historically with slavery and in more recent times with very low social status and lack of education. This feeling about Creole exists even in the minds of its speakers, most of whom would attempt, if they can, to modify their speech in the direction of Standard English in the presence of an English speaker, and would feel insulted if a stranger who is obviously non-Creole-speaking attempts to converse with them in Creole. In this context, even the most Creole-speaking of parents tend to regard Standard English as the language of social mobility, and would tend to think that anyone who suggests the use of Creole or Creole-influenced language in education as advocating the socio-economic repression of the masses. This attitude of Creole and Creole-influenced speakers towards English has been mentioned in Bailey (1964) with reference to Jamaica, but it is an attitude that is to be found in all the officially English-speaking West Indian countries. It is not any way unique to these countries however, as it is very similar to that attitude of non-standard speakers in the USA which Wolfram (1970, 29) describes, and which has been responsible for

the non-acceptance of dialect readers in some "black" English communities.

In effect, it is an attitude that represents a socio-psychological dualism in which the low-status language is stubbornly preserved by its speakers as a part of their identity and cultural integrity, but at the same time these very speakers resist any measures which, by extending the societal role of their own low-status language, might impede their children's acquisition of the accepted high-status language. At the base of the attitude is probably the very pragmatic realization that it is unlikely that the high-status language could ever be completely replaced, and that even if it were possible to replace it, its status in the wider world still makes it a very desirable acquisition.

It may be noted however, that the last-mentioned attitude, whereby parents demonstrate a desire for their children to acquire the high-status language, even to the possible detriment of the home language, is by no means confined to Creole language. Nor, as illustrated by the Wolfram example mentioned earlier, is it confined to black English situations, nor to situations two or three decades ago. In the United States, the same attitude has become evident in parents of Hispanic origin, who have been calling for an end to the bilingual education programmes which the existing language-education establishment considers to be in the best interests of their children. The parents have expressed an overwhelming preference for monolingual education in English (Amselle 1997).

The Hispanic case is significant because it involves a home language and culture that have a long history of high national and international respect and esteem. It is not a case where parental attitudes could have been determined by a history of stigmatization and the search for an identity, as in the case of West Indian Creole. In both cases, like the parent in Craig (1998) who asked:

/aafta yu laan dem fi riid an rait dem Kriiyol, den wa muo?/
After you have taught them to read and write their Creole, then what more?

Parents merely want to be assured that their children are not going to be denied access to what they perceive as a highly valuable goal: SE.

When parents demonstrate a preference for their children to be educated in a language that has a higher utility value than the home language, it would be wrong to assume that communities are abandoning their original cultural heritage. The continuing strength of the heritage can sometimes become manifested in surprising ways. This is illustrated by the case of the Oakland,

California, School District Board in December 1996, when community leaders, frustrated at the continuing language-education failure of African-American children and at not being able to obtain government funds for English as a Second Language (ESL), and wanting for the latter reason to emphasize the uniqueness of black linguistic heritage and its distance from English, shocked the world by reaffirming the thesis of Williams (1975) that "the true language of Black folks" is Ebonics, a "genetically transmitted African language". Nevertheless, it was this same "true language", in the medium of dialect readers, that black communities rejected in the 1970s.

The lesson to be learned from West Indian and North American cases is that countries have to decide how to accommodate, on the one hand, the rights of parents to chose an education for their children and, on the other hand, the rationalist ideal of children's rights to their first language. In order to make the accommodation, countries would need to consider, most carefully, the detailed pros and cons of either retaining a single, traditional, official language or decreeing one or more additional official languages. In many West Indian countries, the choice may already have been made implicitly, through cultural custom, but this does not say that the choice cannot be tested at this or any future time, if there is the ideologically stimulated political will to test it.

Apart from the categorical prescriptions provided in Devonish (1986), the alternatives have been discussed in comprehensive detail in Carrington (for example, 1976, 1993), Craig (for example 1971, 1980), Simmons-McDonald (1996), Roberts (1988) and Robertson (1996). In addition, most of the latter have also explored issues relevant to applications of Creole-focused linguistics in the context of possible policy implementation.

In the studies mentioned, two sets of indications are fundamental. One set (Carrington 1976) analyses the conditions that favour or disfavour the use of any given vernacular as the medium of instruction. The other set (Craig 1980), taking monolingualism either in the vernacular or in the official language as the two extremes, analyses the different types of vernacular/official-language bilingualism that countries may wish to establish, depending on prevailing sociolinguistic conditions in each case.

In relation to the vernacular, the different policy options, including maintaining the *status quo* as an option in each case, individually give automatic approval to one or more behaviours:

That the vernacular be

- not used in education or formal social communication;
- used orally in early education, only for transition to SE;
- used orally for informal social communication;
- used orally for all communication purposes, informal and formal;
- written in a specially designed orthography for the teaching of initial reading, adult literacy, or for general use as a written language;
- written in the spelling system of the standard language that provides its lexis;

and so on. The listing is not intended to be exhaustive.

However, it has gone largely unnoticed or ignored that, while different options require different behaviours in relation to the vernacular, all options require a single, common set of behaviours in relation to the official language, SE. The fact is that, whether SE is the only official language or one of two or more official languages, it has to be used in all the relevant countries with native-like efficiency for a wide range of purposes in speech and literacy. That seems certain to continue into the foreseeable future, and, as already illustrated, social justice demands that goals in relation to SE be made accessible to all vernacular speakers, within whatever is the chosen national policy.

Attention to the common SE part of policy options, however, inevitably entails attention to three sets of factors in any speech community where SE and the vernacular interact and co-exist. These three sets of factors are stated below. Since they involve not only EC and M, which are lexically related to SE, but also FC, which is lexically unrelated, they are stated in a generalized form that involves all first languages:

1. The functional roles of SE and the vernacular or other first languages in the speech community.
2. The conditions imposed by the vernacular or other first languages on the process of acquiring SE and literacy in SE.
3. The use that may be made of the vernacular or other first language in the teaching and learning of SE (in cases where speakers are monolingual in EC or M, or bilingual in EC or M and FC, or monolingual in FC or another language that is lexically unrelated to SE).

These three sets of factors will be further discussed in the rest of this chapter, especially since they involve those ongoing changes in the functional roles of language varieties which, as mentioned earlier, justify re-examination of the use of the vernacular in education.

Before that further discussion is undertaken, it needs to be noted that it is only by attention to stated sets of factors at the level of school classrooms that children's rights to their first language can be realized constructively in education. One consequence of the preceding is that the absence of an explicitly formulated language policy in any country cannot absolve educators from paying systematic and principled attention to the implications of a child's first language. This is so because the previous possession of one or more languages influences the acquisition of any subsequent language, as is shown by studies of the interdependence of languages in work such as that of Cummins (1979b), Rivers (1979), and Genese (1987).

It may be noted also that the principles involved must of necessity be extended to cover, at the level of educational action in schools, irrespective of national language policy, all cases where children's first language differs from, and interacts and co-exists with, the official language. Thus, minorities such as "the minorities who speak American Indian languages in Guyana and Belize, including Garifuna (the language of the 'Black Caribs' of Belize), . . . East Indian speakers of Bhojpuri in Trinidad and Guyana, and French Creole speaking minorities in Trinidad and Grenada", cited in the proposals of Devonish (1986), should not be allowed to continue disadvantaged, as they would be in those proposals even with EC as an official language. The languages of these minorities should in each case be considered alongside of the vernaculars (EC or M, and FC) within the three sets of factors stated above. Relevant to the latter however, some strategies which schools might employ to facilitate the education of linguistic minorities who are not adequately provided for in prescribed bilingual education programmes are discussed in Craig (1996). In the present chapter therefore, the main focus will continue to be on EC or M, and FC (the "vernaculars") as first languages, although rationally, educational provision for FC should entail similar provision for first languages that are unrelated to SE.

In terms of the first of the stated sets of factors, the most obvious indications are that over the years since political independence in the 1960s, the functional roles of the vernaculars of West Indian countries have been expanding significantly. In all countries, political and related social change has stimulated an increased assertion of the traditional native identity and culture. The result is now clearly visible and audible in all forms of artistic creativity, in nationally distinctive entertainment, and in public communication. In a majority of the countries that have a tourist industry, the latter developments have become commercially rewarding. In terms of language use, some statements selected from Shields-Brodber (1997, 63ff) document the situation in Jamaica:

> It is in fact the norm, rather than the exception, to hear speakers switching between the two varieties (*i.e., between Jamaican Creole (JC) and SE*), however formal their public platform (emphasis added) . . . Rather than restricting themselves to SE, many speakers are thus taking full advantage of their linguistic options . . . Some instances of switching are generated as a response to an obvious contextual trigger, and can therefore be predicted; others are only interpretable *post hoc.* . . . Writing is also an agent of expansion, though at a slower pace than that of radio, of the conventionally limited domains of JC. Even in front page newspaper reports, for example, there are attempts to represent, faithfully, the views of those JC-dominant speakers quoted. There are also, at this time, two weekly opinion columns written in JC, one using modified English orthography, the other using Cassidy/Le Page's phonemic system. Another area exhibiting change is the creation of signs in which, for example, Creole-dominant speakers employ non-traditional, creative spelling to transmit their JC as well as English messages (Devonish 1996). Written advertisements addressed to Creole-dominant audiences also regularly incorporate JC vocabulary, idiom and syntax for maximum effect.

The Jamaican situation outlined above shows how public communication has been influenced by the gradual disappearance of traditional linguistic prejudices and inhibitions, and the continuing liberalization of social attitudes. The changes illustrated in the Jamaican situation can be found replicated, in kind, in most West Indian countries. But in countries where the vernacular is dominantly M, rather than dominantly basilect EC as implied for Jamaica in the quotation above, the changes simply cannot be expected to have the same sharpness or vividness of appearance. The fact is that linguistic switching from basilect EC to SE in Jamaica will be far more perceptible and striking, because it spans a much wider linguistic range, than switching from M to SE in Jamaica itself, or in St Vincent, Trinidad, Barbados, Guyana or anywhere else; but indications are that, in all these places, vernacular speech is being heard in a wider range of social situations than it used to be; vernacular forms are increasingly permeating advertisements, graphic signs of all types (personal communication with Richard Allsopp on the data for Allsopp 1996), and even the most formal types of writing. In general the *standard local variety of English*, SE, is absorbing an ever increasing amount of vernacular forms.

It may be noted in passing that, although the discussion above uses the term "switching", the phenomena under discussion seem most often to involve a "mixing" of SE and EC or M, rather than a switching from one to the other. Additional evidence on registers and styles in the vernacular, such as the examples in Patrick (1997), lend support to this view.

In countries with FC, the same influences as just described for EC-dominant countries would have been felt, resulting in FC being used uninhibitedly in a wider range of situations than before. One accompaniment of this is the continuing increase in language mixing, of the kind described in Allsopp (1996, xiii) as "French Creole loans in free operation", in what would otherwise be M or SE discourse. Concurrently with the latter, it would not be surprising however, if pressures for self-assertion on the one hand, and the allure of the SE goal on the other, combine to increase, over time, the proportion of speakers who are bilingual in FC and either M or SE, with a consequent proportionate reduction in monolingual speakers of FC. The latter would explain the proportionate distribution of St Lucian children shown in Simmons-McDonald (1996, 124) where school principals estimate that less than 10 per cent of children entering school in either rural or urban areas are monolingual FC-speakers, whereas 77 per cent of the urban and 88 per cent of the rural children are bilingual in FC and either M or SE. These indications may be consistent with a scenario in which the total use of FC, as well as the incidence of bilingualism in EC or M and FC, are both increasing.

It may be noted in passing, however, that changes such as those described for EC-dominant countries are occurring in English worldwide, and are not confined to Creole-language situations in the West Indies. In this regard, Shields-Brodber's 1997 declaration of a *requiem for English* is currently being replicated in many places – as suggested, for example, in this item (Lindsay Griffiths, "English Goes Global", *Guyana Chronicle*, 5 August 1999) carried by Reuters (London):

> A US–British dictionary published yesterday consigned the Queen's English to history and said the future lay in a colourful new patchwork of words culled from

around the world. "English is now a global language that belongs to all those who speak it", said Nigel Newton, chief executive of Bloomsbury which published the book with Microsoft Corp.

The question that arises, for the West Indies as for the rest of the world, concerns the linguistic mechanisms that must, of necessity, *maintain themselves* in order to ensure that all those who are deemed to be speakers of "English" remain mutually intelligible. Microsoft, with its involvement in the subject of the Reuters item, and its near monopoly of the incipient Information Age, has undoubtedly answered the question for itself already.

In the West Indies, the changes outlined above have taken place since independence and continue. As a result:

1. EC, M, SE are more distinguishable in theory than in reality. The "mixing" that has taken place has given speakers a greater capacity to choose linguistic forms from different categories, in order to achieve specific purposes. The same applies to FC but the distinction between FC and English-based language remains clear, because of the base differences.
2. As a consequence, traditional attitudes to "low" and "high" language have become diluted. Social status is no longer as marked by the use of language. Speakers' choices of linguistic items are now less indicative of "acts of identity" (Le Page and Tabouret-Keller 1985) than of choices of style and register. It is now more possible for SE-dominant speakers to deliver sustained utterances in EC or FC without the traditional inhibitions or any implied pretentiousness; it is also possible for EC- or FC-dominant speakers to do so in relation to SE.
3. The changes have, in effect, been producing a convergence of language varieties in which the relatedness of contemporary EC and SE has been strengthened. If Carrington (1976) is right, this should mean that conditions are less favourable for a discrete form of EC to be adopted as a language of instruction in schools. Nevertheless, it can be expected that the incidental and spontaneous use of Creole-influenced language by both children and teachers will be greater now in school than it has ever been.

In relation to the last point, it is interesting to note in passing that advice originally given to primary schools (Craig 1969) and tested in Jamaica and Trinidad, has now been extended to secondary schools in some places. The advice concerns the need for primary-school children to be allowed to use their Creole-influenced language orally for cognitive continuity and as a bridge to the acquisition of English and English literacy. The ROSE programme in Jamaica (Rickards 1995) has been applying a corresponding approach in some secondary schools but with some additional goals, which if consistently pursued would necessitate certain specific and additional pedagogical inputs at a Grade 7–9 level. Obviously, the SE acquisition problems of primary-school children of two or three decades ago are now being experienced at the secondary level.

The results of changes in the functional roles of language varieties lead to a consideration of the second set of factors outlined earlier: the conditions imposed by the vernacular or other first language on the acquisition of SE and literacy in SE.

In this respect, the position of the FC vernacular vis-à-vis SE – like that of any other first language that is structurally and lexically unrelated to SE – is quite clear. The conditions are those that apply in the teaching and learning of a second or foreign language unrelated to the learner's first language. In theory and practice, these conditions are well-understood and need not be further discussed here. However, the early education of children in a second language, involving the conferment of initial literacy in that second language, raises another set of issues with international evidence, such as that cited in Craig (1977, 317–18), Simmons-McDonald (1996, 125–26), and Shields-Brodber (1997, 62), which indicates the following:

- children's cognitive development can be retarded if their first-language development is curtailed;
- children acquire a second language more easily and competently if they are confident and adequate in their first-language development; and
- initial literacy is best acquired in the first language.

The latter point clearly suggests that monolingual FC-speaking children could be greatly disadvantaged if their early education is in SE.

However, there is also evidence, largely from the cases studied in Lambert and Tucker (1972), and general evidence such as that in Genese (1988), that children educated in a second language may suffer no disadvantage if their learning of the second language comes naturally through their interaction with native speakers and through involvement in activity and content of interest to them. It is also important that they remain secure, confident and progressive in their first-language development, through their home and immediate community culture, like the monolingually educated children in the Canadian immersion programmes (Genese 1988). If similar modifying circumstances can be created for monolingual FC-speakers being educated in SE, then their disadvantage may be mitigated if not removed.

However, in the absence of an adequate early education in FC, or in the absence of modifying circumstances such as those just mentioned, consideration could be given to compensatory action that might relieve the disadvantage of monolingual FC speakers in the West Indies. (Such compensatory action would not have been necessary in the comparable Canadian immersion cases.) Compensatory action might probably best take the form of the oral use of the children's FC in primary education, to match the recommendation in Craig (1969) for the oral use of EC in EC-influenced situations.

In fact, this particular form of compensatory action might also best be taken in the cases of the childhood speakers of minority first languages, discussed earlier and noted in relation to strategies suggested in Craig (1996). For EC-influenced situations, the latter recommendation has subsequently appeared in a syllabus, "Free Talk" in Jamaica (1985) and "Talking Freely" Belize (1995), but whether its implementation is accompanied by the necessary teacher-inputs in other respects remains questionable, as will be discussed.

These issues, however, concern not only monolingual speakers of the FC vernacular and minority foreign languages, but also bilingual speakers of FC and EC or M, and monolingual speakers of EC or M, since all these cases involve early educational acquisition of, and literacy in, the second language, SE.

However, the EC-related cases differ from the monolingual FC because EC overlaps significantly in vocabulary and word order with SE. The precise nature of this overlap and the conditions it imposes on the teaching and learning of SE are discussed in the articles cited above, as well as in Craig (1983) and Craig (1999). In brief, what the discussion shows is that EC-influenced learners find it difficult to perceive grammatical contrasts between their speech and SE; as a consequence, SE does not easily appear to them as a new language and becoming motivated to learn it seems unnecessary to them. These reactions of EC-influenced learners of SE have been noted and commented upon since the 1960s, as shown in the literature cited, and are recognized as being not characteristic of the learning of either a native or a foreign language. This means that orthodox second-language teaching approaches to SE that – whatever the prevailing orthodoxy may be – could be tried with monolingual FC speakers are sure not to be efficacious with EC-influenced speakers. The latter has been repeatedly proven.

As the issues show, it is obvious that the vernacular languages impose significant conditions on the teaching and learning of SE. These conditions may be summarized as follows:

1. As a precondition to the teaching of SE, provision must be made for children's first-language development to be continuous and complete. There are several options for this, ranging from full literacy programmes in the first language, to oral-only programmes in the first language and to reliance on the home culture only for first-language development.
2. If children are monolingual speakers of FC or of a minority language unrelated to EC – whatever the vernacular or other first-language educational option chosen – the principles of teaching a second language, with or without initial literacy, have to be applied to SE.
3. If the vernacular is EC or M, the teaching of SE must be designed to take into account the proven and formidable effects of the vocabulary overlap between EC or M, on the one hand, and SE on the other.

In the light of the discussion so far, it is now possible to consider the third set of factors outlined earlier: the use that may be made of the vernacular or other first language in the teaching and learning of SE.

It will have been noted that the vernacular or other first language may be used in several different, though educationally related, ways. However, whether the vernacular or other first language is used as a medium for literacy, or only orally (as intended in Craig 1969), in Jamaica (1980) and Belize (1995), or through the home culture only (as in the Canadian school-immersion programmes), its use has to be recognized as having the following common and fundamental set of goals:

- exploration and expression of the child's own perceptions, ideas and thought processes;
- through the latter, the maintenance of continuity and the achievement of adequate maturation in the child's cognitive development (Cummins

1979a, 1979b; Long 1990); and
- creation of an adequately rich background of ideas and understanding that can serve as the content of second-language (SE) learning.

It has to be noted, however, that although these goals have been spoken about for some time now in the West Indies, and although, as discussed earlier, have even been extended into the secondary-school level in some cases, it is questionable whether they are being adequately pursued in classrooms. Field experience suggests that teachers remain much too obsessed with the "identity-assertion", "self-esteem", "friendly-relations" and "entertainment" aspects of the use of the vernacular. And this is so at a time when changes in the functional roles of language varieties have reduced the need for the psychological underpinnings of vernacular use to be particularly stressed. As a consequence of the obsessions mentioned, teachers are putting insufficient effort into eliciting from children the challenging topics, themes and intellectual rigour that Labov (1969), for example, demonstrated as possible in vernacular discourse. Teachers need guidance to correct the continuing imbalance.

This guidance should be incorporated into the guidelines for language and literacy programmes in West Indian schools. Apart from the school's use of the vernacular or other first language, however, there is an additional use which would also need to be incorporated into guidelines. This use is necessitated by the difficulty that EC and M speakers experience in perceiving contrasts between their language and SE because of lexical overlap. This use of the vernacular should take the form of procedures for the maximum possible development of *language awareness* among learners, which would be consistent with the now widely recognized fact that language learners can benefit significantly from the development of an implicit as well as explicit awareness of the characteristics of their own language as well as the targeted second language. Contributing to this recognition are studies of language awareness and consciousness raising such as those of Sharwood-Smith (1981) and Fotos (1994). Satisfying the stated need, particularly in EC-influenced learners, would make it easier for those learners not only to perceive contrasts but also to become motivated to acquire SE. The latter, in turn, can be expected to stimulate learners to become more proactive in the application of their own individual learning strategies (Oxford 1990; O'Malley and Chamot 1990; Green and Oxford 1995; Ely and Pease-Alvarez 1996).

Advice to teachers would entail direct use of the vernacular (FC, EC or M) or other first language. However, the overlap of EC or M with SE, also creates a need for a specific set of learner behaviours that are necessary for the acquisition of SE. These behaviours can be most directly evoked by an approach discussed at length in Craig (1999), which would apply procedures for the *perception/reception, internalization/understanding* and *creative utilization* of targeted aspects of use of the second language. These procedures would be independent of those that require the direct use of the vernacular, but they would remain heavily dependent, particularly in early education, on topics, themes, other content, and language awareness derived from the vernacular and its culture.

The combined procedures for the use of the vernacular, the development of language awareness and motivation towards SE, and specific activities in the teaching and learning of SE, embody a set of principles that Craig (1999) has named TESORV (Teaching English to Speakers of a Related Vernacular). As the name suggests, the rationale lies in the lexical relatedness of the learner's vernacular and SE, the targeted second language. TESORV is an eclectic blend of language-teaching approaches: cognitive, structural-contrastive and communicative. The contribution of each approach is determined by specific needs that learners have to have satisfied.

It is important to note TESORV's emphasis on satisfying the needs of specific learners. After the mid-1980s in the West Indies, as discussed in Craig (1999, ch. 4), the implementation of approaches specially designed for Creole-influenced learners often became diluted by the uncritical application of some practices in *communicative language teaching* (CLT) that ignore the specific circumstances of Creole-influenced learners. While some of these practices are valuable if appropriately contextualized, as indeed they are in TESORV, international concern about the shortcomings of CLT, as reviewed, for example, in Celce-Murcia et al. (1997), justify a renewed focus on satisfying learners' specific needs. Such a focus is attempted in Craig (1999), with detailed discussion of the relevant issues, suggestions, crucial syllabus, resources for teachers, and notes towards further study and research. Among the syllabus resources is an outline of a programme, "The Vernacular in Our Lives", which West Indian teachers may be interested in implementing in pursuit of the goals outlined in this chapter.

REFERENCES

Allsopp, R., ed. 1996. *Dictionary of Caribbean English Usage.* Oxford: Oxford University Press.

Amselle, J. 1997. "Adios Bilingual Ed". *Policy Review,* no. 86 (November–December): 52–55.

Bailey, B. 1964. "Some Problems in the Language Teaching Situation in Jamaica". In *Social Dialects and Language Learning,* ed. R. Shuy. Champaign, Ill.: National Council of Teachers of English.

Carrington, L. 1976. "Determining Language Education Policy in Caribbean Sociolinguistic Complexes". *International Journal of the Sociology of Language* 8: 127–43.

———. 1993. "Creole and Other Tongues in Caribbean Development". *Journal of Pidgin and Creole Languages* 8, no. 1: 125–33.

Celce-Murcia, M, Z. Dornvei and S. Thurrell. 1997. "Direct Approaches in L2 Instruction: A Turning Point in Communicative Language Teaching?" *TESOL Quarterly* 21, no. 1: 141–52.

Craig, D. 1969. *An Experiment in Teaching English.* Mona, Jamaica: Caribbean Universities Press.

———. 1971. "Education and Creole English in the West Indies". In *Pidginization and Creolization of Languages,* ed. D. Hymes, 371–92. Cambridge: Cambridge University Press.

———. 1976. "Bidialectal Education: Creole and Standard in the West Indies". *International Journal of the Sociology of Language* 8: 93–134. (Reprinted in *Sociolinguistic Aspects of Language Learning and Teaching,* ed. J. Pride, 164–84, 1979. Oxford: Oxford University Press.)

———. 1977. "Creole Languages and Primary Education". In *Pidgin and Creole Linguistics,* ed. A. Valdman, 313–32. Bloomington: Indiana University Press.

———. 1978–80. "Language, Society and Education in the West Indies". *Caribbean Journal of Education* 7, no. 1 (January): 1–17.

———. 1980. "Models for Educational Policy in Creole-Speaking Communities". In *Theoretical Orientations in Creole Studies,* ed. A. Valdman and A. Highfield, 245–85. New York: Academic Press.

———. 1983. "Teaching Standard English to Non-Standard Speakers: Some Methodological Issues". *Journal of Negro Education* 52: 65–74.

———. 1996. "The Language Education of Creole Speakers in International Urban Society". Keynote address at the Workshop on Creole Language Use in an Urban Setting: New Directions in Education and Society, Miami, March 22–23.

———. 1998. " 'Aftaa Yu Laan Dem fi Riid an Rait Dem Kriiyol, Den Wa Muo?':
Creole and the Teaching of the Lexifier Language". Paper presented at the Fourth
Annual International Creole Language Workshop. Linguistics Program, Miami,
March 19–21.

———. 1999. *Teaching Language and Literacy: Policies and Procedures for Vernacular
Situations*. Kingston: Education and Development Services.

———. 2000. "Lexical Overlap: Its Consequences for Creole-Based Language
Learning". Paper presented at the Thirteenth Biennial Conference of the Society for
Caribbean Linguistics". August, Mona, Jamaica.

Cummins, J. 1979a. "Educational Importance of Mother Tongue Maintenance in
Minority-Language Groups". *Canadian Modern Language Review* 34: 395–416.

———. 1979b. "Linguistic Interdependence and the Educational Development of
Bilingual Children". *Review of Educational Research* 49, no. 2: 221–51.

Devonish, H. 1986. *Language and Liberation: Creole Language Politics in the Caribbean*.
London: Karia Press.

———. 1996. "Vernacular Language and Writing Technology Transfer: The Jamaican
Case". In *Caribbean Language Issues Old and New: Papers in Honour of Professor
Mervyn Alleyne on the Occasion of His Sixtieth Birthday*, ed. P. Christie, 112–18.
Kingston: The Press, University of the West Indies.

Ely, C., and L. Pease-Alvarez. 1996. "Learning Styles and Strategies". Special issue.
TESOL Journal 6, no. 1: 42–47.

Fotos, S. 1994. "Integrating Grammar Instruction and Communicative Language
Use Through Grammar Consciousness-Raising Tasks". *TESOL Quarterly* 28:
323–35.

Genese, F. 1987. *Learning through Two Languages*. Rowley, Mass.: Newbury House.

———. 1988. "The Canadian Second Language Immersion Program". In *International
Handbook of Bilingualism and Bilingual Education*, ed. C. Paulston, 163–74. New
York: Greenwood Press.

Government of Belize. Ministry of Education. 1995. *Teachers' Guides, Language Arts,
Grades 1, 2, 3*. Belmopan: Curriculum Development Centre.

Government of Jamaica. Ministry of Education. 1980. *Foundations of Self-Reliance: A
Curriculum Guide for the Primary Stage of Education*. Kingston: General Education
Unit.

Green, J., and R. Oxford. "A Closer Look at Learning Strategies, L2 Proficiency and
Gender". *TESOL Quarterly* 29, no. 2: 261–98.

Labov, W. 1969. "The Logic of Non-Standard English". In *Twentieth Round Table
Meeting*, ed. J. Alatis, 1–43. Washington, DC: Georgetown University School of
Languages and Linguistics.

Lambert, W., and R. Tucker. 1972. *The Bilingual Education of Children: The St Lambert Experiment*. Rowley, Mass.: Newbury House.

Le Page, R., and A. Tabouret-Keller. 1985. *Acts of Identity: Creole-Based Approaches to Language and Ethnicity*. Cambridge: Cambridge University Press.

Long, M. 1990. "Maturational Constraints on Language Development". *Studies in Second Language Acquisition* 12, no. 4: 251–85.

O'Malley, J., and A. Chamot. 1990. *Learning Strategies in Language Acquisition*. Cambridge: Cambridge University Press.

Oxford, R. 1990. *Language Learning Strategies: What Every Teacher Should Know*. New York: Newbury House.

Patrick, P. 1997. "Style and Register in Jamaican Patwa". In *Englishes Around the World: Caribbean, Africa, Asia, Australasia: Studies in Honour of Manfred Gorlach*, vol. 2, ed. E. Schneider, 41–56. Amsterdam: John Benjamins.

Paulston, C. 1988. *International Handbook of Bilingualism and Bilingual Education*. New York: Greenwood Press.

Rickards, S. 1995. "The Language of Patois". *ROSEGRAM*. Kingston: Reform of Secondary Education (ROSE) Secretariat, Ministry of Education.

Rivers, W. 1979. "Learning a Sixth Language: An Adult Learner's Diary". *Canadian Modern Language Review* 36: 67–82.

Roberts, P. 1988. *West Indians and Their Language*. Cambridge: Cambridge University Press.

Robertson, I. 1996. "Language Education Policy 1: Towards a Rational Approach for Caribbean States". In *Caribbean Language Issues Old and New: Papers in Honour of Professor Mervyn Alleyne on the Occasion of His Sixtieth Birthday*, ed. P. Christie, 112–19. Kingston: The Press, University of the West Indies.

Schneider, E., ed. 1997. *Englishes Around the World: Caribbean, Africa, Asia, Australasia: Studies in Honour of Manfred Gorlach*, vol. 2. Amsterdam: John Benjamins.

Sharwood-Smith, M. 1981. "Consciousness-Raising and the Second Language Learner". *Applied Linguistics* 2: 159–69.

Shields-Brodber, K. 1997. "Requiem for English in an 'English-Speaking' Community: The Case of Jamaica". In *Englishes Around the World: Caribbean, Africa, Asia, Australasia: Studies in Honour of Manfred Gorlach*, vol. 2, ed. E. Schneider, 57–68. Amsterdam: John Benjamins.

Shuy, R., ed. 1964. *Social Dialects and Language Learning*. Champaign, Illinois: National Council of Teachers of English.

Simmons-McDonald, H. 1996. "Language Education Policy 2: The Case for Creole in Formal Education in St Lucia". In *Caribbean Language Issues Old and New: Papers in Honour of Professor Mervyn Alleyne on the Occasion of His Sixtieth Birthday*, ed.

P. Christie, 120–42. Kingston: The Press, University of the West Indies.

UNESCO. 1953. *The Use of Vernacular Languages in Education*. Monographs on Fundamental Education. Paris: UNESCO.

Williams, R. L. 1975. *Ebonics: The True Language of Black Folks*. St Louis: Institute of Black Studies.

Wolfram, W. 1970. "Sociolinguistic Alternatives in Teaching Reading to Non-Standard Speakers". *Reading Research Quarterly* 6, no. 1: 9–33.

Chapter 6

Vernacular Instruction and Bi-Literacy Development in French Creole Speakers

Hazel Simmons-McDonald

Introduction

Language education issues, particularly those relating to the learning outcomes of speakers of Creoles and vernaculars, have provided a focus for discussion and research among educators and linguists in the Caribbean and elsewhere. Studies done in the Caribbean have drawn attention to the problems experienced by native speakers of Creole in learning English as well as to the ways in which education policies have influenced teaching practice and have directly or indirectly determined language learning outcomes. Early concern with this issue by educators and linguists focused on the impact of the language situation on education in selected Caribbean territories. The La Trobe report of 1838 first drew attention to this issue. Later studies paid attention to the language-learning problems of students who did not speak English as the home language. In an early work, Carrington and Borely (1977) drew attention to the deleterious effects of a monolingual English policy on young Creole-speaking children entering school for the first time. Several papers pointed to the need for taking the learner's native language into account in some way (Craig 1971, 1977; Roberts 1983, 1993; Simmons-McDonald 1996, 2001). Carrington (1976) discussed the contexts in which it would be feasible to use vernacular varieties as media of instruction and proposed a set of principles for implementing these varieties in education. Craig (1980) presented different educational models for incorporating vernaculars as media of instruction.

While these and other papers on the subject have drawn attention to the plight of non-native English speakers by placing language and the approach to language teaching at the centre of the debate on development education, few have considered practical procedures for implementing vernaculars in education in the region. Devonish (1983, 1986) presented proposals for standardizing Creole languages and using them to teach English in schools. His discussion focused on general policy and on the benefit to Creole speakers. Craig (1999) presented approaches for developing literacy through the incorporation of a vernacular programme for "maintaining the home language and culture and strengthening the language awareness of pupils" (p. 274) as well as through the use of a combination of principles from established approaches to language teaching, such as the audio-lingual method and the situational, cognitive and communicative approaches. Craig's approach also allowed for the use of contrastive methods, particularly in the area of phonology. Although the principles outlined by Craig include the vernacular, its role appears to be primarily to heighten learners' awareness of language differences, and its recommended use is intended to ease the transition to school for the non-native speaker of English.

Overall, the recommendations for the inclusion of Creole-influenced vernaculars as media of instruction in the Caribbean have been tentative. Despite general acceptance of Creoles and Creole-influenced vernaculars by Caribbean people, there is still a great deal of reserve regarding the use of these varieties in education. The perception that they are "inferior" to English and therefore inappropriate for purposes of education still obtains in many circles, including among teachers and educators in the region. Many educators have resisted the use of these language varieties in education because of a fear that their use as media of instruction might simply reinforce the Creole or non-standard variety and retard the development of literacy in Standard English. Perhaps one of the reasons for the persistence of prevailing negative attitudes towards these language varieties in education is that the results of the studies, particularly those that have shown a positive impact of the native language on learning (even when that language is a Pidgin or a Creole), are not generally publicized in the region.

Several papers included in Tabouret-Keller et al. (1997) discussed the conditions that are conducive to the implementation of vernacular literacy and evaluated several contexts in which such programmes have been successful. Gerbault (p. 148) made the point that literacy acquisition is not language acquisition and that "a person can only learn to read in a language he understands". She went on to say that "in the acquisition of literacy, as in all learning, it makes sense to go from the known (the spoken language) to the unknown (its written representation)". In an article in the same text, Gardner-Chloros remarked that "it is pointless to teach people to master sophisticated literacy skills in a language of which they possess only the barest tools". She further noted that in the case of children "the problem is likely to be compounded if the introduction of the L2 (the second language) and of L2 literacy is at the expense of the normal full development of their vernacular" (p. 219). Studies done in the St Lucian context (Simmons-McDonald 1994, 1999) showed that French Creole speakers in primary school lagged behind their English-speaking peers by at least two years and that some of them did not become sufficiently proficient in English to enable them to continue on to the secondary level.

Some studies conducted in other contexts have reported that the metalinguistic development of learners is enhanced by the acquisition of two or more languages (Bialystok 1991). Cummins (1994, 38) reported that studies he reviewed in 1991 showed that if the conceptual foundation of a child's first language (L1) was well-developed, he or she would be more likely to develop "similarly high levels of conceptual abilities in [an] L2". Swain and Lapkin (1991) reported that comparisons of children who had acquired literacy in two languages with monolingual or bilingual children who had not acquired literacy in their home language showed better performance by the former when they attempted to acquire a third language.

In another paper, Swain pointed out that skills basic to academic progress are most easily learned in L1 (cited in Walker 1984, 165). Walker observed that it "is easier to learn to read in L1 and then to apply this skill to L2 rather than learn to read and learn L2 simultaneously." He indicated that "once the reading skill is automated through L1, more attention can be paid to the acquisition of L2". Siegel (1999) reviewed research in which stigmatized varieties were used in the classroom and concluded that the findings showed that "appropriate teaching methodology incorporating students' vernaculars may actually help them acquire the standard" (p. 721). Siegel (1997) also examined a programme that used Tok Pisin to develop literacy in pre-school children who were native speakers of Tok Pisin. He reported that the use of the Pidgin resulted in greater gains for them than for children who had not been exposed to programmes in which Tok Pisin had been used. He concluded that the Pidgin had not been a hindrance in the children's acquisition of literacy.

Research on bilingual as well as on vernacular education provides ample support for the view that the use of the learner's native language can be helpful to and not disadvantageous for the learner. This chapter reports on a study which was undertaken to examine this hypothesis by implementing a model that made use of French Creole as one of the languages of instruction in St Lucia.

THE CONCEPTUAL MODEL FOR THE FRENCH CREOLE COMPONENT

The French Creole alternative model that formed the basis for the study reported here is one component of a tripartite vernacular instructional model developed by the author (2000) for speakers of the three language varieties spoken in St Lucia, namely St Lucian Standard English (SLSE), St Lucian English-Lexicon Vernacular (SLEV) and St Lucian French Creole (SLFC, also referred to as Kwéyòl). The model is fully described in the 2000 paper; consequently, only a brief outline is presented here. The three components of the model are synchronized and integrated to allow for instruction to be tailored to the language needs of the learners when they first enter school. The model thus seeks to address directly the needs of speakers of the three varieties. The components are designed for simultaneous implementation with groups of speakers from the three different language backgrounds in either a heterogeneous classroom setting or separately, homogeneous groups. All three components are designed to develop a learner's ability to read in the home language and in Standard English. It is essentially a model for the development of bi-literacy and it promotes an understanding of the differences between the language varieties, primarily through an integrated language programme with a rich literature base that makes use of culturally relevant materials.

This chapter reports on a modified implementation of the French Creole (henceforth Kwéyòl) component, based on the proposition that children who speak Kwéyòl as their native language should be helped to develop literacy in it, even as they are exposed to a programme that fosters the acquisition of St Lucian Standard. The expected outcomes for a programme based on the French Creole component are

- the development of proficiency in the second language (SLSE);
- proficiency in the child's native language;
- promotion of the use of the native language for a wider range of purposes, including academic purposes; and
- the development of academic language proficiency[1] in both Kwéyòl and English as a means of fostering bilingualism and bi-literacy in these languages.

Figure 6.1 is a schematic representation of the Kwéyòl component.

Figure 6.1 Kwéyòl Instructional Model

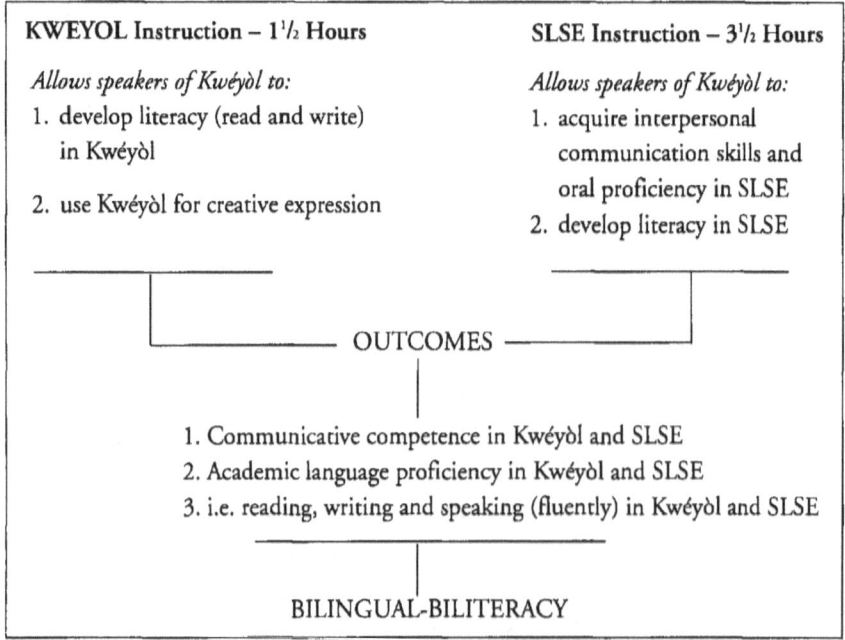

The model provides learners with one-and-a-half hours of instruction in Kwéyòl and three-and-a-half hours in Standard English daily. It therefore promotes the development of early literacy in the first language (the L1) even as learners acquire communicative competence in the L2. During the time devoted to Kwéyòl instruction, learners would be exposed to a programme that, in the early grades (pre-kindergarten to Grade 1), focuses on emergent literacy in Kwéyòl. As literacy in Kwéyòl develops and learners acquire communicative skills in English, the focus in Grades 1 through 6 would shift increasingly to the development of literacy in English. However, the model also allows for continuing literacy development in both languages. The integrated programme provides a framework for the introduction of rich reading selections, including narrative choices in which the characters express themselves in vernacular varieties (in this case Kwéyòl) as well as English, thereby providing a natural context for the judicious comparison of these varieties.

RESEARCH DESIGN

A modified version of the French Creole model was used in the study reported here. Because it was not possible to begin the study with a kindergarten group, as recommended in the model, permission was sought to conduct a limited preliminary pilot study with a small group of learners in higher grades. This meant that the full-scale model could not be implemented over an extended period of several consecutive weeks of instruction, but was done in six intensive sessions each of one week's duration over three terms. The model was modified to allow for forty-five minutes of instruction in Kwéyòl and one hour of English in each session.

A single-subject research design (Neuman and McCormick 1995) was selected for the study as this allowed for the subjects to be used as their own controls. Neuman and McCormick (1995, 4) explained that the goal of single-subject experimental research is "to demarcate each individual's current level or stage of responses at the beginning of an experiment and then to determine the degree to which approaches examined in the investigation change each individual's responses". This design allows for the analysis of every subject's responses, thereby permitting a researcher to do a "personalized" and individual analysis of a subject's performance.

The methodology requires the gathering of baseline data which is displayed on a graph and which is contrasted with intervention data. The baseline allows the researcher to determine and show a subject's behaviour or performance before an intervention is introduced. During an intervention, the subject's performance is measured frequently and repeatedly, and the results are also displayed graphically and compared with the baseline performance. Neuman and McCormick (1995, 5) pointed out that in many cases with single-subject research "a student's changes in response are not contrasted with changes (or lack of changes) of other individuals in the study. And in almost all cases, changes are compared with the student's own pre-intervention level of responding." Neuman and McCormick referred to this as "using the subject as his or her own control and (this) is accomplished by collecting baseline data". They explained further that the term "single-subject" refers to a process rather than to the actual number of participants (p. 4). In short, this design eliminates the need to have a control group: the individuals in the study are their own controls; this is made possible by establishing baseline data and then comparing these results with intervention results.

THE SAMPLE

The sample for the pilot study was drawn from a group of sixty-nine children who had been identified by teachers as having severe reading problems. Reading records of all sixty-nine children on the list were taken, using the reading record system designed by Depree and Iversen (1994). The results of that initial survey revealed that approximately 60 per cent of the children were reading between two and four grade levels below their reading age and that 40 per cent were beginning readers. The profiles of all the children indicated that they needed immediate and intensive instruction in reading. However, because of the limited time available, three of those in the ten-to-twelve age range were considered to be at greatest risk and were selected for the intensive preliminary pilot study.

The subjects were two boys, Ado and Dovi, who were twelve and eleven years old, respectively, and one girl, Uka,[2] who was ten at the start of the study. All three children were dominant Kwéyòl speakers when they entered school, but by the time of the study, they all spoke the St Lucian English lexicon vernacular variety (SLEV) fluently. Table 6.1 shows the profile of the subjects in the sample.

Table 6.1   Profile of Subjects in the Sample

Subject	Age	Sex	Actual Grade Level	Reading Level	% Accuracy – Reading Level at Survey	% Sound-Symbol Correspondences Recognized at Survey
Ado	12	Male	6	Grade 1	85.5	88.5
Uka	10	Female	5	Beginning	-50.0	81.0
Dovi	11	Male	5	Beginning	50.0	84.0

The initial survey results showed that Ado was reading at a beginning Grade 1 level but with considerable frustration. Several of the selections from the readers used at Grade 1, including seen texts, proved to be difficult, and he read them with several lengthy pauses between words and phrases; he omitted several words and made many requests for help. Uka was unable to read and she did not know the sound-symbol correspondences for several letters of the alphabet. She could recognize only a few words from the word lists in the kindergarten books. The -50 per cent reflects a very high level of frustration in reading a selection at the kindergarten level. Dovi's situation at the start of the study was similar to Uka's. He had only a few words in his sight vocabulary and had some difficulty with sound-symbol correspondences in English. Attempts to take reading records in Kwéyòl during the survey proved futile because the children could not read in Kwéyòl and used the English sound representation for the letters that they recognized in Kwéyòl texts. Of the three children, only Ado had participated in an end-of-term reading session in Kwéyòl, organized by An Tjè Nou, the publisher of Kwéyòl texts, who had made available some storybooks with Kwéyòl folk-tales for the children at the school. However, although Ado knew one of the stories, he could not decode the words in the text or read it fluently.

Procedures

The single-subject design required the establishment of a performance baseline for each subject, then the introduction of the intervention, which, in this case, involved teaching the children the sound systems of Kwéyòl and English. This was done during sessions in which one or the other of the two languages was the focus. Phonics instruction was given considerable contextual support within the framework of a rich reading programme. The children were engaged in listening to a variety of selections and were encouraged to attempt to read and talk about the selections that were read to them; they also expressed personal responses to the narratives. The language used as the medium of instruction in a given lesson was used throughout the lesson.

The teaching sessions with the group closely followed the framework outlined in the description of the model. A typical teaching day began with the Kwéyòl session, which lasted for forty-five minutes to an hour. This was followed by a mid-morning break, followed by the English session, which lasted sixty to seventy-five minutes with the whole group. During the afternoon, sessions were scheduled for individual interaction with the children so as to work with them on areas in which they needed attention and to give them opportunities to practice reading, to talk about what they had read and to retell stories. Reading records were usually taken during early morning sessions. Kwéyòl and English were alternated in individual sessions, unless the children asked specifically to read in both languages, which they were sometimes allowed to do.

A typical session usually began with conversation in the relevant language, exchanging news about school, or community activities or anything else they wanted to share with the group. The children then selected the stories they wanted to read (from the stories made available) during the session. Each reading session was preceded by discussion to activate the children's prior knowledge about the selection. If the level of difficulty was within the capability of one of the children, that child would be invited to read. Alternatively, the researcher would read and the children were encouraged to interrupt and comment or ask questions. Discussion was an integral part and always took place before, during and after reading, to help the children construct the meaning of the text. When appropriate, attention was drawn to the letter-sound correspondences that had been the focus of instruction during the week. At the end of the group reading session, the children were allowed to represent their responses to the text orally, in writing, or through drawing and painting. Of the three children, Ado made the most progress with writing and often chose to write his response to the reading. The discussion that followed the reading provided the opportunity to check the children's understanding of what they had read. Questions and opportunities for the children to retell what they had read also provided a basis for checking their understanding. Greater attention was given to reading in this study, but it was possible to check the children's writing and to give them some guidance on sentence construction and other features. Only Ado consistently chose writing as a means of representing his response to what he had read. Uka and Dovi chose drawing more frequently.

THE MATERIALS

A wide selection of reading materials was used in the pilot. The new readers produced by the Curriculum and Materials Development Unit (CAMDU) were the readers of choice in the school. These, as well as selections from the Nelson Readers first, second and third primers and a wide range of stories, including several from the Longman Read Awhile series, were used for English. For the Kwéyòl component, the basic reader *Li ek Ekwi Kwéyòl*, developed by the Summer Institute of Linguistics, was found to be most suitable as the basic instructional text. In addition, a wide selection of stories from the series published by An Tjè Nou was used for group sessions and individual silent reading. Table 6.2 shows the materials used during the study.

Table 6.2 List of Kwéyòl and English Texts Used in the Pilot Study

Kwéyòl Texts	Publisher	English Texts	Publisher
Li ek Ekwi Kwéyòl	Summer Institute of Linguistics	The New CAMDU Series (Grades K–3)	Macmillan
Stories and Fables [A selection of five]	An Tjè Nou	The Nelson West Indian Readers	Nelson Caribbean
		Read Awhile Narratives	Longman Caribbean

The Instrument

The Record of Reading Behaviour, based on the work of Clay and Goodman and developed by Depree and Iversen (1994), was used to take running records of the children's reading behaviour. The records were taken at different points in the study. Selections of seen and unseen texts of approximately one hundred to one hundred and fifty words were used to score two measures, namely the reading level and the self-correction rate. Seen texts were usually selected to test fluency at a given level while unseen texts were used to determine whether a child was able to read text independently at a given level of difficulty.

The reading level was determined first by calculating the error rate, then finding the corresponding accuracy percentage, using either the formula or the conversion table that the authors developed for this purpose. The error types taken into account were omissions, insertions, substitutions and teacher-told items. The self-correction rate was determined first by adding the number of errors to the number of self-corrections, then dividing by the total number of self-corrections. Depree and Iversen (1994, 56) indicate that an accuracy score of 95 to 100 per cent suggests that a child can read the given selection and others of similar difficulty easily and independently. However, a score of 89 per cent or less on a given selection suggests that it is too difficult for the child to read independently and that guided instruction is required. In addition to the accuracy score (fluency measure) and the self-correction rate, the other measures tested in the study included phonological awareness and the ability to recognize words in context and words in lists. Only the fluency and self-correction measures are reported here. The results on phonological awareness and word recognition are presented elsewhere.

Results and Discussion

The purpose of the pilot study was to test the effects of using an alternative model that included Kwéyòl as a language of instruction. The results on two of the measures examined, specifically accuracy (or level of fluency) and self-correction rates, are presented and discussed here. The accuracy percentages for English and Kwéyòl were plotted separately, to show individual performance in the two languages. Performance in both languages was then compared by plotting the accuracy percentages for each on the same chart, showing the trends of development in reading in both languages.

ENGLISH RESULTS

All three children were reading at high levels of frustration during the survey. Ado could read some selections from kindergarten texts with ease, but most of the selections from the Grade 1 text were too difficult. Both Uka and Dovi had minimal competence in reading. They could only decode some individual two- and three-letter words and could not read an entire sentence in the kindergarten reader independently. Table 6.3 shows the words in the children's sight vocabulary at the start of the study.

Table 6.3 Words in Sight Vocabulary at the Start of the Study

Subject	Grade	Words in Sight Vocabulary	Difficult Words
Ado	6	*it, and, that, my, by, he, the*	*for, from, a, feet, he, an*
Uka	5	*at, we, he, is*	*the, got, ran, this, his, up, us, an, am*
Dovi	5	*he, sit*	*us, from, can, to, no, cap, his, not, in*

Figure 6.2 shows the accuracy or reading fluency level for Ado. The first three data points on the figure represent the baseline established after the first few instructional sessions that immediately followed the survey. During these sessions, instruction focused on teaching the children the sound-symbol correspondences for English and on reading selections which emphasized these correspondences. An intensive intervention followed during which instruction proceeded according to the pattern described earlier in the section on procedures. The other data points reflect Ado's performance during the intervention session. In these sessions, attention was given to reinforcing Ado's phonological awareness, developing his word-recognition strategies and his reading practice.

Figure 6.2 Accuracy Percentages for English: Ado

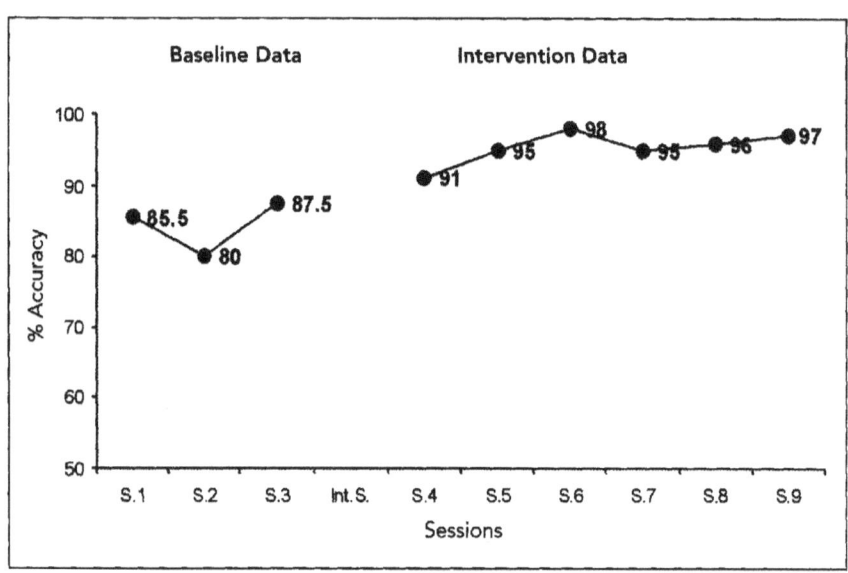

The first two points of the baseline data show Ado's accuracy on more difficult reading selections from the kindergarten reader. The data points at Sessions 4, 5 and 6 show his accuracy percentage on Grade 1 texts. The points at Sessions 7 and 8 show his accuracy on selections from Grade 2 texts and the last data point at Session 9 shows his accuracy percentage on a Grade 3 text. What these data show is that Ado, who had been reading kindergarten and Grade 1 texts with a high level of frustration at the start of the study, was reading Grade 2 and Grade 3 texts independently and with ease by the end of the study.

Uka was reported as having a high absentee rate from school and indeed she missed some instructional sessions and had to have additional lessons. She showed minimal competence in reading during the survey and the individual attention she received during instruction focused on developing phonological awareness and providing her with opportunities to practice decoding and develop fluency. Figure 6.3 shows the accuracy percentages for Uka in the baseline and intervention sessions.

The first baseline data points show an increase from -50 per cent to 85.5 per cent. These figures indicate that Uka experienced considerable difficulty

Figure 6.3 Accuracy Percentages for English: Uka

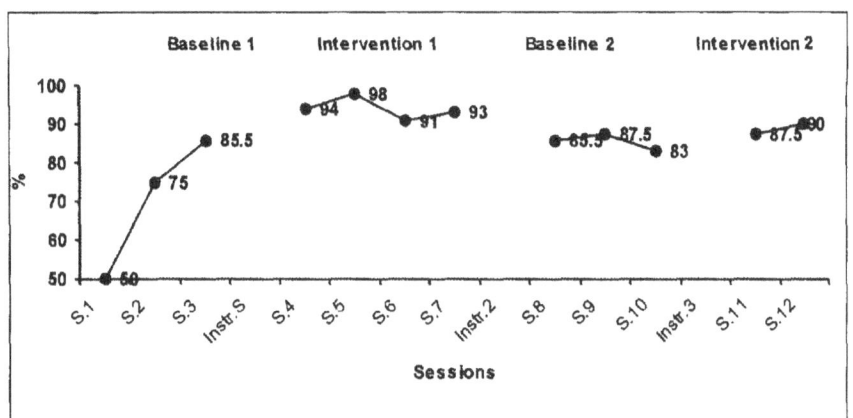

reading basic sentences and simple text in the kindergarten series. However, after intensive instruction her accuracy improved. This is reflected in the data points shown at Intervention 1 where the accuracy percentage was increased with variability in the 90 per cent range. An accuracy score in the range of 90 to 94 per cent indicates that the reader finds the text selections challenging but can achieve greater control over the texts with some guidance. (Depree and Iversen 1994, 57). The data points at Sessions 8 through 10 reflect Uka's attempts to read selections from the Grade 1 readers and from a narrative by Beverley Cleary. A baseline was established within the range of 83 per cent to 87.5 per cent. The increase to an accuracy rate of 90 per cent by Session 12 suggests that Uka had begun to achieve greater control of the reading material at Grade 1 level of difficulty.

Dovi's survey data also showed that he had minimal competence in reading. He was able to recognize some sound-symbol correspondences as well as a few words from the list in the kindergarten series but could not read through a sentence at that level with fluency. The data points at the first three sessions indicate a gradually improving trend after initial instruction. However, the figures show that he still experienced a high level of frustration in reading basic texts at kindergarten level. The data points in the intervention sessions show an improvement in the 90 per cent range, indicating ability to read the texts at kindergarten level with a greater degree of control. In addition to helping Dovi develop phonological awareness and strategies for

Figure 6.4   Accuracy Percentages for English: Dovi

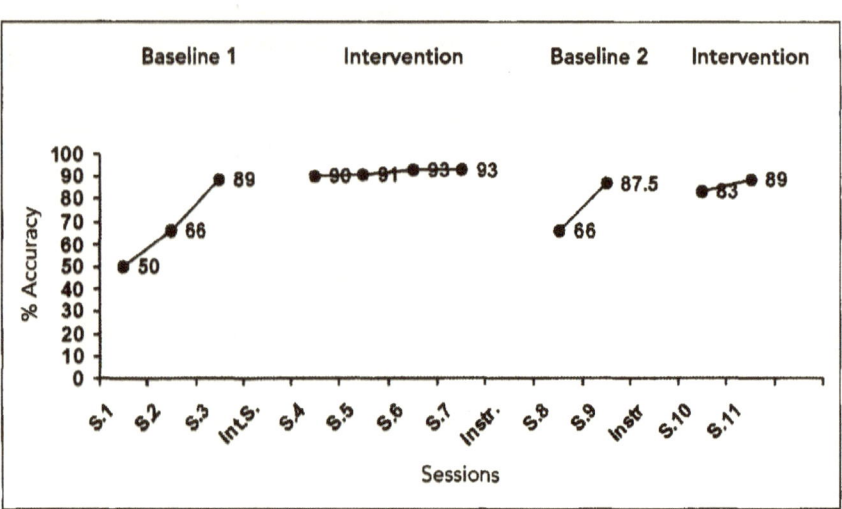

automatic decoding, close guidance was also provided for reading during the intervention sessions. Baseline data also showed gradually increasing accuracy on kindergarten text selections – from 50 per cent to 89 per cent. Figure 6.4 shows his accuracy percentages.

In the first four sessions after the intervention, Dovi achieved accuracy in the range of 90–93 per cent on selected texts from the kindergarten readers' series. A second intensive intervention was introduced after Session 7, when he began to read selections from the Grade 1 series. The data points at Sessions 8 and 9 show his attempts to read texts at Grade 1 during instructional sessions. Sessions 10 and 11 show that he had fluency rates of 83 per cent and 89 per cent. He was reading Grade 1 texts at an instructional level in these sessions, that is, he needed guidance during his reading of these texts. However, a comparison of the first baseline data set with the second (Sessions 8 and 9) show an improvement in that the second set represents his reading at Grade 1 level while the first represented a beginning level with kindergarten-level selections. Although he had slight improvement, the 89 per cent figure at the end of the study indicated that Dovi would continue to need guided reading at the Grade 1 level in order to become an independent reader with a high level of fluency at that grade level. Of the three children, Dovi was slowest in achieving fluency. He was also the least enthusiastic about learning to read.

SELF-CORRECTION RATES

For the most part, Ado's self-correction rate varied between 1:2 and 1:3. A self-correction rate of 1:3 means that he corrected 1 out of every 3 errors he made. A self-correction rate of 1:3 to 1:5 is considered to be a good indicator that the learner is noticing and correcting miscues during reading. In Session 7, when a new and more difficult Grade 2 text was introduced, Ado's self-correction rate was 1:7, which indicated that he was probably paying more attention to decoding and processing more difficult syntactic constructions and therefore paid less attention to his mistakes. The self-correction rates for the three children are shown in Table 6.4.

The self-correction rates shown in the second row of Table 6.4 indicate that Uka worked at the discrepancies that arose during reading. Although she

Table 6.4 Self-Correction Rates in English

Sessions	4	5	6	7	8	9	10	11	12
Ado	1:3	1:2	1:4	1:7	1:2	1:2	1:3	–	–
Uka	1:2	1:3	1:2	1:6	1:3	1:4	1:3	1:1	1:3
Dovi	1:1	1:3	1:2	1:3	1:3	1:4	1:8	1:3	–

achieved 93 per cent accuracy at Session 7, she recorded the lowest self-correction rate of 1:6, which indicates that she ignored some miscues.

Table 6.4 shows that Dovi had a high level of awareness of discrepancies for the most part, except for Session 10 when he did not correct several miscues. The self-correction rate of 1:3 for the final session of the study indicates he had a high level of awareness of the text and of mistakes in his reading even though he did not, in every case, correct his errors.

The Kwéyòl Results

None of the subjects had received any formal instruction in Kwéyòl and, although they knew several stories and could retell them in Kwéyòl, they were unable to read in Kwéyòl or to recognize any of the sound-symbol correspondences in Kwéyòl. Early instructional sessions therefore focused on reading to the children in Kwéyòl and drawing attention to phonics in context as well as providing additional opportunities for recognizing words. The approach was integrated and followed a similar pattern to that used for English. Opportunities for listening, speaking, reading and writing (or drawing) were provided in every session. A typical session began with discussions in Kwéyòl about school, community and personal activities that the children had engaged in on the weekend or on the previous day. After this, a story selected by the children from the An Tjè Nou series was read and a discussion session followed in which the children expressed their responses to the story.

Some of the phonemes proved to be difficult initially. Table 6.5 lists the items that caused problems.

Table 6.5 Kwéyòl Phonology That Caused Some Difficulty

Phoneme	Example	Gloss
j	jip	skirt
dj	djèp	wasp
tj	tjilòt	trousers
ch	chapo	hat
on	mouton	sheep
é	hélé	cry
è	pèl	shovel
ò	sòt	silly
an	ban	bench

Confusion arose most often with é and è because the children did not always pay attention to the acute or grave accents which signalled that a different pronunciation from the neutral [e] was required. They made more mistakes with these phones during the early sessions. Nevertheless, all the children showed high levels of understanding of the Kwéyòl selections and

Figure 6.5 Accuracy Percentages for Kwéyòl – Ado

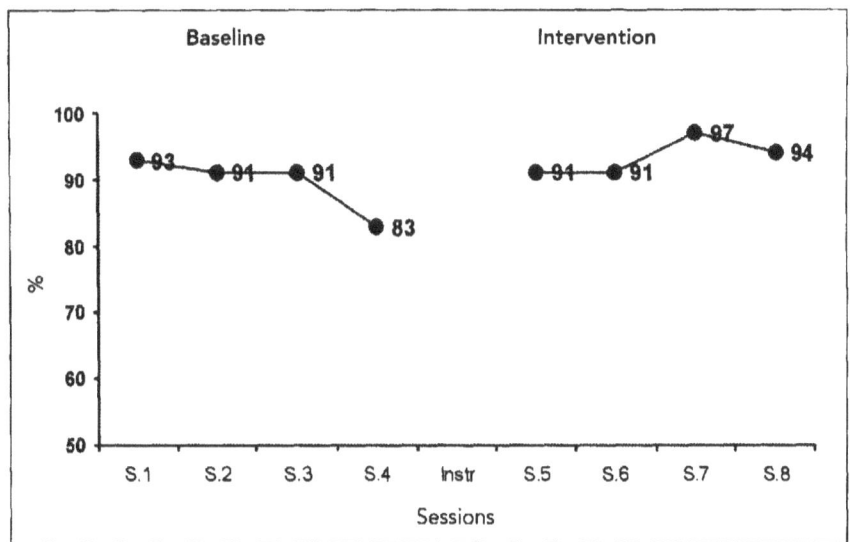

were able to make inferences without much difficulty. The text used for the developing literacy activities was the Summer Institute of Linguistics publication *Li ek Ekwi Kwéyòl* (LEK). The accuracy percentages for each child are shown in Figures 6.5–6.7.

During the intervention sessions, more advanced selections from the LEK text were attempted as well as narratives from the An Tjè Nou series. The last two data points of the intervention series show that by the end of the study Ado had achieved greater independence in reading in Kwéyòl. During group sessions, he increasingly offered to read to the group and did so with confidence. Self-correction rates in Kwéyòl were consistently good (see Table 6.6). With the exception of Session 2, in which the rate was 1:4, the rates were never higher than 1:2. In any case, a self-correction rate of 1:4 indicates a high level of noticing errors. A comparison of these data with the English self-correction rates shows a higher level of noticing errors while reading the Kwéyòl. This suggests that processing in the native language while reading was easier for him. Ado also responded frequently to what he had read by writing in Kwéyòl. The following are examples of Ado's writing in English and Kwéyòl. The errors in the examples are italicized and the correct forms are in brackets.

English Samples

1. Lester and Joe *was* going to catch crabs. Lester was having fun on his *oun*. There was no need for flashlight because the moon was shining *britly.*
2. (Personal response to a poem.) The Grade 3 pupils speak in the poem. The word that best describes the children is hard-working. I like the way they *exprest there filing* (feeling). They do not fight, steal or cheat. The best part of the poem I like is we look so smart from head to feet.

Rough translations are given for the Kwéyòl examples. Self-corrections are italicized. The second examples in English and Kwéyòl were written during the last session and they are more controlled and fluent than the first. The Kwéyòl examples show the difficulty that Ado had with the [é] [è] distinction, but there are fewer errors with these forms in the second sample.

Kwéyòl Samples

1. Zanndoli andjélé Konp*é* Chyen pas *lè* e i *to* (té) vlé Konpè Lapen *poto* (pòté) yo wèspé. Konpe Zanndoli to (té) faché piscè Konpe Lapen pa té ni pus (pyès) wèspé pu li.
(Lizard called comrade/partner dog because he wanted comrade rabbit to have respect for them. Comrade lizard was angry because comrade rabbit had no respect for him.)
2. Man Aynèz té ka wété Labowi. Tifi Man Aynèz té bai . . . Konpè Lapen . . . Konpè Chouval épi Konpè Lapen té vlé mayé tifi man Aynèz. Chouval *téka* (té ka) alé lakay man Aynèz tou *la* (lé) sanmdi. I té ka alé lakay Man Aynèz pou i kozé épi tifi-a.
(Mrs Aynez used to live in Laborie. Mrs Aynez's daughter had given – comrade rabbit – [both] comrade rabbit, and comrade horse wanted to marry Mrs Aynez's daughter. Horse used to go to Mrs Aynez's house every Saturday. He used to go to her house to chat with [or court] Mrs Aynez's daughter.)

Uka's Kwéyòl results also show better performance towards the end of the study. One must recall that Uka could not read either English or Kwéyòl at

Figure 6.6   Accuracy Percentages for Kwéyòl – Uka

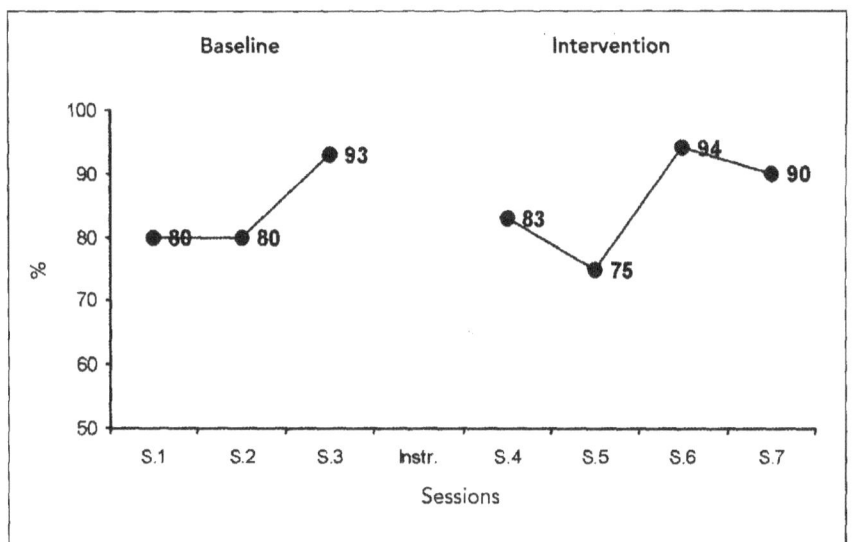

the start of the study. The last data point in the baseline series shows Uka achieving an increasing level of control in reading Kwéyòl. The data points at Sessions 4 and 5 show the accuracy percentages for unfamiliar and slightly more difficult texts. This accounts for the lower accuracy rates of 83 per cent and 75 per cent. However, the accuracy rates of 94 per cent and 90 per cent in the last two sessions are particularly encouraging because they suggest that while the texts read at this level presented some challenges to Uka, she seemed to be moving towards increased control and independence in reading Kwéyòl texts.

In the records taken immediately after the initial instruction in Kwéyòl, Dovi achieved high accuracy – 97 per cent – on the first six reading selections from LEK. The first two sessions and the two following sessions, in which he attempted to read unseen selections from the same text, were used to establish the baseline for accuracy. In the instruction that followed these sessions, Dovi was provided with guided reading sessions to help him develop fluency in reading longer selections from LEK. The accuracy percentages are indicated in the four data points of the intervention series shown in Figure 6.7.

The lower percentages of 87.5 per cent and 80 per cent at Sessions 6 and

Figure 6.7   Accuracy Percentages for Kwéyòl – Dovi

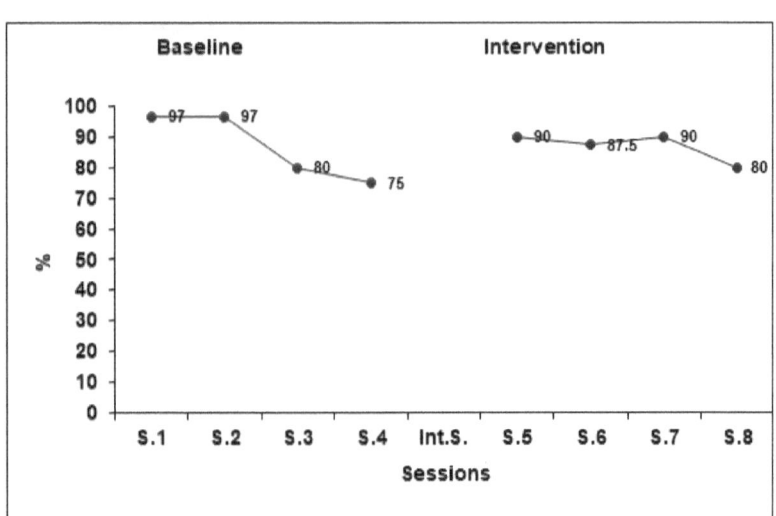

8 reflect attempts to read new, unseen texts from LEK. Unlike the other two children, Dovi did not attempt to read any of the narratives from the An Tjé Nou series on his own although he participated in shared reading activities in which these narratives were read and he joined in the discussions about them. He was more hesitant than Ado or Uka in his efforts to read in English and in Kwéyòl. The reasons are probably related to other factors, including his attitude to and interest in learning as well as physical factors that were beyond the scope of the study. The self-correction rates for Kwéyòl are shown in Table 6.6.

Of the three subjects, Ado's rates were consistently good, ranging between

Table 6.6   Self-Correction Rates in Kwéyòl

Sessions	1	2	3	4	5	6	7	8
Ado	1:2	1:4	1:2	1:2	1:2	1:1	1:2	1:2
Uka	1:3	1:3	1:3	1:12	1:12	1:1	–	–
Dovi	1:1	1:3	1:11	1:4	1:3	1:3	1:2	1:2

1:1 and 1:4. These rates show that while reading he was aware of miscues and other discrepancies and that he acted on them. With the exception of Sessions 4 and 5, in which Uka had high rates of 11 and 12, respectively, she showed a high degree of awareness and corrected errors. Similarly, Dovi had one session (Session 3) in which several lapses were recorded. His level of awareness and self-correction in all other sessions was commendable.

COMPARISON OF ENGLISH AND KWÉYÒL RESULTS

One question the study sought to answer was whether the levels-development of reading ability would be comparable in the native and second languages if a model directly incorporating the native language was used. As a means of comparing performance in both languages, the figures for all sessions in both languages were plotted together for each of the subjects. Figures 6.8 through

Figure 6.8 Accuracy Percentages for Kwéyòl and English – Ado

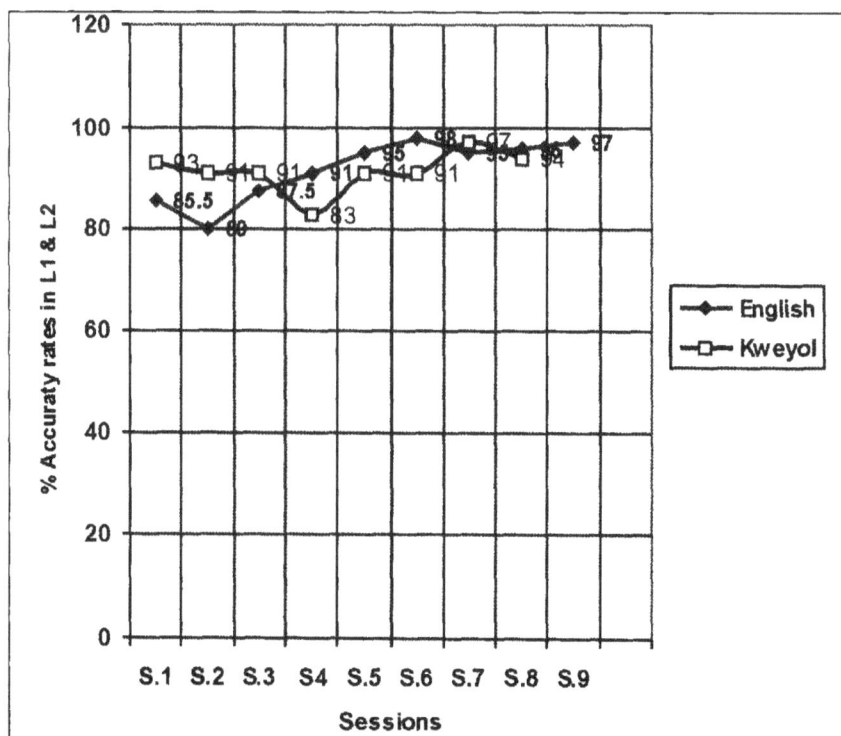

Figure 6.9   Accuracy Percentages for Kwéyòl and English – Uka

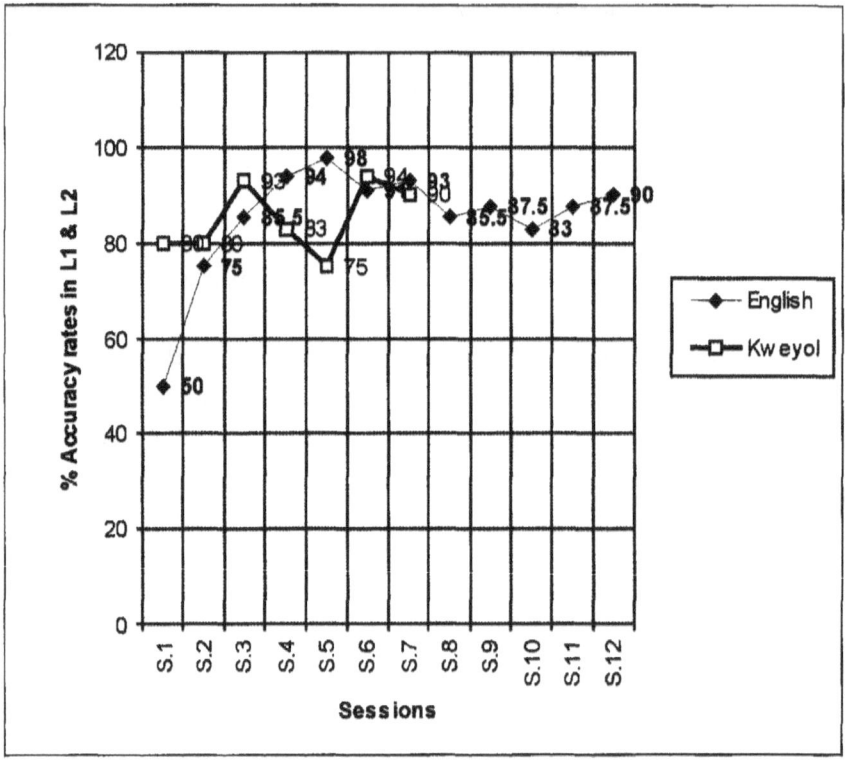

6.10 show these results. The baseline and intervention figures are included in the charts.

The trends in Ado's case (Figure 6.8) show a close correspondence in accuracy in reading in both languages. Accuracy percentages for Kwéyòl are higher at the start of the study, but at the end performance in both languages is on par. Overall, Ado's results show a comparable performance in L1 and L2, which strongly suggests balanced development in reading in English and Kwéyòl. The writing examples also indicated a balanced development in both languages with, perhaps, a stronger performance in Kwéyòl, in which the errors tended to be misuse of the phonemes [é] and [è] and one or two minor spelling errors.

Figure 6.9, which compares the trends for Uka, shows that at the start of the study her accuracy was higher for Kwéyòl than for English. As noted earlier, the low accuracy percentages in Kwéyòl at Sessions 4 and 5 reflected her

Figure 6.10 Accuracy Percentages for Kwéyòl and English – Dovi

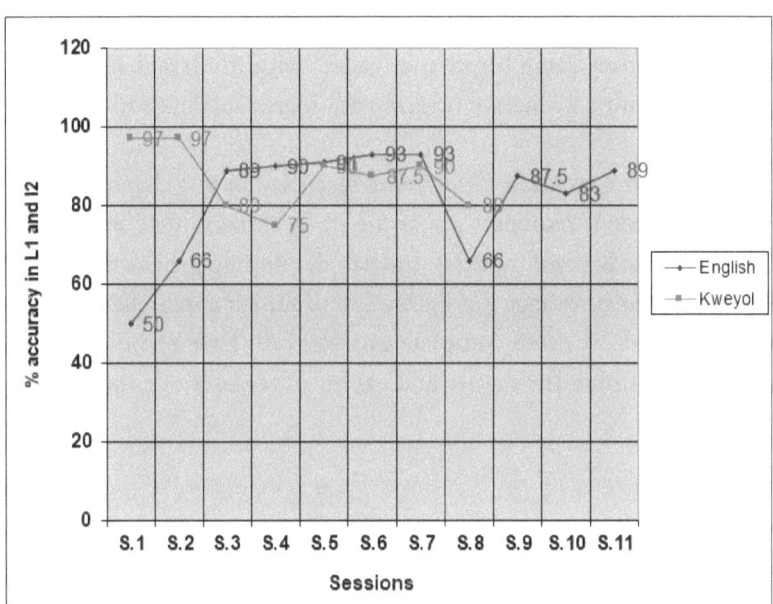

attempts to read more challenging and unfamiliar texts. Note, however, that during those sessions she maintained a high level of accuracy in English and was able to read the English texts on her own and with fluency. In Sessions 7 and 8, Uka's accuracy percentage in Kwéyòl was an encouraging 94 per cent and 90 per cent, respectively, which indicates increasing control over the material and a movement towards independence. The data also show that by the end of the study Uka's accuracy percentage in both languages was similar: in the 90 per cent to 94 per cent range, which represents an ability to read with fluency.

In Dovi's case, performance in both languages was somewhat inconsistent. All the same, the data points show an overall improvement in levels of accuracy in both languages. Earlier in this chapter, it was noted that lower accuracy scores were recorded when the children attempted to read more difficult unseen texts. The percentages towards the end of the study reflect their attempts to read texts at higher levels of difficulty. In Ado's case, the figures reflect his attempts to read texts three grade levels higher than at the start of the study. In the cases of Uka and Dovi, the figures reflect their attempts to read materials two grades higher than at the start of the study. In other words, they improved from being beginning readers with minimal competence in English to becoming bi-literate readers with increasing levels of accuracy in both languages.

Although comprehension is not being discussed in this chapter, a preliminary look at student responses across the study showed high levels of comprehension of the Kwéyòl material. Indeed, developing proficient literacy in Kwéyòl seemed to encourage the application of similar comprehension strategies with English. A more complete analysis will have to be undertaken in order to determine the nature and extent of transfer of comprehension strategies.

Conclusion

Considering the limited time frame of the study, the results are encouraging and support findings from other studies that instruction in the native language does not hinder the literacy development of learners in the L2. In fact, in this study, the use of Kwéyòl actually seemed to help the development of reading ability in English. Although the study use a scaled-down version of the French Creole model, Ado, Uka and Dovi developed fluency in reading texts at least one grade level higher than their levels at the start of the study. All three had been listed as being at risk at the start of the study and had only limited word recognition abilities at the kindergarten level. In the case of Ado, his gains in accuracy in both languages exceeded expectations and, by the end of the study, he was able to read texts at Grade 3 level, that is, two grades higher than at the start of the study, and he went on to sit the Common Entrance Examination and gain a place in a secondary school.

Although little has been said here about the integrated and culturally rich literature that the model advocates, it was clear from student responses in instructional sessions that such an approach fully engages the learner and encourages development across language domains. Further implementation of the French Creole component as well as initial studies with the English-lexicon vernacular and Standard English components of the model need to be undertaken to determine whether such a model can help to reclaim Kwéyòl and extend its use in a nation in which policy for over a century has led to its endangerment and which has also set in motion a trend that, if not halted, will lead to its eventual demise.

Acknowledgements

An earlier version of this chapter, with the title "The Effects of Vernacular Instruction on the Development of Bi-Literacy Abilities of Native Speakers of French Creole", was presented at the Fourteenth Biennial Conference of the Society for Caribbean Linguistics at the University of the West Indies, St Augustine campus, in August 2002. I am grateful to the Campus Research Committee of the School for Graduate Studies and Research at the Cave Hill campus for providing financial support for the preliminary study on which this chapter is based. I am also grateful to Ms Marietta Edwards and Dr Martha Isaac for their help in screening the students prior to the study.

I am pleased to dedicate this chapter to my friend, colleague and mentor, Dr Pauline Christie, who provided valuable guidance during our years of service for the Caribbean Examinations Council and also during my early years as a lecturer at the University of the West Indies. I am grateful for her friendship.

Notes

1. Cummins (1979a, 1979b) discussed the concept of cognitive academic language proficiency and the importance of this "school" language for academic success. The acronym CALP (Cognitive Academic Language Proficiency) is widely used in the literature. This chapter uses the simple term "academic language", which essentially refers to the same concept.
2. Pseudonyms are used for the children to preserve anonymity.

References

Bialystok, E., ed. 1991. *Language Processing in Bilingual Children*. Cambridge: Cambridge University Press.

Carrington, L. 1976. "Determining Language Education Policy in Caribbean Sociolinguistic Complexes". *International Journal of the Sociology of Language* 8: 127–43.

Carrington, L., and C. Borely. 1977. *The Language Arts Syllabus 1975: Comment and Counter-Comment*. St Augustine, Trinidad: University of the West Indies Multi-Media Production Centre.

Craig, D. 1971. "Education and Creole English in the West Indies". In *Pidginization and Creolization of Languages*, ed. D. Hymes, 371–92. Cambridge: Cambridge University Press.

———. 1977. "Creole Languages and Primary Education". In *Pidgin and Creole Linguistics*, ed. A. Valdman, 313–32. Bloomington, Indiana: Indiana University Press.

———. 1980. "Models for Educational Policy in Creole-Speaking Communities". In *Theoretical Orientations in Creole Studies*, ed. A. Valdman and A. Highfield, 245–65. New York: Academic Press.

———. 1999. *Teaching Language and Literacy: Policies and Procedures for Vernacular Situations*. Georgetown, Guyana: Education and Development Services.

Cummins, J. 1979a. "Cognitive/Academic Language Proficiency, Linguistic Interdependence, the Optimal Age Question, and Some Other Matters". *Working Papers on Bilingualism* 19: 197–205.

———. 1979b. "Linguistic Interdependence and the Educational Development of Bilingual Children". *Review of Educational Research* 49: 222–51.

———. 1994. "Knowledge, Power and Identity in Teaching English as a Second Language". In *Educating Second Language Children: The Whole Child, the Whole Curriculum, the Whole Community*, ed. F. Genesee, 33–58. Cambridge: Cambridge University Press.

Depree, H., and S. Iversen. 1994. *Early Literacy in the Classroom: A New Standard for Young Readers*. Auckland: Lands End Publishing.

Devonish, H. 1983. "Towards the Establishment of an Institute for Creole Language Standardization and Development in the Caribbean". In *Studies in Caribbean Language*, ed. L. Carrington et al., 300–316. St Augustine, Trinidad: Society for Caribbean Linguistics.

———. 1986. *Language and Liberation: Creole Language Politics in the Caribbean*. London: Karia Press.

Gardner-Chloros, P. 1997. "Vernacular Literacy in New Minority Settings in Europe". In *Vernacular Literacy*, ed. A. Tabouret-Keller et al., 189–221. Oxford: Clarendon Press.

Gerbault, J. 1997. "Pedagogical Aspects of Vernacular Literacy". In *Vernacular Literacy*, ed. A. Tabouret-Keller et al., 142–85. Oxford: Clarendon Press.

Neuman, S., and S. McCormick, eds. *Single-Subject Experimental Research: Applications for Literacy*. Newark, Del.: International Reading Association.

Roberts, P. 1983. "Linguistics and Language Teaching". In *Studies in Caribbean Language*, ed. L. Carrington, 230–44. St Augustine, Trinidad: Society for Caribbean Linguistics.

———. 1993. "Affective Factors in the Use of Creole in the Classroom: The Resolution of a Paradox". Paper presented at the Society for Pidgin and Creole Linguistics Conference, Amsterdam.

Siegel, J. 1997. "Using a Pidgin Language in Formal Education: Help or Hindrance?" *Applied Linguistics* 18: 86–100.

———. 1999. "Stigmatized and Standardized Varieties in the Classroom: Interference or Separation?" *TESOL Quarterly* 33, no. 4: 791–28.

Simmons-McDonald, H. 1994. "Comparative Patterns in the Acquisition of English Negation by Native Speakers of French Creole and Creole English". *Language Learning* 44, 29–74.

———. 1996. "Language Education Policy: The Case for Creole in Formal Education in St Lucia". In *Caribbean Language Issues Old and New*, ed. P. Christie, 120–42. Kingston: University of the West Indies Press.

———. 1999. "Developmental Patterns in the Acquisition of English Negation by Speakers of St Lucian French Creole". In *Studies in Caribbean Language II*, ed. P. Christie, B. Lalla and V. Pollard, 75–99. St Augustine, Trinidad: Society for Caribbean Linguistics.

———. 2000. "Language Education and the Vernacular Speaker: A Model for Multilingual Competence." Paper presented at the Thirteenth Biennial Conference of the Society for Caribbean Linguistics, Mona, Jamaica.

———. 2001. "Competence, Proficiency and Language Acquisition in Caribbean Contexts". In *Due Respect: Papers on English and English-Related Creoles in the Caribbean in Honour of Professor Robert Le Page*, ed. P. Christie, 37–60. Kingston: University of the West Indies Press.

Swain, M., and S. Lapkin. 1991. "Heritage Language Children in an English-French Bilingual Program". *Canadian Modern Language Review* 47, no. 4: 635–41.

Tabouret-Keller, A., et al., eds. 1997. *Vernacular Literacy.* Oxford: Clarendon Press.

Walker, A. 1984. "Applied Sociology of Language: Vernacular Languages and Education". In *Applied Sociolinguistics*, ed. P. Trudgill, 160–220. New York: Academic Press.

Chapter 7

ISSUES OF FACE-SAVING IN THE PRE-SCHOOL CLASSROOM

VALERIE YOUSSEF

INTRODUCTION

Over the last thirty years there has been an increasing focus, in both sociolinguistics and language acquisition, on the development, not just of grammatical forms and vocabulary, but also of conversational norms (for example, Snow and Ferguson 1977; Romaine 1984; Holzman 1997). In terms of young children, this has largely gone on in the context of interaction between the child and his or her primary caregiver, and discussion has focused mainly on the different communicative strategies which children bring to school with them and the effect of these strategies on early schooling (for example, Heath 1983; Roberts 1988). This study, however, focuses on a range of conversational norms, some of which may be established for use in the pre-school itself, given particular features of its interactional arrangement. Further, this study illustrates the way in which a three-year-old child can display acute sensitivity and responsiveness to his or her own face needs and develop defensive strategies for face-saving. These strategies might well impede the child's progress in school, since the strategies are essentially non-cooperative and would be perceived as impolite, even rude, by teachers. The study seeks to sensitize educators to the potential for cementing negative conversational traits in young children through interactional practices which may be well-intentioned, but are nevertheless destabilizing.

BACKGROUND TO THE STUDY

The Language Acquisition Milieu

It is necessary to review briefly language acquisition in Caribbean speech communities. It is now well-established that the language acquisition milieu of children in the Caribbean is unique, given the way in which Creole varieties commonly interface with lexically related Standard varieties. The fact that there are two or three overlapping language varieties available means that persons readily develop what I have elsewhere labelled "varilingual" competence (see, for example, Youssef 1991c, 1996). This kind of competence may entail commanding the contact codes fully but may equally entail having only partial control of one or more of the codes, according to the relative levels of exposure to each. A closely related acquisition scenario is that of Hispanic Americans who grow up with mixed exposure to Spanish and English in a variety of North American settings (see, for example, Zentella 1997; Field 1994). One result of this kind of language acquisition experience is that speakers may believe they know the Standard when in fact parts of its rule system (Craig 1971, 1983), and indeed, part of its lexicon (see Allsop 1996), are substantially different from those of the Creole and may not have been acquired. The more decreolized the language varieties become, and the more mixed the contexts of usage, the more potential there is for mixing between the contact systems and confusion about where one ends and the other begins. A false sense of familiarity with the Standard can result and can have an effect on both adults and children in their attitude towards acquiring the Standard variety.

As early as 1971, Craig noted the demotivation that can result from the speaker's partial knowledge of the Standard code, giving him a false sense of security, and the association of the Standard code with an alien culture towards which the child may have hostile, or at best ambivalent, feelings.

Later, he noted that "teachers should be flexible in relation to their goals for the sounds of spoken SE and concentrate on the meaningful use of English vocabulary and on the linking of English language activity to the natural interest of learners" (1983, 74).

Craig believed that some purpose for learning Standard English could be salvaged by its being effectively related to the students' own language milieu. With no clear direction for the implementation of a language policy, however, educational situations remain very mixed, dependent on the views of the educators in any single school. Statements like that of Craig can be misinterpreted if educators are not aware of the clear methodology and strategies that go along with it (for example, as offered in Craig 1999).

When we consider the success that bilingual programmes have had in achieving additive bilingualism, for example, the programmes reviewed by Baker and De Kanter (1983) and Cummins (1983), we want to argue more strongly for Creole having a consistent place within the curriculum and for a policy of at least transitional bilingualism (Craig 1976), but many parents continue to be bent on mainstream assimilation for their children through the exclusion of any form of the vernacular from the classroom. Educators argue increasingly for language awareness teaching from the primary school level (Robertson 1996, 118), but large pockets of resistance remain entrenched. Where there is entrenched resistance to recognizing and valorizing the Creole vernacular and culture, negative teaching strategies can result not only in the cultural dislocation of the child, but also in inculcating negative motivation and negative attitudes about language and language use from the earliest stages.

This study focuses on one child's experience in a nursery school in Trinidad and Tobago, where Standard English (SE) is held up as the norm; it does not suppose the situation described is unique to Trinidad and Tobago, however, but has the potential to occur wherever there is insensitivity to the cultural and communicative norms that children bring into the classroom.

The Development of Communication Skills

It has been noted that infants in their first year, prior to the production of any vocabulary, learn to babble a response when their caregiver speaks to them and then leaves a natural conversational pause. Conversations go on at the babbling stage with the child responding and inserting his or her turn into the interactional frame (Holzman 1997, 66–67). It may well be that the urge to communicate conversationally is a primary one, which develops in the course of time and according to the norms of the community in question. Indeed, the desire for social interaction per se may be a powerful constrainer of developing language in itself, quite apart from the need to have one's desires met (expressive function) or to give and take information (referential function).

Middle-class American (Nelson 1981) and British families (Wells 1978, 1985) customarily seek to stimulate their children lexically from an early stage through the constant pointing out of objects, the supplying of labels and, very often, a question-seeking repetition of the vocabulary item. These families often employ a strategy prevalent in the school system, that of requesting known information from the child, a curious use of the question indeed, if we consider its primary purpose to be seeking new information. An example would be to ask: "What's this?" When the child and teacher are looking at a picture of a boy kicking a ball, the child is expected to respond: "A boy", or even "A boy kicking a ball", even though both child and interlocutor already know the information.

Certain classes and cultures, it has been claimed, have less time to stimulate their young children, who are more surrounded by adult talk that they pick up on as best they can. In these contexts, children are spoken to more as adults, with a body of shared knowledge and experience established between them and whoever is speaking. Loose associations have been made then between the lower class and an implicit code, and the middle class and an explicit code (see, for example, Bernstein 1972; Heath 1983), with the latter identified as more compatible with the school classroom mode. The two kinds of exposure have been linked to different styles of language acquisition (cf. Peters 1980; Nelson 1981; Youssef 1994), and the styles themselves have been associated with particular circumstances at home. Nelson suggested that first-born children are more likely to have the "active teaching" kind of nurturing which encourages them to develop speech analytically and later children are more likely to be left to themselves, acquiring language in formulaic chunks and subsequently breaking these down and developing along the analytic route. All children display some of each style but in different relative proportions.

In addition to interactional norms being different, there may be different rules for extra-linguistic communicative features like eye contact, which may similarly have a negative impact on the child who is not always accustomed to meeting the eye of the speaker and may be suddenly expected to do so in the classroom (Roberts 1988). If we add to this the problems raised by a Creole-speaking child's knowledge of Creole rather than English grammar and lexicon, then we have to recognize that one-to-one conversation in the classroom may become very problematic indeed if it is not met with sensitivity to the contrastive norms of the contact interactional systems.

Conversational Norms

To explicate fully the conversational strategies used in the course of the interaction between teacher and child, we will first consider some theoretical positions on conversation. Taking the conversational unit as the basis of linguistically manifested social cooperation through which parties to the communication interact and support one another, we must consider the rules of Sacks et al. (1974) for turn-taking in conversation and Grice's (1975) conversational maxims. We must also examine the importance of politeness in the context of its face-saving potential as primarily elaborated by Brown and Levinson (1987).

Talk is our main means of cooperating in order to achieve personal and social ends. That cooperation depends on taking turns at talking, in accordance with the culture-specific norms to which we are exposed. Sacks (1974) first commented formally that speaker change recurs and that it is not usual for more than one party to talk at a time; transitions between turns are usually brief. A current speaker selects who speaks next. Conversations not only have typical structures but also most normally entail typical openings, closings, and topic maintenance and shift strategies, which allow for repair of problematic turn-taking. We know that these norms are more strictly adhered to in formal conversations and that control usually rests with the more empowered speaker.

The Gricean observation that conversation is driven by a cooperative principle has long been accepted. Briefly, the right amount of talk must be supplied, the talk must be genuine, it must be relevant, and it must be clear (Grice 1975, 45). In addition, however, speakers offer a "face" to others through conversation and speakers cooperate in maintaining mutual face in their interactions. It may be that the need to maintain face is itself universal and that Grice's maxims should be adapted to make allowance for this. Many times, for example, we may be less precise or clear than we need to be informatively if we are to respect a hearer's face needs as well as our own. Brown and Levinson's (1987) theory of politeness builds on Grice's work and places politeness in the mainstream of universal communication theory in perceiving it not just as a social requirement but also as the critical means of maintaining face. Brown and Levinson focus crucially on the need for maintenance of *positive face* – one's good self-image and that of the other party and one's right connection to others – and *negative face* – the non-violation of an individual's rights to agency and autonomy. These face needs are strongly constrained by societal and cultural mores.

In most classrooms, the rules adopted are those associated with a power differential among participants. Professional-client interactions are similar to teacher-student ones: the teacher dominates and controls the talk through questioning techniques.[1] The teacher decides the topic of conversation and who shall speak. As already noted, the teacher already knows the answers and moreover has the right to evaluate answers according to what he or she considers appropriate to the situation. Wardhaugh (1992, 306) argues that the teacher, in fact, "owns" the conversation, having the right to control topic, turn-taking and even beginnings and endings. He notes:

> teachers actually get to comment on the contribution of others with the intent of making such conversations fit a predetermined pattern. We should think what would happen if we tried to manage an ordinary conversation in such a manner: if we insisted on selecting topics and insisted that others keep to them and to our definitions of them . . . began or ended the talk to suit our own external demands . . . told X that what he was saying was irrelevant . . . Children must learn about such ownership and such learning may not be at all easy.

What is clear is that the transition to the classroom must be a challenging one for any child. The classroom's norms and requirements are at odds with those of most home environments. Where a child's language and culture are different from the school's focus norms, conflict can clearly develop, particularly if the differences are not mediated by a sensitive teacher who recognizes the need for the child to have his or her own norms valorized as well as those held up in the classroom. Without recognition of these factors, the face-threatening dynamic becomes very high and, from the very outset, the child may retreat from positive communication.

THE STUDY

An Individual in the System

The child under study, Kareem (K), is the first-born child of university-educated Trinidadian parents. Superficially, he might have been expected to accommodate fairly readily to the classroom by virtue of his home interaction. His parents, to some extent, defied the stereotypes, however. They chatted with the child but had little time for pouring over books with him and were concerned that he should develop the language varieties of his environment, both Trinidadian Creole (TC) and Trinidad Standard English (TSE), as naturally as possible. His language development was predominantly analytic, with pockets of formulaic speech, notably in areas in which there was some difficulty in disambiguating between Creole and Standard forms (see Youssef 1991a, 1994).

Kareem was recorded regularly as part of a longitudinal study of the development of the Verb Phrase in three Trinidadian children (Youssef 1990), and it is as part of that larger study that data was gathered on some conversational norms he employed in the classroom.

THE CHILD'S DEVELOPING COMMUNICATIVE COMPETENCE

Data Collection Settings

Up until the age of two years, ten months, Kareem was exposed to the Creole at least eight hours per day, seven days per week as he spent this time with his Creole-speaking caretaker. The rest of the time was spent with his parents at home, where interaction varied between the Creole and an informal Standard, with considerable motivated mixing, according to topic and situation. At age two years, ten months, however, he was using the TC code almost exclusively, and his normal conversation, as he interacted with his different caregivers, crystallized around talk of his immediate activities or events that had happened or might happen in the future. Those in his own home were more activity-oriented and involved him in asking a large number of questions around such activities as washing clothes; those in his caretaker's home often involved discussion of what he had done or was going to do with his family and in these discussions the caretaker had the dominant questioning role. Conversations recorded at home were more naturalistic in that his mother would simply leave the tape-recorder on as she went about her household business with Kareem's help; the caretaker encouraged him more to talk about his everyday life, actively interviewing him for purposes of tape recording. From age two years, ten months, he entered a nursery school where the staff insisted on the use of TSE; he also began recordings in my home where he heard some TSE and some upper-mesolectal TC. His use of TSE started to increase, but he was not entirely constrained towards SE in recordings at my home. As he became a friend of the family, he would sometimes mix TC with TSE. Since I knew that he enjoyed activities around housework, we mostly engaged in that kind of activity while recording.

It was observed, through the recordings, that Kareem developed sensitivity to TSE use after entering the prescriptively TSE-speaking nursery school and that he reduced overt Creole markers even in Creole contexts. On account of this, I resolved to do some recording in the school setting. This would hopefully allow for assessment of the extent of usage of TSE in that environment and the reason for his reducing his Creole output elsewhere. Between age two years, ten months, and three years, eight months, it was observed that he came to use certain TSE variants exclusively in SE-appropriate contexts, for example request forms like *can I?* and *may I?* (see Youssef 1991b) and that his overall usage of a range of TSE markers, including present continuous *be +-in(g)* and SE *-ed* increased sharply. In the same period, he developed TC əz as an apparently camouflaged alternant to TC dʌz for habitual marking (see Rickford 1980), and his usage of the context-specific SE simple present for the same function gradually increased. Writing in 1991, I commented: "Kareem was not just sorting his linguistic world but also the social milieu in which he found himself . . . He reduced his overall usage of TC forms and made some modifications towards SE as societal exposure led him to recognize that in certain environments it was the requisite form" (1991b, 89).

I set out to observe communication in the setting that had apparently induced this code-switching phenomenon.

The Data[2]

Compared to conversations in other settings, the conversation between Kareem and his teacher that I observed and recorded was in some senses unique. It was the only conversation where he was focused on an activity he was clearly uncomfortable with and where he was visibly restless throughout.

Just before the recording session in question he was asked if his teacher liked him to talk in a special way. He replied as follows:

> 1. She say, "How *do you* speak? *Nicely, quietly, softly and correctly.*"

When I asked him what "correctly" was, he replied:

> 2. Because she *means* that's right.
> *Correctly's* talkin nice and not shoutin.

Apart from the informational content that he gave, Kareem used an SE question form for the first time in 1, as well as SE adverbial marking *-ly*. In 2, he used third singular *-s,* and *is* with a following adjective. In the same recording, he produced eight tokens of third singular *-s* on the SE simple present pattern, and four were used in reference to his teacher and information he had learned in school. Apart from these examples, there were the following:

> 3. The red and the green *says* go.
> 4. And the red *says* stop and the yellow *says* be careful.

These were the only tokens of this SE feature to be recorded up until age four years, zero months, indicating to me that he very much associated "talkin nice" with the use of TSE and the use of Standard features with school and school-related topics. Not only was he context-sensitive to an extent that was allowing him to develop stylistic variation extremely early (Youssef 1991c), his acquisition of SE was also proceeding apace.

The Conversation and Its Analysis

Descriptive Procedures

As space does not allow for presentation of the entire discourse, I will pinpoint sections in Kareem's interaction with his teacher where he appeared to become uncomfortable. As the discourse is examined, it will become clear how Kareem endeavoured to preserve face by employing specific conversational strategies. I will also highlight elements in the conversation which appear to have been unusual in his interactions.

General Interaction Characteristics

Kareem was a talkative child, often questioning, and he exhibited different levels of compliance and non-compliance in normal circumstances. It was not usual for him to have someone else entirely control the conversation or activity; he was, in contrast, accustomed to asking questions himself and sometimes even setting or shifting the topic or activity. There were minimal constraints on both the child and his interlocutors in the natural course of their everyday encounters.

In the classroom, however, the dynamic was somewhat different. As his teacher chatted with him, she necessarily set out to control the situation in a manner to which he was not accustomed. This might not have been problematic had there been a fit of understanding and reference frame between teacher and student.

Phase 1

First, Kareem was asked to comment on pictures of other children in a book which represented a foreign cultural experience – picnicking in the English countryside. He was thereby involved in moving from using language to describe contexts that were physically and socially familiar to those that were not familiar. It was not that he had never done this before, but certainly it was not normative for him.

Immediately the conversation began; he was asked to comment on the obvious: to display knowledge which in other contexts might be taken to need no explanation:

> 5. T. What are they?
> K. Children.
> T. And what is this?
> K. A horsie.

As noted earlier, this type of questioning is typical of early school but depends on the child's familiarity with and acceptance of it. The naming game continued on the teacher's terms but gradually degenerated in the course of Example 7 below:

> 6. T. John is a what – is he a girl or a boy?
> K. A boy!

> 7. T. What? Tell me, what's that?
> K. A book!
> T. What other toys can you see?
> K. Uh?
> T. Look at the toys. Tell me some of the toys you can see?
> K. Over the river and through the wood.
> T. No. What are some of the toys that you can see, Kareem?
> K. OK. Um (1) So much toys.
> T. Tell me, what's this?
> K. Why they're not scattering it?
> T. Well they are very tidy children.
> K. Tidy? Mm. Why them not dirty?
> T. Well (1) they are – they are not untidy. They're playing with their toys in a very orderly fashion. What toy is this?

Kareem tried a nonsense answer (*Over the river and through the wood*) and then, told that he was wrong (*No*), attempted a response, but it seemed that the objects were sufficiently unfamiliar that he did not have labels for them; thus he improvised (*OK. Um, so much toys*) and finally countered with a *why* question, which stressed his recognition that the children he was being asked to describe were simply not realistic for him (*Why they're not scattering it?*). If we consider Grice's maxims, as far as Kareem is concerned, we can see immediately that the teacher is neither relevant, nor clear. Nor is she sufficiently informative. As a result, his positive and negative face needs are threatened since he finds himself in a situation where he cannot answer some questions, undermining his sense of self, and is not interested in other questions. He is being imposed upon against his will.

As the naming game continued and as Kareem continued not to have labels for the objects he was asked to identify, the activity became one in which he *repeated* the label the teacher supplied:

> 8. T. And a toy (.2) boat.
> K. A toy boat.
> T. And what's this one here?

When he attempted to get away from the repetitive *toy* sequence, he was again told that he was incorrect, but this time he disputed the teacher:

> 9. K. If you put it in the sea it will be real.
> T. Well, no.
> K. Oh yes.
> T. If you put it in the sea it will be a toy boat sailing.

All in all, to signal his discomfiture with the teacher's topic, he had at this point used the following strategies:

- ignored or not answered a question,
- gave a nonsense answer,
- asked his own questions,
- interrupted to change the subject, and
- contradicted the teacher's pronouncement that he was wrong.

All of these responses could be seen to threaten the teacher's positive face, since its preservation demanded that her students answer her questions readily and not contradict anything she said. Some more traditional teachers in Trinidad and Tobago continue to prefer that their students not ask questions and, generally, teachers are affronted by questions that they deem irrelevant.

Phase 2

At the next stage in the encounter, the teacher tried relating the environment of the story to Kareem's own more familiar environment, which could have been successful had she not approached this in a culturally insensitive manner:

> 10. T. So do you have toys like these children too?
> (Silence.)
> T. What are some of the toys that you have?
> K. I have old toys at home.
> T. Old toys? Well, what kind of old toys?
> (K ignores the question. Mutters, inaudible)
> K. And who toys these are? Huh?
> T. These are not toys over there.

It appeared that by asking Kareem about his own toys the teacher had violated his face again. His sensitivity to the question is clear in his silence and his response (*I have old toys at home*). Finally, as the teacher pursues her questioning, he breaks her control again, first by not answering and second by asking the teacher a question (*And who toys these are?*). His demanding *Huh?* must have been an additional affront for her in its insistence.

A final problem in the naming game occurred when Kareem tried to cooperate by describing an item he clearly did not recognize. When he identified the object with something with which he was familiar, the teacher denied his imaginative powers and he was told that he was incorrect:

> 11. T. And this? What's this? This long string in her hand.
> What's that called?
> K. That's the (1) the clip.
> T. That's a skipping rope.
> K. But (5) these sides are fish.
> T. No.
> K. Yes. And we seein a mouth.
> T. No. That's the handle of the skipping rope. So do you have toys like these?

Again here Kareem was told that he was incorrect (*That's a skipping rope*), but he persisted in disagreeing with the teacher (*But these sides are fish*). Finally, she had to change the topic to escape their disagreement (*So do you have toys like these?*). Again, his positive face was violated by his being told that his answer was wrong. In turn, his failure to agree infringed on the teacher's positive face, leading her to change the topic back to his toys.

Phase 3

Although it must now be clear that Kareem showed a clear preference for the familiar and environmentally real, the teacher insisted that he move into a storytelling mode:

> 12. T. You tell me the story.
> K. Your washing machine plug in like this?
> T. Yes.
> K. I want to see.
> T. Well, not now. Tell me the story first, OK?
> K. Where the white thing to put in the washing machine? (2) Uh?
> T. Yes, begin telling me the story.

Here, the teacher was controlling the topic against the clear wishes of the child and according to what she perceived to be appropriate. Immediately, he changed the topic (*Your washing machine plug is like this?*).[3]

At one stage, he attempted to develop the topic by asking questions himself to find out more about an unfamiliar object (*To do what? And what's this hand to do?*) But at this point, it is as if the teacher does not know the answers and is discomfited (*Well. It's sort of. . .*) Ultimately the teacher returns to her focus, the story telling:

> 13. T. This is a cash register.
> K. To do what?
> T. Well (2) It's sort of (1)
> K. And what's this hand to do?
> T. To wind it.
> K. To wind what?
> T. The cash register. Will you[
> K.]Why to wind it?
> T. Will you please tell me the story?

Following this relatively disempowered request from the teacher (*Will you please tell me the story?*), as Kareem gained control through the strategies he was now using, he did tell the story very indistinctly and very rapidly, diverting back to the environment as soon as he heard an unusual noise outside:

14. K. So the giant stepped down back and Jack
went back down. Underneath the beanstalk (.).
Where that comes from? (Noise outside.)

At this stage, the exercise had largely become one of non-cooperation, since the conflicting interests of teacher and student were disrupting almost every turn of the conversation.

Phase 4

Finally, the validity of Kareem's Creole lexicon was brought into question:

15. T. So where is this dog?
T. He lives in this little house here. What is the house called?
K. He could fit in there?
T. He could fit in the house. What is the house called?
K. A cage.[4]
T. A kennel.
K. Not a cage?
T. No.
K. Who own is a cage?
T. Well, maybe a lion lives in a cage when he lives in the zoo.
T. What does he eat?
K. Kennel – um foodie.
T. What kind of food?
K. Um spoil food.
Spoil food.
Ripe food. Ripe food. Ripe food.
. . .
T. And they eat dog chow. Or sometimes bone. Or sometimes rice.

16. T. What's in the basket? What do you think is in the basket?
K. A ball.
T. Anything to eat in the basket, maybe? What – what kind of thing?
K. Um doubles. What is doubles? (A Trinidadian Indian fast food.)
T. I don't know. You tell me.
K. Food with bake and channa. Like Shanna.
(The name of a girl in the class.)

Here, according to the standards she wanted to impose, the teacher appeared to be deciding what was correct and relevant. Instead of explaining to the child that British SE has different names for *doghouse* and *dog food* than the names he was accustomed to using, she explicitly told him that he was wrong. In the case of the *doubles* in the picnic basket[5] and even the label *cage* for a *doghouse*, the teacher feigned ignorance, clearly violating the Gricean maxim on truth. In the end, since she had demonstrated unfamiliarity with the terms he was using, the child seemed to feel he must explain the local terms *channa*[6] and *doubles*. In her usage, the teacher had breached the Gricean maxim on clarity, but the child seemed to be trying to make up any deficit on his side by explaining *channa* through its similar sound to the name of a child in the class.

In the following extract, Kareem went into a question-answer sequence which occurs regularly in the classroom when students are asked their names. At first, the teacher and Kareem are talking at cross-purposes because the teacher thinks he is still talking about *channa*. Subsequently the teacher understands the "routine" he is following:

17. K. But what is shanna, what?
    T. Something to eat.
    K. No.
    T. What?
    K. I sayin sha/na. Shanna what?
    T. Shanna. Channa is something you eat.
    K. But I sayin sha (.5)na. Shanna what?
    T. Shanna.
    K. Shanna.
    T. Channa.
    K. No Shanna. Shanna what?
    T. Shanna. Channa is something you eat.
    T. But I sayin sha/(.5)na.
    T. Shanna is the name of a little girl in your class.
    K. What? Shanna what? Shanna Ramphalie or what?
    T. Oh I see. You mean what her surname is. She is (1) – I can't remember her surname.
    K. You have to write it and see?
    T. Yes. I have to look in her bag and see. I can't remember her surname. (1) What's your name?

> K. You have to look in my bag and see.
>
> T. No, but I want you to tell me. What's your name?
>
> K. I not telling you because you have to look in my *bag and see*.
>
> T. Well, OK then (1) Would you like to[
>
> K. [I want to play with Dominic's toys *now*

Here we see Kareem using a strategy the teacher has demonstrated: insisting on a response to a question that she does not fully understand. By this, he reverses the control of the conversation, employing a strategy that she has been inflicting on him, much to her discomfiture. He controls by asking a question and persisting in that line of questioning, despite the teacher's clearly not comprehending what she is being asked. When the teacher finally turns the question on him, matching a difficult question with another question, he supplies an evasive answer – *You have to look in my bag and see* – which matches her last response. His response is interesting because, as in the teacher mode, he has taken up the technique of asking questions to which he already knows the answers but deliberately not supplying these answers. The teacher's positive face needs are now violated since she has to acknowledge that she does not have the information required. At this stage, the teacher herself resorts to disempowered strategies to get him to tell the story – pleading, using *please* and finally reminding him of his prior commitment to the task. All these strategies undermine her further by taking her out of her teacher role; she uses the kinds of devices a child might use with an adult:

> 18. Please tell me the story or I'll become very sad.
>
> 19. You told me that you would tell me the story about Jack today.

IMPLICATIONS OF THE STUDY

What emerges from this analysis of Kareem's interaction with his teacher is that the conversational strategies employed by the latter are at least as negative in their effect on the child as the language variety in use. In the broader study from which this data is drawn (Youssef 1990), I focused on the development of code-switching in the context of Trinidadian children encountering speakers of different language varieties; quite clearly in this case, however, the problem of Creole versus Standard lexicon is exacerbated by the insistent *interactional* demands made on the child.

If we return to the Gricean maxims of quantity, quality (genuineness, truth), relation (relevance) and manner (clarity), we find that the teacher violated at least the latter two maxims. Further, the quality of her interactional control is also questionable for, in the very act of deciding what answer she should accept, she determined truth. We have a typical case of the type of teacher control described by Wardhaugh (1992), and it does indeed prove that "such learning may not be at all easy". In discussing the supportive features of the environment in developing conversational interaction effectively in young children, Wells (1978) mentions "a warm responsiveness to the child's interests and a recognition of the child as an autonomous individual with valid purposes and ways of seeing things" (McTear 1985, 212). This is the antithesis of what emerged in the extract under discussion here.

Clear conversational norms used by teacher/interrogator and student/interrogated are as follows:

For the interrogator:

1. The person in power asks the questions.
2. The questions may be difficult to answer and may be repeated despite the difficulty; this is in opposition to the conversational rule that repair mechanisms for difficult turns are available and freely used to ensure the smooth running of a conversation (Sacks et al. 1974); clearly the insistence on response violates the child's positive face.
3. The response may be assessed by the interrogator/controller and judged; this is in opposition to an acknowledged concern in the literature on conversation and the face needs of others, beginning as early as Goffman (1955). Part of our cooperation as social beings entails respecting the face the respondent displays to us as well as not violating his or her rights and freedoms in any way (Brown and Levinson 1987). There is a need to support the addressee's sense of selfhood (positive face) and not to impose or infringe on his or her agency (negative face).

The findings on teacher/interrogator strategies match those identified by Heath (1983) for the African-American working-class children she studied. That study identifies the following communicative problems for children in the classroom:

1. the teacher's use of pragmatically directive interrogatives,
2. the teacher's use of questions to which he or she knows the answer, and
3. the teacher's use of questions which relate to content information derived from books.

It seems unsurprising that out of all this the interrogated child displays the following non-cooperative norm set of his own to deal with the above:

1. ignoring a difficult question,
2. countering it with another,
3. giving a nonsense answer,
4. giving an unsatisfactory answer, on a model supplied by the interrogator, and
5. adopting the teacher's own strategies to assert himself as the one empowered in the interaction.

These develop as a counter to the working out of meaningful and constructive communication, indicating that it is not necessarily just the clash of cultural-linguistic norms that hamper classroom interaction: interactional norms are used specifically as defence mechanisms for dealing with the teacher's line of questioning. Once the teacher is alerted to the problems entailed in his or her interactional style, more meaningful interaction can be worked out and a gradual transition to teacher-controlledness may be made less difficult.

When topic choice and topic control are considered, and this means focusing on "the meaningful use of English vocabulary and on the linking of English language activity to the natural interest of learners" (Craig 1983, 74), it becomes clear that it would have been possible to deal with the same topic material constructively by highlighting the points of similarity and difference between the English and Caribbean notions of *river, picnic, toy, kennel* and so on. The child would have recognized that his answers were not wrong but that the labels linking physical objects to their symbolic representations needed to expand in reference range to encompass language use in other English-speaking countries. There is, after all, nothing wrong with learning about other territories as long as they are not assumed superior to one's own.

The teacher in this case seemed insensitive to the extent and nature of differences among language varieties serving a range of English-speaking cultures. In fact, in indicating that Kareem gave wrong answers, the teacher put the foreign language variety and culture above the indigenous one, creating a problem for Kareem's sense of self. Although relatively few foreign concepts and lexical items were involved in this interchange, Kareem's responses registered his alienation and a possible sense of instilled inadequacy in his own background. This alone can explain his embellishment of his background to include a swimming pool and his non-response and evasion on the issue of his own toys. This sense of inadequacy did not stem from any experience outside of the school; his parents were proud of their own culture and life experience and were concerned that he should be too.

Kareem's evident boredom with the repetition of *Jack and the Beanstalk* could have been alleviated with a switch to a local folk-tale – an Anansi story, for example – which could have been presented in the Creole and contrasted with the Standard code of the English storybook. Undoubtedly, we need to look at such options for biculturalism and multiculturalism and whatever levels of bilingualism and varilingualism (Youssef 1990, 1991c) may be appropriate to the demands of particular classroom circumstances. The acting out of particular scenes in each variety could well have been carried out through the contrastive use of modes.

As part of the longitudinal study of development of the VP in Kareem, it was found that his productive competence in the Creole declined in the course of his stay in the school. It seems that he became self-conscious about his home language and his home environment at this time. Proper respect for both might have been ensured by the inclusion of a place for both in part of the curriculum focused on local history, geography, norms and culture.

Overall, the child's responsiveness to the means of controlling and redirecting the conversation presented to him by the teacher was acute. But children should not have to defend their face needs to such an extent; a less articulate child would have been left helpless in the same encounter. The study evidences the child using a range of non-cooperative tactics, including, finally, an affront to the teacher's face tantamount to what the child suffered – all this in the framework of spoken interaction, supposedly man's means of maximizing cooperative activity and social bonding. Children are often accused of being rude to the teacher, slow or uncooperative (Gumperz 1981, 9), and this has often been blamed on their home background when it may well have been that they were using strategies for self-defence in the classroom. They may not learn them all there, but their circumstances in the classroom cause them to maximize their use in that setting.

It has sometimes proved difficult to assess effectively children's psychological set towards various aspects of their education; one further implication of this study is that conversational analysis can provide meaningful insights in this arena.

NOTES

1. Where there are power differentials between parties to an interaction, items like questions may both empower and disempower: they may be used to control the course of an interaction in the former case and used to sustain a conversation in the latter.
2. Transcription symbols used in this data set are as follows:
   (0.4) Pauses in number of tenths of second.
   = Equals signs, one at the end of a line and one at the beginning of the next, indicate no gap between the two lines.
   [Left brackets indicate the point at which the current speaker's talk is overlapped by another's talk.
   ] Indicates overlapping talk by new speaker.
3. The washing machine was one of Kareem's favourite "toys"; he loved to wash with his mother and operate the machine.
4. *Cage* is the TC label for "doghouse".
5. Kareem's description of this popular Trinidadian Indian fast food was quite accurate.
6. *Channa* is the TC label for "chickpeas".

REFERENCES

Allsop, R. 1996. *Dictionary of Caribbean English Usage*. Oxford: Oxford University Press.

Baker, K., and A. De Kanter. 1983. *Effectiveness of Bilingual Education: A Review of the Literature*. Washington, DC: US Department of Education Office of Planning and Budget.

Bernstein, B. 1972. "A Sociolinguistic Approach to Socialization; with Some Reference to Educability". In *Directions in Sociolinguistics: The Ethnography of Communication*, ed. J. Gumperz and D. Hymes, 465–97. New York: Holt, Rinehart and Winston.

Brown, P., and S. Levinson. 1987. *Politeness: Some Universals of Language Use*. Cambridge: Cambridge University Press.

Craig, D. 1971. "Education and Creole English in the West Indies: Some Sociolinguistic Factors". In *Pidginization and Creolization of Languages*, ed. D. Hymes, 371–91. Cambridge: Cambridge University Press.

———. 1976. "Bidialectal Education: Creole and Standard in the West Indies". *International Journal of the Sociology of Language* 8: 93–136.

———. 1983. "Teaching English to Non-Standard Speakers: Some Methodological Issues". *Journal of Negro Education* 52, no. 1: 65–74.

———. 1999. "Teaching Language and Literacy: Policies and Procedures for Vernacular Situations". Paper presented at the University of the West Indies' Fifth Biennial Cross-Campus Conference on Education, St Augustine, April.

Cummins, J. 1983. *Heritage Language Education: A Literature Review*. Toronto: Ontario Ministry of Education.

Field, F. 1994. "Implicational Universals and the Origins of Mixed Codes: When Languages Combine". Paper presented at the Tenth Biennial Conference of the Society for Caribbean Linguistics, Georgetown, Guyana, August.

Goffman, E. 1955. "On Face-Work: An Analysis of Ritual Elements in Social Interaction". *Psychiatry* 18: 213–31.

Grice, H. 1975. "Logic and Conversation". In *Syntax and Semantics 3: Speech Acts*, ed. P. Cole and J. Morgan, 113–27. New York: Academic Press.

Gumperz, J. 1981. "Conversational Inference and Classroom Learning". In *Ethnography and Language in Educational Settings*, ed. J. Green and C. Wallatt, 3–25. Norwood, New Jersey: Ablex.

Heath, S. 1983. *Ways with Words*. Cambridge: Cambridge University Press.

Holzman, M. 1997. *The Language of Children*. Oxford: Blackwell.

McTear, M. 1985. *Children's Conversation*. Cambridge: Cambridge University Press.

Nelson, K. 1981. "Individual Differences in Language Development: Implications for Development and Language". *Developmental Psychology* 17, no. 2: 170–87.

Peters, A. 1980. "Language Learning Strategies: Does the Sum Equal the Whole of the Parts?" *Language* 53: 560–73.

Rickford, J. 1980. "How Does *doz* Disappear?" In *Issues in English Creoles*, ed. R. Day, 77–96. Heidelberg: Julius Groos Verlag.

Roberts, P. 1988. *West Indians and Their Language*. Cambridge: Cambridge University Press.

Robertson, I. 1996. "Language Education Policy: Towards a Rational Education Policy for Caribbean States". In *Caribbean Language Issues: Old and New*, ed. P. Christie, 112–19. Kingston: The Press, University of the West Indies.

Romaine, S. 1984. *The Language of Children and Adolescents: The Acquisition of Communicative Competence*. Oxford: Basil Blackwell.

Sacks, H., E. Schegloff, and G. Jefferson. 1974. "A Simplest Systematics for the Organization of Turn-Taking for Conversations". *Language* 50, 696–735.

Snow, C., and C. Ferguson. 1977. *Talking to Children: Language Input and Acquisition*. Cambridge: Cambridge University Press.

Wardhaugh, R. 1992. *An Introduction to Sociolinguistics*. Oxford: Blackwell.

Wells, G. 1978. "Talking with Children: The Complementary Roles of Parents and Teachers" *English in Education* 12, no. 2: 15–38.

———. 1985. *Language Development in the Early Years*. Cambridge: Cambridge University Press.

Youssef, V. 1990. "The Development of Linguistic Skills in Some Trinidadian Children: An Integrative Approach to Verb Phrase Development". PhD diss., University of the West Indies.

———. 1991a. "Can I Put – I Want a Slippers to Put On": Children's Development of Request Forms in a Code-Switching Environment". *Journal of Child Language* 18: 609–24.

———. 1991b. "Variation as a Feature of Language Acquisition in the Trinidad Context". *Language Variation and Change* 3: 75–101.

———. 1991c. "The Acquisition of Varilingual Competence". *English World-Wide* 12, no. 1: 87–102.

———. 1994. " 'To Be or Not to Be': Formulaic and Frame-Based Acquisition of the Copula in Trinidad". *First Language* 14: 263–82.

———. 1996. "Varilingualism: The Competence Behind Code-Mixing in Trinidad and Tobago". *Journal of Pidgin and Creole Languages* 11, no. 1: 1–22.

Zentella, A. 1997. *Growing Up Bilingual*. Malden, Mass.: Blackwell.

This page intentionally left blank

Section 3

Language and Caribbean Society

This page intentionally left blank

Chapter 8

CREOLE REPRESENTATION IN LITERARY DISCOURSE
Issues of Linguistic and Discourse Analysis
Barbara Lalla

THIS CHAPTER SEEKS TO DEFINE issues raised by the representation of Creole in literary texts. A crucial framework for such discussion is the relationship between ideological perspective and code choice.

As Fowler (1986), Simpson (1993) and others have noted, ideological (as distinct from spatio-temporal) perspective is the attitudinal orientation of the speaker to the topic. Whereas spatio-temporal perspective is conveyed mainly through deixis, ideological perspective is encoded in a variety of ways, such as through modal systems, transitivity, lexical choice and code choice. Ideological perspective interrelates with the speaker's perception of his or her identity and, among linguists, code choice is well-recognized as linked with issues of identity. The significance of the link between code choice and identity in Creole language situations is well-known (see Morgan 1994). However, in exploring sociological dimensions of identity, linguists have drawn little on the evidence of literary discourse, where the natural link between code choice and identity in part defines context, contributes to the construction of setting and represents a dimension of ideological perspective.

The essays in Morgan's collection do not explore implications for identity associated with Creole permeation of literary canons, although Alleyne laments marginalizing practices that have prevented Creole speakers from developing "styles, registers, or strategies of discourse such as political speech making or presentation of papers before professional societies or before corporate board meetings, all of which require planned, deliberate discourse" (1994, 16). In the same collection, Winford discusses how switches relate to such factors as group solidarity, and he suggests probable implications of intrumentalizing the Creole (1994, 53), but he does not take into account subtle inroads of Creole into the canon of world literature in English. More recently, Roberts's (1997) study contributes historical depth to our understanding of scribal discourse in the Caribbean, but it focuses on literacy rather than on the development of creative literary discourse. Cooper and Devonish (1992) discuss creativity in Caribbean language but concentrate on orature in Jamaican rather than on the inroads of the Creole into literature.

Literary analysis, on the other hand, scrutinizes issues of identity for their cultural implications but rarely grounds critical interpretation in analysis of discourse. In this way, detailed critical analysis of language – characteristically analysis of style rather than linguistic description – tends to support the critique of an individual work or author rather than reveal characteristics of Caribbean literary discourse on the whole.

The significance of code choice in Caribbean creative writing invites serious consideration by both linguists and critics. Creative writers who locate the situations or events they describe in the Caribbean have long treated code choice as a crucial component to setting. Setting, which Prince (1987, 87) defines as the spatio-temporal circumstances of events and situations presented in narrative discourse, is frequently constructed, at least in part, by markedness of code choice,[1] and the Caribbean setting has been no exception to this pattern. Markedness in code choice is also a crucial component of characterization and in the construction of character, so the Creole occurs as the marked code both within the Caribbean setting and elsewhere. Creole and non-Creole speakers and writers from within the Caribbean and from abroad have long associated code choice in Caribbean discourse with notions of realism. Creole features that mark Caribbean setting, characterization or perspective are drawn from every level of linguistic analysis:

- lexical items or lexico-semantic features, as in *ole higue;*
- phonological features conveyed by a variety of orthographical means, such as alveolar stops rather than dental fricatives (*widdout rhyme, widdout reason,* Brathwaite, "The Dust");
- morphological features, such as absence of inflectional morphology for tense or person in verbs (*When sunset, a brass gong, / vibrate through Couva,* Walcott, "The Saddhu of Couva"); and
- syntactic features, such as serial verbs, word order in questions, absence of auxiliary in negative constructions and thematization (*Portia saying / is life she facing,* Matthews, "Portia Faces Life").

A technical description of Caribbean literary discourse might involve collecting features drawn on (in the creative process) to mark Caribbean language, measuring their frequency, stating their distribution, and describing their variation in form and method of representation. Moreover, a description of Creole features in literary discourse requires support of a linguistic theory that takes account of the specific needs of such description. For example, phonological description must facilitate an evaluation of orthographic systems to convey definitive Creole features without alienating the Standard English reader whom most writers wish to accommodate. In the process, some current approaches to linguistic description may require adjustment. For example, formulations such as the phrase "absence of" in the list of examples above, normally frowned on as Anglocentric, are naturally evoked where a discourse selects Standard English as the unmarked code and Creole as the marked code. Another area for development is definition. In attempting to construct a cognitive frame for discussing vernacular literacy, Tabouret-Keller acknowledges the inaccuracy of terminology and the vagueness of notions such as *literacy, vernacular, mother tongue* and so on, but insists on the need to develop a coherent cognitive frame for discussion (1997, 220). The urgency of defining such terms as *literary discourse* is obvious, but need not halt analysis. After all, creolists are still working on the definition of *Creole.*

The occurrence of Creole in literary discourse has in the past been constrained by genre or discourse type. For example, Creole was more likely to occur in comic discourse and in dialogue, rather than in formal monologue or in narrative. Early writers, such as the anonymous writer of *Marly,* and such as Michael Scott, indicated Creole speech by metanarrative comment or, at most, they included relatively short utterances. These indications of Creole amounted to a token of "otherness" – an index of distance from normative and familiar behaviour. Inclusion of Creole was a means of encoding conceptual distance between speaker/narrator and subject/character. The comedy of such Creole inclusions was the comedy of distortion. In such circumstances, contrast with the Standard was crucial, but accuracy in observation of the Creole was not. Rigid constraints hedged the occurrence rather than the quality of such utterances.

Major changes of distribution have taken place in the occurrence of Creole across genres and discourse types. Such changes in pattern of code choice (where the choice includes Caribbean language) is associated with change in context, in the circumstances external to the text involved. These changing circumstances are multidimensional. The geography of Creole increases constantly as the Caribbean diaspora widens and as producers and consumers of its literary and oral discourse increase in number and geographical distribution. The literate population of the Caribbean increases in number and distribution through social classes. The situational constraints on Creole discourse diminish.

These geographical, social and situational dimensions of contextual change effect major change in the discourse itself. The socio-historical changes have reshaped creative discourse of the Caribbean to a mesh of operations that include the exploding of canons, the engagement in counterdiscursive interaction and the rewriting of situations, settings, characters, even whole texts, from alternative perspectives. This mesh of activity amounts to a dynamic literary context for further discourse. In this literary context, generic constraints on code choice in written Caribbean discourse have all but collapsed.

As Creole use expands over domains, spreading more into public use rather than being restricted to private domestic use, Creole also spreads into written use rather than remaining exclusively in oral use or, even, in written representation of oral use. In other words, Creole in scribal discourse is no longer restricted to representation of dialogue. The correlation with certain variables like intellectual/cultural prestige changes as the choice of Creole is privileged (for ideological reasons) by performers who enjoy mass appeal and by intellectuals who engage in formal analysis of Creole or of the popular culture for which Creole is the medium.

This multidimensional change in the context of Caribbean literary discourse has definable linguistic implications. Changing circumstances external to the text not only permit more and more extensive use of Creole but also increasingly demand greater and greater accuracy in Creole representation. This increase in quantity and quality of Creole representation has crucial implications for reader comprehension.

The degree to which a literary text is comprehensible to its readers – its *legibility* – is a function of several features. Prince (1982, 133) defines legibility as "the measure of ease with which a given text can be interpreted". He notes that the legibility of a given text can be computed in terms of the number, complexity and diversity of the operations required for the text to make sense. Prince also argues that legibility declines if chronological order is difficult to infer, if statements decrease in transparency (through sarcasm, ambiguity, and so forth), if characters change names or share names, if perspective shifts or if knowledge is required of some additional linguistic code. In literary discourse, the inclusion of Creole has positive or negative implications for legibility, depending on the linguistic competencies of the reader. This consideration constrains Creole representation in a number of ways.

In the first place, legible representation of Creole requires the writer to choose the variety of Caribbean English-based Creole to be represented. Indeed, Creole representation requires the writer to choose whether the regional variety characteristic of a particular territory should be presented or whether a more general sense of the Caribbean should somehow be conveyed. One writer may wish to create an imaginary island in the Caribbean. Another may wish to represent the variety of a particular group which is culturally, rather than geographically, defined. Dread Talk, for example, is closely associated with Jamaica historically, but has increasingly cut across geographical boundaries in recent years. So specificity of territory cannot be assumed. The strictures articulated by Tabouret-Keller et al. (1997, 11) regarding vernacular literacy apply:

> Any attempt at a universally valid sociolinguistic model for vernacular literacy must face the complexities not only of variation in political and economic circumstances from country to country, from region to region within the same country, from ethnic group to ethnic group within a region . . . but also those of linguistic variation, and the degree of standardization needed.

The importance of decisions about which Creole is to be represented is that features characteristic of one group may be quite unfamiliar to readers from another group. Over-precision in representing a variety may thus reduce legibility even among Caribbean readers. (Linguistic theory can support creative writing in the Caribbean in developing procedures to facilitate writing Creole in a form that non-technical audiences can read, where the Creole occurs alongside, perhaps alternating with, the official language.)

The extent to which the Creole is to be reflected also affects legibility, and the extent varies from text to text. The Creole may be indicated through reference only, through metadiscursive comment, such as "he spoke in the manner of his slaves". Alternatively, some writers actually reproduce Creole in amounts that vary from occasional words, to scattered quotations, to dialogue, to narrative.

Representation of Creole does not take place in a vacuum. Legibility often requires some accommodation of the surrounding/supporting text. Issues of installation include the problem of ensuring balance between accuracy in representation and comprehensibility of the utterance. To ensure comprehension of utterances in the unofficial code rather than the official (assumed to-be-familiar) code, some writers depend on glosses, either on the page or in end matter. On-the-page glosses may be overt, marked by quotes or included in parentheses.

Interestingly, reversal is beginning to occur in the distribution of codes as maintext or gloss. That is, Creole may now be offered as the gloss for Standard English, rather than the other way around. One Caribbean writer in the United States who habitually conveys alienation from the Caribbean does not always produce an exact equivalence between the Creole gloss and its Standard English text: "He said he did not think I would come to see him ('Me hear you a come but me no tink you a come fo' true')" (Kincaid 1997, 9). Alternatively, writers weave glosses in by apposition. In either case, equivalence between codes is explicit. However, many writers depend on context, clarifying through implicature material in the code that may be unfamiliar to some readers.

The importance of strategies for installation arises from the pivotal significance of legibility in representing the Creole in a literary discourse which has, traditionally, been in Standard English. At first glance, the question is, How much of the marked code can safely be included? On more careful consideration, the question turns out to be, How far (in an attempt to be realistic) can a writer go in reproducing the marked code? This is really a question not about the length or frequency of Creole expression but of the degree of precision possible in markedness of code choice. In a very real sense, precision in representation may be inversely proportional to legibility.

However, some representation is often motivated by the desire for realism in setting or characterization. The problem is that representation of the Creole in literature can never actually be realistic, any more than any scribal representation of oral discourse can be more than impressionistic. Creole features may be included with accuracy (just as, conversely, there is room for inaccuracy, for erroneous representation) but can hardly be maintained with rigorous precision. To pretend otherwise is to fall into the reproductionist fallacy (see Slembrouck 1992, 103). However, for the impression of Creole speech (virtual realism?) to be achieved by the reader who is a non-speaker, or for the mental shift to be made for the reader who is a speaker, some features from the marked code must be included. The question is: which features and on what basis?

As a consequence of two conflicting values, *virtual realism* and *legibility*, inclusion of Creole in literary discourse raises issues of selection. We know that features may be selected to varying extents from the different levels of linguistic analysis. However, there appear to be conflicting parameters for selection. Some features may be selected because they are *shared* by both marked and unmarked codes. These shared features maintain legibility. Other features are selected because they *contrast* marked and unmarked codes. (Indeed, these are the features that mark the marked code!) These contrasting features sustain readers' awareness that Creole is being represented.

Shared features are not to be dismissed as unworthy of note – particularly those that only appear to be shared. There are significant issues of overlap. Le Page notes the significance to vernacular literacy of the move from viewing languages as discrete systems to viewing them as linguistic continua (1997, 5). In the Creole occurring in Caribbean literary discourse, some items (words, phrases, sentences) are identical in form and in function across the codes; however, others share the same form but contrast in function. The spelling is the same, but the pronunciation is known to be different to the Creole speaker. Or, the pronunciation of the word or the combination of words is identical, but the meaning contrasts across codes. Only the Creole speaker knows.

One result of such partial contrast and partial overlap between representation of the codes is ambiguity. However, for the reader who is competent only in English, such ambiguity remains covert (with the potential for impoverishment in interpretation). On the other hand, the implication for the reader who is a Creole speaker is *braata* meaning. In cases of partial overlap, then, the readership of Caribbean literary discourse is covertly divided and the Creole speaker treated, in effect if not by design, preferentially.

Cooper and Devonish argue persuasively for the privileged status of orature in Jamaica (especially in association with music culture), demanded by performance, supported by electronic development and ratified by the international acclaim of reggae. However, parallel developments in the affirmation of national identity through language are emerging in scribal discourse.

When features shared by both codes are orthographical, words or sentences may become unambiguous through pronunciation by the speaker of one code or the other. In such instances, plurality of meaning resides only in the written text. This possibility makes an issue of medium, makes the choice of writing itself a requirement for plurality of meaning in the text. Ambiguity in code choice may be thematically significant, but also may relate to ambiguity of identity or to hidden meanings in an interface between cultures. What does this imply about the nature of what Brathwaite has termed *nation language*? Brathwaite's coinage has been variously applied to Caribbean English-based Creole, to specific Creoles in the Caribbean, to Caribbean speech in general, and to Caribbean discourse that foregrounds the African heritage in vocabulary, in metaphor and so on. Cooper and Devonish (1992, 70) ascribe precision to the term *nation language,* but define it by limited reference to a characteristic literary, in fact metrical, feature of traditional British verse – that is, in terms of lack of iambic pentameter. Elsewhere (Lalla 1996, 198), I have argued for *nation language* as necessarily comprising a total competence that would include code-shifting. Creative writers in the Caribbean today so frequently manipulate code choice to exploit ambivalence of meaning that such exploitation may be viewed as a dimension of their competence.

Such plurality of meaning and such semantic density is especially available in written text, where it is retrievable only to the Creole-speaking reader. This dual constraint on medium and readership works in parallel to the empowerment of orature recognized by Cooper and Devonish. Not only does the culture promote the oral and the immediate (performance), it increasingly privileges a scribal discourse in which Standard English is intercepted by Creole.[2] At the same time, because Standard English readers unfamiliar with Creole will be unaware of the alternative or additional meanings, actual legibility is limited for such readers. In fact, legibility is, at least in part, only apparent – virtual rather than actual – where the exclusively Standard English reader is concerned.

In addition to the possibility of *virtual legibility*, at any point where Creole is included in the literary text, comprehension may actually collapse. This collapse, both real and apparent, may perhaps be termed *illegibility*. Paradoxically, incomprehensibility at specific, limited points of the text may not necessarily be detrimental to the intended meaning of the total text. Where the Creole comprises a brief concentrate of features that contrast the marked code sharply from the unmarked code, lack of comprehension may be the desired end. Historically, legibility has varied in importance in Creole representation.

Illegibility of text, in fact, functioned in some nineteenth-century writing as a means of conveying incomprehensible surroundings.[3] Part of the hero's alienation from civilization was exposure to uncodified language. In such texts, particularly of the travel narrative type, Creole dialogue sets apart the speaker (black or white) from civilized society by confronting the reader with an unfamiliar marked code. The Creole speaker's meaning was not an intrinsic component of global meaning in this type of text. On the contrary, illegibility involved the reader in the non-Creole speaking protagonist's wilderness experience (see Lalla 1996).

The importance of legibility in Creole representation depends on the seriousness with which the author views the speaker-within-the-text. (Is what the speaker has to say worth understanding?) The installation of Creole in comprehensible form and with significant meaning in written discourse challenges what some would term the linguistic imperialism of English. Phillipson (1992, 47) offers a working definition of linguistic imperialism, with reference to English, as "the dominance of English . . . asserted and maintained by the establishment and continuous reconstitution of structural and cultural inequalities between English and other languages". The dimensions of the challenge are suggested by Collins's assessment of Selvon's *Lonely Londoners* as a landmark in the 1950s because it was completely in Creole.[4]

"Partly because of its linguistic daring, this has become a seminal work in Caribbean literature. Since then the more widespread use of Creole in literary works reflects changing perceptions" (1998, 91).

Reduction of ideological barriers to Creole in literature of the anglophone Caribbean has proceeded parallel to national sentiments that have intensified ideological imperatives to vernacularize literature. Ideological change has not only affected Creole representation quantitatively, but qualitatively. Ideological perspective constrains selection, representation and installation of Creole features, and ideological change has therefore influenced the accuracy and precision with which Creole is represented in scribal discourse. In this way, ideological perspective has constrained degree of legibility. Not surprisingly, the degree of accuracy in Creole representation can be seen to have increased over the history of Caribbean literary discourse. Increasing accuracy has intensified realism in setting and characterization. This increasing *accuracy* appears to correlate with the following:

- increasing authorial competence, where more and more authors have native-speaker competence rather than non-speaker curiosity;
- increasing reader competence, where readership is affected by the growing incidence of literacy in readers with native-speaker competence in the oral language (though these readers are primarily readers of SE) and by the growing incidence of speakers without native-speaker competence but with at least limited exposure (through parents or acquaintances, or through oral performance or Caribbean literature) that takes Creole to an international audience; and
- changes in authorial perspective, especially on the plane of ideological perspective, and in associated authorial assumptions about audience/reader perspective.

The validity of these correlates is generally demonstrated by comparing representation of Creole in current Caribbean literature with representation in older texts and with current texts that perpetuate the attitudinal orientation of nineteenth-century Eurocentricism. (Objective testing and documentation of these correlates requires extensive historical and comparative textual analysis of a large and growing corpus.)

Apart from accuracy, *precision* constitutes another index of realism. Precision continues to be constrained by the desirability of an international market. This hinges on accessibility of the text to the international audience to whom most writers wish their work to be legible. Written discourse in international English resists departures from the unofficial code because uniformity is the business of a standard language and because of the pressure that Phillipson identifies as linguistic imperialism. These pressures constrain precision in Creole representation in that they control the number of definitive features to be conveyed. To judge realism in Caribbean discourse on the basis of degree of detail in Creole representation is to fall into reproductionist fallacy, as representation hinges on a relatively frugal selection of features. This selection, in turn, rests on a balance of two (contradictory) criteria:

- similarity to official language to preserve control of international audience, and
- contrast with official language to convey distinctiveness of discourse and so to suggest otherness or affirm identity, and construct setting or character.

It has been noted that the extent and accuracy with which Creole can be represented naturally correlates with the degree of competence in Creole that can be expected of a writer, on the basis of the writer's exposure to the language. However, while the most competent writers are accurate, they do not necessarily record Creole features in detail. Moreover, there is also a movement, as Caribbean literary discourse develops, in the clarity of the distinction between Creole and English. In earlier texts, the marked code (Creole) is hermetically sealed from the main discourse, which is in the unmarked code (English). More recently, Creole discourse has come to carry the full weight of narrative perspective in some texts (like Selvon's). Now, writers frequently alternate between Standard English and Creole. When Creole is thus drawn on substantially for the main discourse, the "sealing" between the codes tends to break down. In such instances, code-switching occurs with little or no flagging. Contrasts between the codes are muted so that movement between codes is unobstrusive. The precision with which the Creole is marked may actually decrease, facilitating some ambiguity about which code is in use ("is the university of hunger the wide waste", "they come like sea birds", Martin Carter).

The correlation between competence on the one hand and, on the other, the quantity and quality of representation can be outlined as follows:

Degree of Competence	Quantity and Quality of Representation
No exposure, or indirect exposure (knowledge second-hand or imaginative)	Metadiscursive indication of Creole utterance; orthographical indication of well-known phonological differences; occasional, scattered words; brief quotes; proverbs; inaccuracies; flagging. Creole sealed from English.
Limited competence	Brief dialogue; isolated monologue, for stated purpose of illustration; orthographical indication of phonological differences; accurate representation of a few chosen features (like final vowel in *killee, wantee*) and tendency to labour these few; probable flagging. Creole sealed from English.
Competence	**Type 1** Substantial dialogue; non-contiguous distribution; increased precision – accurate representation of wide range of features; some words used in narrative with gloss; flagging limited but implied through gloss or orthography. Creole sealed from English. **Type 2** Narrative in Creole, or codes interwoven; accurate representation; reduced precision, especially in representation of phonology; flagging non-existent; code ambiguity exploited. Creole "unsealed".

A writer may exploit ambiguity of code choice to indicate ambivalence about identity or, more probably in recent years, to convey choice and so to indicate power. By suppressing detailed representation, the writer may also play on indeterminacy of meaning. Because features shared by both codes facilitate the literary exploitation of anomaly and plurality of meaning, the representation of Creole (particularly by orthographical means) may actually be muted to preserve subtleties of play between Creole and Standard meanings.[5]

The development of such subtleties in representation reflects radical change in ideological perspective. Traditional perspective, centred in English as the unmarked code, tended not to recognize competence in Creole but to view Creole as a lapse in Standard English competence in (black) Caribbean speakers and a lapse in Standard English performance in white settlers/residents. An illuminating approach to the alternation of Creole and Standard English in creative writing is that of Myers-Scotton (1993, 92, following Gumperz and Hymes 1972), who treats code-switching as a skilled performance rather than as an interference phenomenon. The Caribbean creative writer can not only effect a shift in ideological perspective by selecting Creole as the marked code, but can also exploit overlapping features of the two codes in which he or she has competence in order to maintain parallel alternative meanings – a sentence that may be a Standard English question or a Creole statement, a verb phrase that may be timeless present and simultaneous description or narrative, or may be past perfective and narrative ("they come from the distant village of the flood" in Carter's "University of Hunger") (see Lalla 1999). In such cases, provided phonological detail remains unspecified, and as long as the discourse is scribal, alternative meanings are available, interpretation remains open and the discourse accommodates the potential for an ideological perspective that is complex, multifaceted.

In operating through alternation and ambivalence of code, current creative discourse of the Caribbean presents a mine of information on the changing relationships between code choice, social identity and the attitudinal orientation of the speaker.

Acknowledgements

Adapted from a paper presented at a Conference of the Society for Caribbean Linguistics, St Lucia, August 1998.

Notes

1. "The theory behind the markedness model proposes that speakers have a sense of markedness regarding available linguistic codes for any interaction, but choose their codes based on the persona and/or relation with others which they wish to have in place. This markedness has a normative basis within the community, and speakers also know the consequences of making marked or unexpected choices" (Myers-Scotton 1993, 75).
2. This interface is to be distinguished from errors arising through interference between Creole language structures and Standard English language structures. The exploitation discussed above is associated with bilingual competence.
3. Notably in *Marly, or The Life of a Planter in Jamaica* (1828) and in Michael Scott, *Tom Cringle's Log* (originally serialized in *Blackwood's Magazine*, beginning in 1829; first published in book form in 1833).
4. It might be more accurate to describe the work as representing a discourse completely in Creole.
5. On the creative process of negotiating the slippage between the codes, see Collins (1998, 93).

References

Alleyne, M. 1994. "Problems of Standardization of Creole Languages". In *Language and the Social Construction of Identity in Creole Situations,* ed. M. Morgan, 7–18. Los Angeles: UCLA Centre for Afro-American Publications.

Anon. 1828. *Marly, or The Life of a Planter in Jamaica.* Glasgow: Griffin.

Collins, M. 1998. "Writing and Creole Language Politics: Voice and Story". In *Caribbean Creolization: Reflections on the Cultural Dynamics of Language, Literature, and Identity,* ed. K. Balutansky and M. Sourieau, 89–95. Kingston: The Press, University of the West Indies.

Cooper, C., and H. Devonish. 1992. "A Tale of Two States: Language, Lit/orature and the Two Jamaicas". Paper presented at the International Group for the Study of Language Standardization and the Vernacularization of Literacy Workshop, Creativity in Language, Sèvres, France.

Fowler, R. 1986. *Linguistic Criticism.* Oxford: Oxford University Press.

Gumperz, J., and D. Hymes, eds. 1972. *Directions in Sociolinguistics.* New York: Holt, Rinehart and Winston.

Kincaid, J. 1997. *My Brother*. New York: Farrar, Straus, Giroux.
Lalla, B. 1996. *Defining Jamaican Fiction: Marronage and the Discourse of Survival*. Tuscaloosa: University of Alabama Press.
———. 1999. "Conceptual Perspectives of Time and Timelessness". In *All Are Involved: The Art of Martin Carter*, ed. Stewart Brown. Leeds: Peepal Tree Press.
Morgan, M., ed. 1994. *Language and the Social Construction of Identity in Creole Situations*. Los Angeles: UCLA Centre for Afro-American Publications.
Myers-Scotton, C. 1993. *Social Motivations for Codeswitching*. Oxford: Clarendon.
Phillipson. R. 1992. *Linguistic Imperialism*. Oxford: Oxford University Press.
Prince, G. 1982. *Narratology: The Form and Functioning of Discourse*. Berlin: Mouton.
———. 1987. *Dictionary of Narratology*. Linton: University of Nebraska Press.
Roberts, P. 1997. *From Oral to Literate Culture: Colonial Experience in the British West Indies*. Kingston: The Press, University of the West Indies.
Simpson, P. 1993. *Language, Ideology and Point of View*. London: Routledge.
Scott, M. 1833. *Tom Cringle's Log*. Reprint. London: Gibbings, 1894.
Slembrouck, S. 1992. "The Parliamentary Hansard 'Verbatim' Report: The Written Construction of Spoken Discourse". *Language and Literature* 1, no. 1: 109–19.
Tabouret-Keller, A., et al. 1997. *Vernacular Literacy*. Oxford: Clarendon Press.
Winford, D. 1994. "Sociolinguistic Approaches to Language Use in the Anglophone Caribbean". In *Language and the Social Construction of Identity in Creole Situations*, ed. M. Morgan, 43–62. Los Angeles: UCLA Centre for Afro-American Publications.

Chapter 9

IS THE PAIN IN YOUR BELLY BOTTOM?
Extending the Boundaries of Jamaican Creole to Non-Native Users

KATHRYN SHIELDS-BRODBER

> Among other things, Creole has been deliberately cultivated in recent times by some who would not formerly have been associated with the use of it in public.
> – Pauline Christie, "Trends in Jamaican English"

INTRODUCTION

The question that provides the title for this chapter is likely to appear curious to most speakers of English; while the interrogative is syntactically well-formed, as far as English is concerned, *belly bottom* is not a recognizable lexical item in that language and is a Jamaican Creole (JC) calque. Similar integration of JC vocabulary and syntax within spoken or written texts intended to be and otherwise identifiably English is discussed in Christie (1998). The quotation with which this introduction opens provides her explanation: it is attributable to the deliberate cultivation and use of JC by speakers and writers of the time[1] from whom such usage would not have previously been expected in public. Christie identifies these as including "some children of professionals and others of similar social backgrounds who have been attracted to Rastafarianism and have adopted Dread Talk (see Pollard 1980) which, despite its lexical and morphological innovations, utilizes a phonology and syntax which are basically Creole" (1998, 24).

Christie's analysis is presented in the context of two sociolinguistic assumptions traditionally associated with the use of Creole in Jamaica: that the variety is correctly relegated to the domain of private, informal interaction and that it is primarily characteristic of non-educated speech. The presence of Creole, on such an increasingly, regular basis, in the public-formal and sometimes also conservative sources of Christie's data[2] is therefore remarkable. Further, as Christie also notes, the fact that the quoted speakers or writers are not only educated, but also likely to have intended to produce formal English, is a significant index of sociolinguistic change in Jamaica. Evidence of the pervasiveness of this change, which has spanned more than twenty years, with increasingly widespread impact, can be found in the sociolinguistic makeup of some of Jamaica's leaders. Speakers who employ the strategy regularly now include some of the best educated and distinguished local leaders of the highest social background, who present themselves as productively bilingual in Standard English (SE) and JC.

The radio doctor who is the subject of this chapter is a member of the class, with an important distinguishing feature: she is a non-native speaker of JC – a medical doctor of English origin, who has lived and practised in Jamaica for several years and provides advice on radio for phone-in callers. The focus of this chapter, therefore, is on the ways in which she demonstrates communicative competence by incorporating JC in her usage, in an attempt not only to clarify callers' problems and explain the solutions which she has to offer, but also to gain the confidence of her callers and the wider Jamaican audience for which the programme is intended. The informant is presented as a current example of the extent to which a non-native speaker may feel obliged to adapt to local linguistic norms, in order to ensure effective communication in contemporary Jamaica where JC has gained substantial legitimacy in the domain of public-formal discourse.

THE SOCIOLINGUISTIC DEMANDS ON A RADIO DOCTOR IN JAMAICA

Medical advice programmes have gained increasing popularity on radio in Jamaica, especially during the 1990s, with phone-in programmes of duration of fifteen minutes in the early days, and up to the current norm of one hour. Doctors on such programmes discuss, and often also offer a diagnosis for, problems communicated by an anonymous phone-in patient, whose call may last three to five minutes on average, but may continue for up to fifteen minutes, depending on the doctor's assessment of the problem.

Obviously, radio doctors operating within such time constraints do not normally attempt a full medical exegesis of problems raised by their phone-in patients. Instead, they spend airtime assuaging the fears of and providing comfort for those callers who appear unnecessarily worried or emphasizing the need for an immediate visit to a medical practitioner for those who require this course of action. Further, callers not only report physical ailments, they also bring to public notice social and psychological concerns which are discussed on air. Thus, the radio doctor may be required to fill the general role of counsellor and is called upon, in many instances, to employ a holistic approach to advice.

Radio doctors have to perform many functions simultaneously: they must listen to the symptoms which their radio patients elect to share, elicit details deemed necessary for an informed, and, on occasion, persuasive discussion, and suggest a diagnosis or course of action to be followed. This must be achieved in a relatively short time and in such a way that those who provide medical advice exude professional integrity, which gains and maintains the confidence of callers. In other words, radio doctors must, in a short time, put up or shut up in a context where not only callers, but also other overhearers, are making a judgement.

The effectiveness of a such a transaction – the public exchange and negotiation of personal well-being and medical details – hinges on clarity in language. Radio patients, on the one hand, must describe, clearly and succinctly, the problem or problems they are experiencing. The medical advisor, on the other, must elicit a comprehensible explanation and then present, equally clearly, an analysis and proposed follow-up action. For clarity to be achieved, doctor and patient will need to speak the same language.

In Jamaica, the phone-in radio population moves, as does the public in general, with varying degrees of freedom and stylistic variation, between two varieties: JC and SE. There are many correspondences between the lexico-semantics and syntax of JC and the local informal varieties of SE used by the general population, especially when its members perceive that they are called upon to discuss issues of a personal nature in English. While some, older, more conservative callers are likely to try to produce their most SE so as to conform to public-formal convention, many younger ones, also intending to produce English, may initially struggle with that variety, before reverting to their normal, informal, heavily Creole-influenced style to achieve clarity.

Hosts of talk radio must not only be aware of likely linguistic and stylistic variation in the language used by the population in everyday oral contexts, but also be able to understand and respond effectively and appropriately to their callers without alienating them. The significant ambiguity, for example, which can arise from lexico-semantic variation, has to be anticipated, as does the psychological gulf that may be established if, by diverging from patients' usage on a regular basis, doctors appear too distant from their phone-in patients. For a non-native doctor, the linguistic adjustments that have to be made to achieve effective communication with phone-in patients are likely to be major.

The radio doctor whose usage is examined here also has to provide clear evidence of her awareness of the linguistic constraints that hosting a medical advice programme is likely to impose, especially in a Creole language context that is non-native to her. She is required to demonstrate an awareness of possible lexical and other differences between her language and that of her phone-in patients, identifying, for example, the contexts in which they have attached local meaning to English words and expressions relating to parts of the anatomy, or to their intimate relations. She must also be able to define and explain medical jargon – not only in English, but in local terms as well – making decisions about the need to modify her own language and style in order to achieve, when desirable, accommodation to the usage of her callers.

Speech accommodation theory, "devised to explain some of the motivations underlying certain shifts in people's speech styles during social encounters, and some of the social encounters arising from them . . . in order to elucidate the cognitive and affective processes underlying speech convergence and divergence" (Thakerar et al. 1982, 207), provides an obvious explanation for the accession to the linguistic abilities and sensibilities of her callers that this doctor-informant will need to make. Coupled with her attempts at convergence with what she perceives to be their usage, these efforts will be aimed at reducing manifest dissimilarities between her audience and herself, achieving social integration and mutual approval in the process. Naturally, she will diverge linguistically when she intends to dissociate herself from her audience (Giles 1980; Giles and Smith 1979).

BRIDGING THE COMMUNICATIVE GAP WITH NON-NATIVE CREOLE USE

While not attempting to deny the general influence of her non-Jamaican origin, this radio doctor makes clear that she intends to operate as an insider, accommodating to the pronunciation patterns, vocabulary choices and grammatical constructions that she perceives as characteristic of the usage of her phone-in patients and of the wider society. Perhaps her most unsuccessful efforts relate to cadence and rhythm; however, these elements are not the focus of this chapter. There are numerous occasions where it is clear, from her linguistic behaviour, that she expects to be accepted as an integrated member of the local community. This section discusses some of the phonological, morphological, lexico-semantic, syntactic and discourse decisions the doctor makes in her quest to achieve linguistic and psycho-social accommodation with her audience. Her primary strategy is to integrate Creole, in various ways, within an otherwise English frame.

The Phonological Integration of /aarait/ as a Discourse Marker

One way the doctor signals her insider status within the local community is in her employment of local phonology. The particle /aarait/ is an obvious example, because she usually inserts it early in the exchange and uses it to punctuate her advice thereafter. When employing the particle, she consistently adheres to JC phonology.

The doctor uses /aarait/ for a number of discourse purposes. One of these purposes, the reinforcement of a previously stated idea, is illustrated in Example 1, below. The particle is accompanied by utterance-final rising intonation:

1. Baby's nurse complains about having to bottle-feed her charge.

Doctor: I don't know what's causing that.
I don't think it IS the bottle.
But you're right she should not be on the bottle still =
Caller: = A three [year old
Doctor: [It's better –
It's better never to start a bottle
/aarait/?
because as you know the bottle carries
germs.

16692/30A

Interesting to note in Example 1 is that the caller, who identifies herself as a baby's nurse, uses English to express her concerns about her employer's practice of bottle-feeding a three-year-old child. The doctor's reply, apart from the phonology of the particle, is English. This concession to Creole, which, in relation to the particle, appears automatic on the doctor's part, achieves accommodation, therefore, not to the usage of the nurse, but to that of the wider listening audience.

On many occasions, callers are insecure about what their next course of action should be or about ways of coping with their immediate situation. In Example 2, the caller, who recently has given birth to a stillborn baby, explains her concerns about her slow progress in coming to terms with her grief. She proposes a solution that she is considering as a means of accelerating the process: starting a new baby. The doctor emphasizes the need to take time, not to accelerate the process, but to let it take its course. She suggests that the caller should have named the baby and kept mementoes of her. However, being sensitive to the fact that her caller may not be in a psychological state to appreciate her advice, she uses the particle /aarait/ to soften the force of her response, while providing reassurance for the caller.

2. Caller questions her rate of recovery after having a stillborn baby.

Doctor: So in answer to your question
it doesn't sound to me as if
you've ahm completely

| | grieved the baby yet.
| | You can't do that,
| | and I wouldn't rush
| | into having another one.
| Caller: | Okay
| Doctor: | /Aarait/?
| | So I would if I were you,
| | think on that baby.
| | Did you have a photograph or anything
| | to remember her by?
| Caller: | No
| Doctor: | /Aarait/
| | It would have helped if you had.

16692/06A

The repetition of the particle, with the addition of a short explanation, not only marks the close of the exchange, but also reinforces the reassurance which the doctor provides.

Callers' constant need for reassurance is the impetus for several of the instances in which the doctor employs /aarait/. In Examples 3a and 3b below, the particle also functions as a request for the caller to acknowledge that the explanation is understood.

3a. Caller complains about stomach pains.

| Doctor: | What the doctor's
| | going to say is,
| | you got a stomach ulcer,
| | and that's very easy to treat.
| | /Aarait /?

16692/132A

3b. Doctor diagnoses a bladder infection and suggests a visit to a doctor.

| Doctor: | Well then it's more likely
| | that you have a germ
| | in your bladder.

	It's very common
	and very easy to treat.
	So you need to see the doctor?
Caller:	Okay
Doctor:	And the doctor will give you
	some antibiotics,
	and maybe do a urine test.
	/Aarait/?

16692/171A

In Examples 1 to 3, the Creole phonology of the particle contributes to the feeling that, even though the interlocutors are strangers, the interviewer, in her dual role of interviewer/doctor, is attempting to establish an easy, open and trusting on-air relationship with her callers/patients. This relationship will also extend, of course, to the wider listening community.

The "Belly Bottom" Syndrome: Lexico-Semantic Variation in the Noun Phrase

To understand and to be understood by her callers, an obvious and successful concession which this radio doctor has had to make to local parlance is to incorporate Jamaican vocabulary within otherwise SE utterances. She achieves this in various ways. In Example 4, she repeats the information provided by the caller, with one modification: she specifies, in local vocabulary, where she believes the pain to be.

4. Caller complains about a pain in the side.

Caller:	Good morning doctor.
Doctor:	Morning.
Caller:	Okay.
	I am having a little pain
	in my left hand side
	at the lower bottom?
	at the lower side?
	I am wondering if it is the appendix now.

Doctor: You're getting a pain
in the left side
of the lower abdomen
so-called belly bottom.
Is that right?

16692/311A

The doctor's use of a local gloss makes it clear to listeners where she thinks the pain is; it also underscores her willingness to define the location in terms listeners can understand and they themselves would use – hence, *so-called*.

There are many instances of the doctor initiating the integration of local words and expressions in the primarily English explanations she often proffers. Example 5 illustrates her reference to *belly bottom,* inserted in the normal run of a primarily English conversation.

5. Caller asks about the cause of pregnancy.

Doctor: What causes pregnancy?
Getting @@@
Having intercourse with a man.
Caller: Yes.
Doctor: and the semen
the sperm and the semen from your man.
Caller: Yes.
Doctor: ahm coming up and meeting up
with the egg that you produce
inside your *belly bottom*
and the –
if the sperm manages to get
to the egg and fertilize it. . . .

16692/267A

As Example 5 indicates, she appears to accept as normal the local meanings associated with parts of the human anatomy and not to be averse to establishing those shared norms in discussing her callers' problems. In Example 6a below, she displays a similar ease when, once again unprompted, she supplies the appropriate local term, as she questions her caller:

6a. Doctor establishes caller's position in the family.

Doctor:	Are you the youngest or the oldest in the family?
Caller:	The youngest.
Doctor:	How many other girls?
Caller:	One.
Doctor:	How old is she?
Caller:	Thirty.
Doctor:	Thirty.
Caller:	Yes.
Doctor:	So you're the *wash belly*?
Caller:	Yes.

26620/257

In Example 6b, perhaps to make the idea of an injection palatable, she initiates the local cognate *jook* in an extended explanation which is otherwise English:

6b. Doctor reassures an anxious caller complaining about ugly warts on her neck.

Doctor: If you go to a dermatologist
the dermatologist will probably be able
to just burn them off.
[*section omitted*]
All they'll do is,
if it's a big one,
they'll just give you
just a tiny *jook* of local anaesthetic
at the base of it.

19620/262A

Further, as Example 7 below indicates, she is certainly not afraid to acknowledge the local, expanded meaning[3] connected to a SE word (in this case, referring to the anatomy) and embraces that meaning effortlessly as she seeks clarification from her caller. The phrasing of her question here underscores her Creole interpretation of *stomach* as *chest*. This she indicates by association, juxtaposing *stomach* in the first part of her question to *not breathing properly* in the second.

7. Caller questions whether she may have asthma.

Caller:	I think I have asthma.
Doctor:	Does your *stomach* get tight
	So you feel like you can't breathe properly?

16692/153A

By not merely responding to local talk, but also initiating it, the doctor is able to earn credibility and establish her position as a bona fide member of the community.

During her interrogation of phone-in patients who may use, with a local meaning, a word shared by standard and local varieties, the doctor has to be certain which meaning the patient intends. She may simply introduce the local cognate,[4] or she may specifically ask for clarification, as in Example 8 below:

8. Caller complains that her stomach feels weak.

Doctor:	The next thing I want to know
	Is what you mean by
	You stomach feel weak.
	Do you mean it's difficult to breathe?

28620/62A

Her choice of the appropriate uninflected Creole form of the second person pronoun (a parallel to the caller's *mi stomak*) as a modifier is the syntactic adjustment she makes in keeping with her JC interpretation. The doctor receives many calls about sexual issues; however, in order to discuss such calls intelligently, she must recognize when sexual connotations are implied, as is the case in Example 9 below.

9. Caller is worried about getting pregnant.

Caller:	I've been trying to get pregnant for a while now
	Because I have this guy I've been *talking to*.[5]

19620/517

The confidence this doctor feels about her knowledge of Jamaican vocabulary sometimes leads her to go beyond merely selecting an appropriate item. She may decide not just to cite a local word, but also to offer a definition to a caller who, though obviously Jamaican, may not have recognized its reference. This is illustrated in Example 10:

10. Caller complains of shaking in the body.

Doctor:	The twitching in the body
	is directly –
	the – the anxiety that causes the twitching.
	You know when you see people have a *quinty*[6]
	You know what they call a *quinty*?
Caller:	No
Doctor:	/aarait/
	Quinty is an old Jamaican word.
	which means
	when the little –
	when the corner of the eye
	starts to jump
	you've seen that haven't you?

19620/407

She may also volunteer an evaluative response to the local phrases she introduces, which, as in Example 11, may not always seem appropriate:

11. Doctor interviews a psychiatrist about death.

Doctor:	One thing I wanted to bring up as well
	/ded lef bizniz/
Psychiatrist:	Hhhh?
Doctor:	A love that term, /ded lef bizniz/
	Yeh!

19620/188A

The disjuncture created between the doctor's selection of a JC expression and the expectations of the psychiatrist, an English-speaking, educated addressee, is explained by the doctor's obvious appeal to her outgroup referees (Bell

1991): those in the audience whom she identifies as her target, but whose language is not hers.

Compounding in Noun and Verb Phrases

One characteristic of Jamaican Creole is its propensity for word compounding. This feature is often transferred to local English so that a non-English compound may occur within what otherwise could be adjudged as conforming to metropolitan SE norms. In Example 12, the doctor mistakes a perhaps less-used English compound, which still has currency in Jamaica, for a Creole form and then hypercorrects in order to make it morphologically English (an analogy with *at nights*, perhaps?):

12. Caller thinks she may have asthma.

Doctor: You may still have asthma
if asthma is in the family
an' you have a chronic cough
an' it come on at *night-time*.
Does it come on *night-times*?

16692/ 150A

A particularly favoured compound in Jamaica is the noun + particle construction. One may give an untidy place a *clean up*, or take a *washout*. The doctor frequently employs this construction as a means of establishing, or responding to, more personal, informal interaction:

13. Caller seeks advice about an unruly two-year-old.

Doctor: SHOW 'im that
every time he does something nice
and he's quiet
and he is respectful
or he's pleasant
/aarait?/
that you'll give him a *hug up*
and do something nice with him.

23597/507B

The use and creation of multi-word verbs is another interesting feature of the doctor's production. In Jamaica, there is a tendency to convert to multi-word structure verbs which in English are normally transitive or monotransitive. So, for example, in local parlance, one may *hug up* another, one may *eat up* one's food or *wash up* one's foot. The local tendency to create new verbs with phrasal structures is particularly strong at this time, with the current phrase being to *big up* (to encourage/praise) someone. So the doctor's exhortation to her caller to *love up* her unfaithful partner (Example 14) is entirely in vogue and in keeping with local practice. It also engenders an appropriate tone of familiarity:

14. Caller admits to finding out about her boyfriend's affair.

Doctor: So listen
          cool down on him.
          Either you've got to forgive him
          or go on an *love im up* again
          or else you have to go away and don leave him
                                                                    23597/313B

A similar process is inherent in her selection, in Example 15 below, of a phrasal structure, *strengthen up* in place of SE transitive *strengthen*.⁷

15. Caller complains of experiencing back pain.

Doctor: If you walk
          an' *strengthen up* yu back muscles
          from the walking
          you'll find that the back
          will get stronger
          and stop paining you
          so much.
                                                                    23597/337B

In Example 16, she reprimands her caller in SE, then, for reinforcement, employs the JC prepositional verb *to business about*. Again, the doctor initiates JC integration.

16. Doctor reprimands diabetic caller for inadequate nutrition while breast-feeding.

Doctor:	You don't seem to realize,
	when you're breast feeding my dear,
	you need to eat a breakfast,
	and a big bowl o' porridge,
	and two hours later,
	you probably need
	to eat something again.
Caller:	An' get big an' fat.
	A mean the [porridge has to sweeten] sugars.
Doctor:	[no no no no]
Doctor:	[Listen love]
Caller:	[Okay]
Doctor:	Don't *business about*
	the big an' fat for now.
	Feed your baby,
	eat according to your appetite,
	and adjust the insulin
	according to your blood

16692/394A

Further Creole Influence in the Verb Phrase

The doctor incorporates Creole elements within her discourse for a variety of purposes. As a rule, she does not attempt to produce extended utterances in JC; however, there are many instances in which the verb phrase undergoes an adjustment towards JC norms and marks the doctor's attempt to accommodate to her local callers.

Invariant verbs are part of the doctor's repertoire and a feature she recognizes as characteristic of JC. In local interaction, especially of an informal nature, non-inflected verbs may also be integrated within what is intended to be SE. In Example 17, the doctor presents a proposed explanation for the caller to offer to his girlfriend and presents it in the words that she thinks it likely that he will use. She then incorporates the preceding JC structure within her intervention, closing the linguistic gap between herself and the caller.

17. Caller is worried about bumps all over his body and has been hiding from his girlfriend.

Doctor:	Why don't you ask her if she minds seeing it.
	I bet you'll find that she'd rather have you
	even with the bumps,
Caller:	Yeh
Doctor:	than have nobody.
Caller:	Yeh
Doctor:	So why don't you talk to her about it.
	Call her up first of all
	and tell her, "the reason
	you don't see me is because
	a cover up wid bump an'
	it look ugly an' I feel shy",
Caller:	Mhm
Doctor:	and see what she say

16692/252A

Of additional interest in Example 17 is the doctor's mirroring of the uninflected verb in her own comment, which closes the example.

The doctor adopts *serial constructions* as a means of establishing immediacy, or, as illustrated in Example 18 below, for emphasizing the seriousness of her directive:

18. Caller complains of back pain.

Doctor:	/Aarait!/
	You get any exercise
Caller:	No
Doctor:	*Start go walk*

23507/335B

She also employs these constructions in order to put an insecure or hesitant caller at ease. In Example 19, for instance, the doctor uses a serial construction in order to converge with what she believes to be the more comfortable usage of her caller, thereby reducing the psychological distance she perceives between them.

19. Caller complains of burning in stomach.

Caller:	A jos . . .
	iim .
	a kaan sliip
	an .
	ma stomak kiip bornin mi
	bot aafta it finish
Doctor:	*It staat burn* again?
Caller:	Yah
Doctor:	You see something is burning
	a hole in your stomach,
	and something is making you
	kaan sliip at nights.

16692/55A

In this instance, the doctor makes cause with the caller before reverting to SE (and invoking her professional status) for the explanation, within which, interestingly, she incorporates the caller's *kaan sliip* rather than choosing SE *unable to sleep* – perhaps as an indication of their psychological reconnection.

A *double negative* is used in what constitutes an inter-sentential switch to JC in Example 20. The doctor, having been persuaded of the correctness of her criticism, switches to JC for emphasis. The tag that follows attenuates the force of what the caller may consider a reprimand and thus politely puts the ball back in the caller's court.

20. Caller admits to covering her own nipple with an artificial one.

Doctor:	Does the baby not manage
	to suck on hard
	an' suck it out –
	bring the nipple out.
Caller:	Out an' get full.

Doctor:	Ah?
Caller:	He sucks it out.
Doctor:	Good.
	Well that's fine then.
	You *don' need no nipple*
	over the top.
	Do you?

16692/411A

The *marking of duration* is another area in which the doctor achieves JC integration within her otherwise standard usage. In Jamaica, even in formal situations, many speakers avoid the perfect aspect construction. Thus, it is customary to hear in newscasts, scripted speeches and so on, as well as to read in newspapers *He is here for ten years,* or *It is here since 1978* (in which present tense and adverbial combine). In fact, there is hardly any use of the perfect aspect where it would normally be expected in English – to indicate duration from a time in the past and extending to the present. In Example 21, the doctor completes the caller's adverbial with a construction parallelling the JC *dis lang taim a doon / neva si yu* (SE *it has been a long time since I've seen you*) and achieves a synergy between them.

21. Caller responds to doctor's question about church.

Doctor:	You go to church?
Caller:	. . . No but yeh I used to go to church
	but *from this long time*
	I don't? =
Doctor:	= You *don't go*

16692/411A

What bears repetition here is that the doctor's accommodation to local norms is not necessarily in response to a caller's usage, but is often an attempt to incorporate her wider Creole-speaking radio audience – the potential overhearers (Bell 1991) to her programme. By converging with what she assumes to be their linguistic expectations, she attempts to enhance the effectiveness of her radio advice, bridging the gap that could be reasonably anticipated between a local mass audience and a non-native host.

Two Contexts of Divergence

Defining and Explaining Medical Conditions and Related Jargon

When defining and explaining medical conditions, the doctor rarely attempts to integrate JC within SE. Often, she introduces the medical term, defines it and explains its significance entirely in English, as illustrated in Examples 22–24:

22. Doctor responds to caller's explanation of her relative's symptoms.

Doctor:	I think she's probably having mild hy-per-ven-ti-lation which is when we get so worried we don't even know to breathe properly.

19620/517A

23. Caller describes nervous symptoms.

Doctor:	What you have is what we call Psychogenic dyspepsia That sounds – that sounds awful. That means that your [nerves
Caller:	[cause sometimes [[I feel so cold like I'm going to die]]
Doctor:	[[are causing a stomach upset]]

16692/89A

24. Caller complains of itching.

Doctor:	Well that sounds like what we call PO-DO-POM-PI-LIX which is a sort of eczema or dermatitis

19620/273A

Perhaps, instinctively, the doctor recognizes that in providing medical definitions, she needs to preserve her legitimacy and mystique as a professional, and therefore diverges from everyday Creole-influenced usage. This would explain her practice of introducing medical jargon in the first place, rather than simply providing the explanation without it. Linguistic accommodation to callers, then, is relegated to putting callers at ease and eliciting comprehensible explanations of their symptoms; it does not extend to the explanation of medical jargon.

English for Issuing Reprimands

One other context in which JC usually finds little place is in the radio doctor's extended reprimands of her callers. In such instances she does not mince words and estranges herself from their sentiments in no uncertain terms. Example 25 provides one instance where she converges initially, then as she ascertains the facts, she diverges.

25. Doctor upbraids caller for trying to get pregnant.

Doctor: I myself am wondering
          why a 22-year-old
          with a relationship
          with just a year and a half
          is so anxious about getting pregnant
          so quickly.
          An' that worries me because
          I wonder whether the need
          for a baby is
          a bit immature
          an' isn't really
          a need to form a family
          with this man
          and more a need to have a –
          "Oh I want a nice baby for myself"
          or "Oh I want to give him a baby . . ."
          That sounds a bit hard, doesn't it?

19620/547A

Example 25 is interesting because the doctor remains in SE even when, in closing the conversation, she mitigates the force of her reprimand with an acknowledgement of its harshness.

Negotiating Identity and Meaning in a Non-Native Setting

From the examples, it is possible to identify two general levels of linguistic adjustment the doctor makes to her SE usage as she communicates using her second language. She produces JC substitutes for SE lexical items and displays semantic awareness of the differences between varieties, which will allow her not only to produce appropriate local cognates when required, but also to respond meaningfully to their use by callers. She also integrates JC syntactic structures within SE – which requires greater linguistic skill on her part – especially when she initiates the introduction of a non-English structure and uses it effectively, rather than merely copying or matching one produced by a caller. She demonstrates an even higher level of proficiency in her second language when she is able to participate with a caller in the joint production of a JC utterance. This reflects a level of processing and internalization of that structure – a thinking in the language. This is an achievement to be acknowledged, given the inherent potential challenge of such an activity for a non-native speaker.

The radio doctor must also demonstrate receptive competence in JC. From the beginning of a call, she must indicate an understanding of some of the lexical, phonological and syntactic characteristics of that language, but especially of the lexico-semantic peculiarities in relation to medical issues. Most important, she must also demonstrate communicative competence in JC, to achieve clarity as she articulates and negotiates meaning with her radio patients.

Since negotiating meaning does not occur in a vacuum, but depends on the extent of shared linguistic resources of the participants in the process, the doctor must make on-the-spot judgements about her callers' linguistic abilities, with which she then elects to converge or diverge. Information-checking and clarification questions usually promote convergence, which then facilitates the social intercourse required. In this regard, the sociolinguistic composition of her target audience of over-hearers can never be far from her consideration.

What the examples also suggest, however, is that the doctor's divergence from the sentiments either expressed or implied by a caller, or known to be held by the wider local community, will lead to her divergence from local JC norms. This will, of course, establish her as an outsider in those contexts. Recourse to outsider status is also her option when she wishes to remind callers of her professional persona and therefore remind them of the authenticity of her advice.

This points to the need for the doctor to establish social and professional legitimacy in a language not her own but indispensable to her purpose. Thus, the negotiation of multilevel identity is fundamental to her effectiveness. This radio doctor has gone a far way in her journey towards this goal.

ACKNOWLEDGEMENTS

An earlier version of this chapter was presented at the 2000 conference of the Society for Caribbean Linguistics. The database comprises recordings from radio programmes aired between 1992 and 2000.

NOTES

The key for examples above is as follows: [ ] enclose simultaneous speech; ? is appeal/rising intonation; = is latching, that is, no perceptible gap between end of turn of one speaker and the beginning of that of the next; @@@ is laughter. Italics are used to highlight the feature in focus. Cassidy–Le Page orthography is used for JC.

1. Her analysis was first presented in 1982, informed by data collected between 1977 and 1982.
2. These included the leading newspaper, news broadcasts, commentaries, announcements and interviews with public figures in the electronic media, as well as essays by university students.
3. This is an implicit acknowledgement of the fact that lexical items referring to the anatomy and shared by SE and JC are likely to differ semantically. Thus, by expan-

sion, JC *foot* and *hand* include SE *leg* and *arm* respectively, while *stomach* in (JC paradigm *stomach, belly, belly bottom*) is often used with reference to SE *chest*.
4. See Example 4.
5. Similarly, a loss of *nature* in Jamaica refers to a reduction in SE *libido*.
6. I have never heard the "y" added. The more usual /*kwint*/ (interestingly, not entered in either the *Dictionary of Jamaican English* or *Jamaica Talk*) is the cognate for SE *squint* and is a verb.
7. The use of an uninflected pronoun in the complement adds to the Creole authenticity of the phrase. See also Example 5, where she uses the phrasal prepositional, *meeting up with* in lieu of the more usual transitive meeting.

References

Bell, A. 1991. *The Language of News Media*. Oxford and Cambridge, Mass.: Blackwell.

Christie, P. 1998. "Trends in Jamaican English". *UWILING Working Papers in Linguistics* 3.

Giles, H. 1980. "Accommodation Theory: Some New Directions". In *Aspects of Linguistic Behaviour*, ed. S. de Silva. Oxford: Blackwell.

Giles, H., and P. Smith. 1979. "Accommodation Theory: Optimal Levels of Convergence". In *Language and Social Psychology*, ed. H. Giles and R. St Clair. Oxford: Blackwell.

Pollard, V. 1980. "The Social History of Dread Talk". Paper presented at the Third Biennial Conference of the Conference of the Society for Caribbean Linguistics, Aruba.

Thakerar, J., H. Giles and J. Cheshire. 1982. "Psychological and Linguistic Parameters of Speech Accommodation Theory". In *Advances in the Social Psychology of Language*, ed. C. Fraser and K. Scherer, 205–55. Cambridge: Cambridge University Press.

Chapter 10

ASOU DOWN-THERE
Code-Mixing in a Bilingual Community
— MARTHA ISAAC

> In all cases of intimate contact between different communities there is likely to be multiple linguistic input to the children's language systematization, and the children will produce for their peer groups initially at least a diffuse and varying output. What happens next is a transactional focusing among peer groups, agreements on the social marking of tokens being exchanged, the emergence within each generation of sets of linguistic attributes assigned to different groups within the community, the use of these differentially to mark their own identity within the community.
>
> – Robert Le Page, "You Can Never Tell Where a Word Comes From"

The current manifestations of code-mixing in St Lucia seem to suggest a comfortable acceptance of the dual codes[1] which characterize St Lucian life. The quotation from Le Page captures some of the varied dimensions of utilizing dual codes in a bilingual speech community. Additionally, the notions he expresses, such as transactional focusing and identity marking, are expressed by several authors: Kachru (1978), Thomason and Kaufman (1988), Gardner-Chloros (1995), Milroy and Musyken (1995), Tabouret-Keller (1995), Poplack (1998), Myers-Scotton (1995, 2000), and Winford (2003).

In this chapter I discuss the origin of the expression *asou down-there*, and examine the notion, proposed by Le Page (1998) and Romaine (1989), that although it is inevitable that individuals make linguistic choices, those choices are not necessarily consciously made but may be the result of a collective cultural and social experience. I will also explore the notion of interference, as well as some definitions of language use in bilingual situations and the implications of these phenomena for education and language development.

Code-Mixing

Code-mixing is described variously as the alternate use of two codes in a fully grammatical way in the same discourse, or even in the same sentence, (Poplack 1998) and as a rapid form of language switching that enables a speaker to signal two identities (Le Page 1998). Interestingly, Trudgill (1998, 23) defines code mixing as "the process whereby speakers indulge in code-switching between languages with such rapidity and density, even within sentences and phrases, that it is not really possible to say at any given time which language they are speaking".

Code-mixing, code-shifting and code-switching appear to be used interchangeably, although some writers attempt to distinguish between them. Code-mixing is often used to refer to lexical input of one code within another and code-switching to the smooth transitions from one code to another involving larger grammatical segments by a single speaker within a conversation. Poplack (1998) uses code-switching for the alternate use of two codes in a fully grammatical way, in the same discourse, and even in the same sentence. According to her, the use of other terms such as code-mixing or code-shifting to describe the same phenomenon is not problematic.

Kachru (1978) uses the term code-mixing to refer to the use of one or more languages for the consistent transfer of linguistic units from one language into another and reserves the term code-switching for instances in which different codes are used for different occasions or correspond to different stages in an interaction (p. 28). Myers-Scotton (2000) subsumes both types of alternation, that is, intrasentential as well as intersentential under the term code-switching. Gardner-Chloros (1995) views code-switching as a fuzzy-edged concept because speakers make binary choices, operating in either one code or another at any given time.

Confounding of Bilingual Behaviour

Linguistic behaviour in bilingual communities is variably described as code-switching, code-mixing, borrowing, incomplete language acquisition and interference. According to Gumperz (1982), these are all used as evidence of code-switching. The realities of bilingual behaviour seem to defy conceptual frames. However, many writers are searching for a heuristic to harness this variable linguistic behaviour. Some conceptual frames are briefly mentioned below.

1. For Winford (2003, 103–5), it is not easy to point out the particular social factors that regulate the linguistic outcomes of contact situations. Against a background of contact languages, his work examines, among other things, the various bilingual mixtures to which the label code-switching has been applied.
2. The concepts "projection" and "focusing" characterize the work of Le Page and Tabouret-Keller. Le Page (1998, 72) explains that individuals are envisaged using the linguistic systems that they themselves have created in order to project unto others the universe as they envisage it, including their own place in it.
3. The Matrix Language Frame model proposed by Myers-Scotton (1995, 235) ascribes the terms matrix language (ML) and embedded language (EL), respectively, to the language that plays the dominant role and to the others that constitute the bilingual or multilingual character of the community. The matrix language is the less marked language[2] and comprises most of the lexicon and syntactic apparatus of one language, usually the target. There is insertion of single words or phrases from the other, the EL. According to Winford, the mixture provides a third constituent.
4. Thomason and Kaufman (1988) view the sociolinguistic history of the speaker, not the structure of the language, as the determinant of linguistic outcomes in contact situations. Contact situations provide the broad canvas against which bilingual behaviour is analysed. The authors claim that while linguistic considerations are secondary, focus remains on systematizing the linguistic facts rather than the social influences (p. 36).

5. For Kachru (1978), the theory of code-mixing has yet to be viewed within a theoretical model. He discusses code-mixing in terms of Firth's (1957) framework of "context of situation". Kachru attempts to relate form to the immediate cultural context, considering that in order to provide linguistically and contextually adequate explanations for code-mixed language types, it is useful to relate these language types to contextual functions.

Interestingly, Kachru's framework seems the most appropriate for the situation that I present here. Although he refers to a largely multilingual context, he addresses a dual system comprising first, the target, and second, other languages. I retain the broad canvas of the contact situation as the background for this discussion and relate bilingual behaviour to the ethnography of communication, as proposed by Hymes and used by Saville-Troike (1989).

With some bias in the debate over terminology, I have retained the term code-mixing, using Kachru's definition (1978, 31): "It involves functioning in a disystem, and developing another linguistic code comprising formal features of two or more codes."

Code-mixing is therefore used here to refer to the smooth, simultaneous use of elements of both codes in a discourse segment in the bilingual territory of St Lucia. The codes referred to are French Creole, along with either of the two varieties of English used in St Lucia, and conversely – as some of the data will show – English with French Creole. While I have adopted Kachru's description of code-mixing with some adaptation, namely, using it in a primarily bilingual context (as distinct from the multilingual Southern Asia about which he writes), concerns of other writers who are attempting to define a framework also inform my discussion of the phenomenon.

Of interest, among others, is Robertson's (1982) suggestion of a post-Creole continuum, as described for Berbice Dutch, where informants used lexical items from Berbice Dutch with English. In a MPhil thesis, Isaac (1986) addressed the notion of calquing from French Creole, which created a basilectal form that is gradually decreolized towards the target, English. Robertson's description of that phenomenon in Berbice Dutch suggests that decreolization (De Camp 1971) does not necessarily preclude contexts where the existing languages do not share a common lexicon. Robertson (1982, 5) notes:

From a purely non-theoretical standpoint, Berbice Dutch, at least, provides strong evidence that the Creole may undergo relexification towards the new target language and may participate in the general decreolization movement towards the new target. The evidence shows that the process is characterized by a smooth rather than abrupt transition.

ASOU DOWN-THERE

The annual New Year's Day fair in St Lucia is a traditional cultural event. Originally held on the Derek Walcott Square in Castries (a park in the centre of the city, formerly known as Columbus Square) the event was commonly referred to as *asou square,* literally translated "on the square". In recent times, the venue was changed twice, first to a playing field north of the city, and later, much further north, to a beachfront on Pigeon Point. Despite these varied locations, the name *asou square* remained, defining a cultural event to which every St Lucian could relate.

It is interesting that the code-mixing in naming the cultural event was never as stark as the naming when the venue was changed again, this time to the south of the city in the Cul-de-Sac Valley. The location, it would seem, made it important for people to state that, far from the park facilities which characterized other venues, this venue in the muddy Cul-de-Sac Valley was different and referred to as "down-there". However, the locative *asou,* carrying nuances of an event and entertainment which are accessible largely to a St Lucian sensibility prevailed, and increasingly over the New Year's holiday of 2000, there was reference to *asou down-there.* The coining of this expression is an example of code-mixing. Poplack notes, however, that "the smaller the switched constituent, and particularly at the level of the lone lexical item, it is more difficult to resolve the question of whether we are dealing with a code-switch or a loan word (1998, 49). This consideration prevails as I examine the data. Notwithstanding this distinction, the mixing of codes in St Lucia can be described as just that – code-mixing – without any suggestion of "unprincipled chaos" (Myers-Scotton 2000).

Another expression I heard for the first time during that period was *mwen box* – literally "I box", meaning "I am filled"/ "I've had more than enough to eat." The expression has an interesting origin. It was explained by the nineteen-year-old male who used it as an analogy coming from the banana boxing plant. When the box has been filled with its quota, the expression *mwen box* expresses completion of that task. The analogy is used with eating. The boxing of bananas for export provided the image and cultural dimension, resulting in the code-mixing or coining of these lexical items. There appears to be a collective understanding, within which meaning is expressed and understood, and the expression is accepted (Le Page 1998).

Cultural Domains and Identity

Le Page (1998) proposes the notion of projection, focusing and diffusion as a contribution to a theoretical framework for contact situations. He argues that it is important to start not from reified discrete systems but from observable language use and by recognizing the individual as the sole locus of language use. Acts of identity, he claims, are the means, given the colonial heritage of territories such as St Lucia, for people to find ways to acknowledge and define their heritage – individual language use being a clear manifestation of this. Myers-Scotton (2000, 138) assumes all linguistic code choices are indexical of a set of rights and obligations holding between participants in a conversational exchange. Any code choice points to a particular interpersonal balance, and it is partly because of their indexical value that certain dialects, languages and styles are maintained in a community. There is a tacit understanding that this juxtaposition of codes does not violate conversational maxims (Grice 1975), but invites interlocutors to negotiate meaning within a dual code exchange. Given the historical import of *asou down-there*, one can assume a certain social, cultural and political import. The conversational implicatures (Grice 1975) generated are part of a "collective unconscious". The speech community has a sense of "script"– the medium of dual codes is simultaneously a tool and an index (Myers-Scotton 2000, 141).

The globalization of English as projected and focused usage and the standardizing nature of Quirk's grammar, referred to by Le Page, cause Creoles to be viewed as aberrant in nature. Devonish (1986) calls for the acknowledgement of a Creole as an autonomous language, but this leaves unattended the problem of how to deal with the interlanguage or interdialect varieties that continually develop when languages co-exist. Clearly, consideration of the linguistic implications of the co-existence of Standard and Creole varieties in Caribbean societies must of necessity include the various ways in which new varieties involving both codes are created. Code-mixing in St Lucia might very well be the creation of another variety, indexing a St Lucian sensibility, identity and cultural context within which meaning is negotiated.

INTERFERENCE PHENOMENA

Can these expressions be considered interference phenomena? The cultural and social interaction – or the absence of that interaction – within the community determines the extent and direction of interference. The sociolinguistic history of the speakers, not the structure of their language, is the primary determinant of the linguistic outcome of language contact. Linguistic interference is therefore conditioned by social factors. Both the direction of interference and the extent of interference are socially determined, as, to a considerable degree, are the kinds of features transferred from one language to another.

A common feature in interference phenomena is borrowing – the incorporation of foreign features into a group's native language by speakers of that language. The native language is maintained but is changed by the addition of the incorporated features; invariably the first elements to enter the borrowing language are words (Thomason and Kaufman 1988, 37). The motivations for lexical borrowing depend on a range of social factors that vary from one contact situation to another: the need to designate new things, persons, places and concepts (Weinreich 1953).

For a long time, the concern with interference phenomena in St Lucia has been with its manifestation in schools. The following are still general concerns: that insufficient exposure to English within the dual contexts of home and school makes acquiring the target language difficult and that the pedagogy of the language classroom should effectively clean up the English expression of students. Despite these considerations, code-mixing is prevalent among students who have successfully completed secondary and tertiary education, as in the case of the nineteen-year-old referred to above.

Notions of interference can be viewed as twofold: that which is positive – an expected and acceptable understanding of the inter-influence of languages in contact situations such as bilingual contexts (Le Page 1998; Trudgill 1998) – and that which is considered negative and causes greater concern – the idea that the less "prestigious" language gets in the way of learning the target or the "prestigious" language (Weinreich 1953) or that interference is a result of incomplete second language acquisition (Poplack 1998).

Writing about interference in St Lucia, Isaac (1986) outlined possible French Creole features in the written English of fifth form students. This was actually the use of lexical items: instances of calquing and structures which did not manifest conventions of Standard English. The study was informed by the work of Weinreich (1953), who proposed the comparative analysis of languages as a means of studying types of interference.

Winch and Gingell (1992), working with eleven-year-olds in primary schools in St Lucia, suggest that what was considered interference phenomena by St Lucian educators was actually an inter-language, in which the seeming errors were similar to those made by British children learning their mother tongue.

In the case of Isaac's 1986 research, it is considered that given the appropriate pedagogical guidance, fifth form students who are in a grade which marks the end of their secondary school education should have the capacity to control and manage their written production of the target language. For pragmatic purposes, the learning of English in Britain is different from that of learning English in a bilingual St Lucian community. Even though the diasporic nature of some contexts in Britain create bilingual communities that can be considered similar to some Caribbean communitites, the situations are not comparable.

By age seven, most of the defining characteristics of the native language have been learned. In St Lucia that would depend on the home code, which may be French Creole or a variety of English close to or far removed from the standard. The interlanguage, then, would be a complex mix of individual choice as well as societal influence. In the St Lucian context it would be unwise to dismiss the non-standard elements of students' writing as simply a neutral interlanguage akin to that of children of monolingual communities. However, such a proposition need not be ignored; it may provide the basis for further research but should not lead to diluting the intensity of the research on sociolinguistic implications of our bilingual, bidialectal environment. Contradictory findings in the research on language acquisition in bilingual situations make it difficult to be conclusive about the competence of students in bidialectal or bilingual contexts (Krashen 1996). The linguistic environment remains a constant factor.

MOTIVATION FOR CODE-MIXING

Crystal (1997) proposes that code-switching may take several forms. In the midst of conversation, speakers change from one language to another for a number of reasons – as an expression of solidarity, to exclude others and/or to increase the impact of their speech by using it in an effective manner.

The world of technology has spawned new words and new vocabularies. The creative input of young people to language development is evident in the short-lived expressions used to mark their identity as teenagers. Words such as "safe" and "dis" have specific meanings among young people. This feature adds to the dynamism of language development.

The expressions *asou down-there* and *mwen box* are examples of typical mixing and both allude to the cultural and social matrices of St Lucian life. If the dynamism of language is acknowledged, it will be acknowledged too that the standard and target varieties will constantly undergo change. The varieties of English across the world (Pennycook 1994) attest to the fact that English will be coloured by the culture and social life of a particular nation or community.

A pertinent question then is "What are the boundary lines?" Bailey's (1971) search for dialect boundaries would be less fruitful today, when complex interactions are manifested through complex linguistic processes such as those discussed thus far. The English of St Lucian children will always be coloured by the language with which it shares its environment – the ecosystem. Teachers must be cognizant of that and should teach children to be conscious of the sociolinguistic environment as well as to learn the conventions of both languages. It may be possible to define a St Lucian standard variety of English, but the consequent varieties of mixing of linguistic items from both codes present a new challenge for which boundary definitions are unpredictable and most likely improbable.

The Creole names of certain plants do not have known English equivalents. A student writing about a *latannyé* bush is using the linguistic competence available to him or her. This would be an instance of lexical borrowing. In order to increase students' options, an area of research in Creole worthy of consideration is the translation of certain cultural and social French Creole lexical items and expressions.

The production of dictionaries of French Creole (Mondesir 1992; Frank 2001) is a step in this direction, but just as the code-mixing referred to at the beginning of this chapter is an option available to, and used by, individuals, even with the presence of lexical translations, individuals may select code-mixing as an apt form of expression, a sort of *mot juste* depending on the audience or the realization of speaker intention.

WHAT'S IN A NAME?

In a search for cultural identity individuals often modify their linguistic behaviour. Labels are difficult and problematic in this area of dual and multiple codes. Code-mixing, code-switching and interference are terms which name that process – the creation of varieties to express identity or to index some social or cultural circumstance. As Le Page (1998) argues, the locus of language is the individual and it is at the level of the individual that issues of language choice and use must be addressed. The linguistic choices made by individuals in bilingual contexts may be referred to as code-mixing, code-switching or interference; whatever name is selected, these choices are rooted in cultural and social understandings and are pragmatic indicators of a discourse peculiar to that context.

The following are examples of code-mixing by a group of fourth form St Lucian students. They were asked to indicate their familiarity with the expressions *mwen box* and *asou down-there* and to indicate similar expressions which they used.

Although code-mixing is seen to result from the cultural and social expression of a bilingual territory, it is evident too that certain expressions are used where there is no access to syntactic or lexical components in either language. These self-reported examples can only be analysed at the level of what students claim to say. Some of these may be considered borrowing – the insertion of lexical items from English which are largely nominal in function. The larger question of the reasons for these insertions is not addressed and can only be surmised at this point. There are Creole words available for the majority of these nouns (Examples 1–14), while English lexical items in Examples 1–9 are commonly used in French Creole. Poplack (1998) notes that mixed expressions are used where there is no access to syntactic or lexical components in either language. Are these examples then the result of partial knowledge of the Creole? According to their teachers, these students are competent users of Creole in their casual interactions. These expressions are possibly simply a mode of discourse.

French Creole with English   **Gloss**

1. Koté *roll-on* mwen   Where is my *roll-on*? [deodorant]
2. Alé *brush* dan'ou   Go *brush* your teeth
3. Acheté an *brush* dan   Buy a *toothbrush*
4. Dan'ou ni *lipstick*   There is *lipstick* on your teeth
5. Ko *bag* mwen   Where is my *bag*?
6. Gadé *clock*-la   Look at the *clock*
7. Alé an *shop*-la   Go to the *shop*
8. Dubout *van*-la   Stop the *van*
9. Mi an *van*   Here is a *van*
10. Achté an *toy* ban mwen   Buy a *toy* for me
11. Mwen ka alé an *bank*-la   I am going to the *bank*
12. Pwan *macaroni* ban mwen   Take some *macaroni* for me
13. Koté *pony tail*-la   Where is the *pony-tail* holder
14. Ban mwen an pack *macaroni*   Give me a packet of *macaroni*
15. Sòti *there*   Move away from *there*
16. Koté *you come from*   Where have *you come from*
17. *The* gauché *girl*   The left-handed girl
18. Mwen *hungry*   I am *hungry*

The choices reflect the cultural and social expression of a bilingual territory, a way of speaking and sharing meaning accessible to those familiar with the community.

Use of Metaphor

19. Mwen té *nice*	I was *nice* (high/intoxicated)
20. Mwen *ceiling*	I am as "high" as the *ceiling* (high/intoxicated)
21. Mwen *brokes*	I am *broke* (I have no money)

The use of metaphor is interesting and adds to the social and cultural interpretation of meaning. Clearly, as seen in Examples 19, 20 and 21, a literal translation does not convey the intended meaning. The metaphorical expression noted here is distinct from metaphorical code-switching, which signals a change of topic (Gumperz 1972; Wardaugh 1992). Participants are often unaware of which code is being used; their main intent is the communicative effect of their code choices. In fact, they build on their own and their audience's sense of "script" and cooperative maxims are not violated. The lexical items "nice", "ceiling" and "brokes", in the examples above, do not convey literal meanings; rather they have connotative value which signals other kinds of experiences accessible to members of the local cultural context. They invite interlocutors to negotiate meaning in the context of use and generally accepted community norms.

English with French Creole	**Gloss**
22. The forest provided much needed fruits such as *bwa gwié*	Fruit (similar to a berry)
23. A piercing scream was coming from a *latannyé* bush	Plant used for making local brooms
24. My brother had told me all about *gengajé*	An evil spirit
25. Some got *jèp* bites	Wasp
26. I decided to make a *flambeau*	An open flame torch made from local materials

In Examples 22–26, the absence of a recognized translation for common French Creole lexicon may account for their occurrence. Current dictionaries (Frank 2001) provide some of these translations. The classroom use of these dictionaries would provide a significant option for students. However, as I have mentioned earlier, providing access to English translations of French Creole lexical items may not preclude the option of a mixed structure.

Thus, multiple linguistic input is an integral part of language use in St Lucia. At the lexical level, it may be the use of a lexical item for which there is no known English or French Creole equivalent, depending on the code primarily used. Here pedagogical assertions and boundary settings become important for mastery of the target. The assessment of that mastery is usually the terminal examination at each level of education. When two languages co-exist, the possibilities are infinite, and code-mixing, code-switching or interference phenomena will characterize language use in such a territory.

It is imperative, therefore, to know the cultural contexts of dual code patterns (Poplack 1998). That way the apparent conceptual simplicity of questioning the juxtaposition of lexical items can be supported with empirical adequacy in an ethnographic study (Hymes 1974). This chapter explores the phenomenon of code-mixing as a first stage in the process of finding empirical support.

CODE-MIXING AS A DISCOURSE MODE IN ST LUCIA

Code-mixing appears to be a mode of discourse in St Lucia. The mixing of codes as exemplified in phrases such as in *asou down-there* occurs in several contexts – in formal as well as in less formal discourse such as parliamentary debates, newspaper articles, political speeches and face-to-face interactions. As Gumperz (1982) asserts, there has to be some shared understanding of a term or a concept that makes the writer confident that the use of a lexical item from another code would be the most apt form of expression. That is what is best for the audience, without violation of cooperative principles since there is a sense of "script" which makes communicative intent unambiguous. The following are examples taken from St Lucian newspaper articles.

Examples	Explanatory Notes
27. Political pinez	The title of an article by columnist Jason Siflet. The Creole word *pinez* means "bedbug" and is used to describe persons

	who make, according to Siflet, "artistic and satirical commentary on the songs sung at the various calypso tents preceding the final calypso competition". The extension of this reference to the political arena is the text of this article (*Mirror*, 8 June 2001).
28. I hope that de green hope dat de alliance have is *espwa mal papay*.	The forlorn hope of the male pawpaw tree that will never be fertile and bear fruit ("Cocky & Stocky", *Crusader*, 9 June 2001). A satirical reference to a new government opposition party.
29. Government making *opiage* with people money. De bread sharing *vikivy* (*Queek Quack*, 9 June 2001).	*Opiage* – making games, treat money like it has no value, to squander it (informant explanation). *Vikivy* – anyhow/ad hoc.

In each example, the writer has depended on the shared cultural and social knowledge within the community. Shared presuppositions are established: individuals interacting in bilingual contexts do not ordinarily engage in code-switching before they know whether the listener or reader's background will render it feasible or acceptable. It was noted earlier that Kachru (1978, 31) proposed that individuals function in a disystem, and, as a consequence, develop another linguistic code comprising formal features of two or more codes. This is what I consider to be gradually taking place in St Lucia. I have already noted the empirical inadequacy of this position. However, I do not intend to provide empirical support at this point. I do intend to note the behaviours, to consider their implications and, consequently, to carry on further work to answer questions of attitude, motivation and intention – in fact, to examine the pragmatics of code-mixing in St Lucia.

Attitudes

An area of further investigation would be to examine the reasons for individual code-mixing or switching. Is it an attempt at employing the most apt word? Is it a mark of identity? Is it an obfuscation of meaning aimed at outsiders? Or is it simply an assumption that shared understandings and shared languages within the community make this a natural form of discourse. Raising these questions also raises a number of implications.

IMPLICATIONS

Pedagogical

Bailey (1971) asserts that the question of linguistic boundaries – in fact of what constitutes a variety – is important for those of us who teach. Against the contemporary backdrop of multiple codes, the conceptual and philosophical independence of the professional familiar with the sociolinguistic context must, necessarily, drive the pedagogy. Theoretical frameworks such as contact situations, the matrix language frame or the context model (proposed by Kachru) should inform pedagogical practices. The ethnography of communication proposed by Hymes allows exploration of the contexts of usage, alongside the norms of the community.

Language Policy

It is as important to establish language policies which address the developmental issues as well as status of respective languages.

Corpus-Building of Creole

Language planning philosophies are expressed in dichotomous terms, determining the status of the languages as well as developing the language to suit the tasks required of its status. Corpus-building (Wardaugh 1992) involves standardization as well as vocabulary expansion. Many French Creole terms do not have readily identified translations and may need to be accepted in English. There should exist a reference library of target language equivalents for the flora and fauna of the territory. For example, the dictionary meaning of *latannyé* bush is a description of its function. The biological name is provided, but no equivalent (Frank 2001). This French Creole term will simply be accepted into English usage.

Language mixing characterizes not only the speech and writing of young people, but also the work of established writers such as Derek Walcott and younger St Lucian poets such as Robert Lee and Kendal Hippolyte. Whether language mixing is called "interference phenomena", or "code-switching" or "mixing", it constitutes a natural linguistic process which provides an opportunity for continued linguistic research.

Conclusion

I have attempted to show that an utterance comprising a juxtaposition of aspects of different codes is both a medium and a message (Myers-Scotton 2000). The emergence of such a medium in the St Lucian context appears to be a new discourse strategy. However, empirical support would be required to explain the motivation for this strategy. This notion of a third variety is not new and has been discussed (Kachru 1978; Myers-Scotton 2000). It is worthy of consideration that this new variety may be part of a continuum of varieties within a post-Creole continuum (Robertson 1982), however this can be problematic, given the established contexts of post-Creole continua (De Camp 1971; Bickerton 1975).

The discussion here has considered the elusiveness of designations and the fact that they do not always capture the empirical realities of linguistic behaviour in bilingual contexts. Consequently, while designations provide a conceptual handle, they are not necessarily ironclad; therefore, designations and their description have to fit a specific set of realities.

There are pedagogical implications and language-planning imperatives in all of this. Code-mixing in St Lucia is a pragmatically determined medium of communication.

NOTES

1. The term "code" is used, according to Myers-Scotton, as a "cover term for linguistic systems at any level, from separate languages to dialects of a single language to styles or substyles within a single dialect" (1998, 3).
2. According to Myers-Scotton, a marked code is indexical of other than expected rights and obligations (2000, 138). The particular linguistic variety used in an exchange carries social meaning since linguistic codes index rights and obligations holding between participants in an exchange. In the St Lucian context, English is a less marked variety; as the official language it is the expected code of interaction.

REFERENCES

Bailey, B. 1971. "Jamaican Creole: Can Dialect Boundaries be Defined?" In *Pidginization and Creolization of Languages,* ed. D. Hymes, 341–48. Cambridge: Cambridge University Press.

Bickerton, Derek. 1975. *Dynamics of a Creole System.* Cambridge: Cambridge University Press.

Crystal, D. 1997. "Code-Switching as a Countenance of Interface". *Internet TESL Journal* 3, no. 10 (October).

De Camp, D. 1971. "Toward a Generative Analysis of a Post-Creole Continuum". In *Pidginization and Creolization of Languages,* ed. D. Hymes, 349–70. London: Cambridge University Press.

Devonish, H. 1986. *Language and Liberation: Creole Language Politics in the Caribbean.* London: Karia Press.

Firth, J.R. 1957. *Papers in Linguistics, 1934–1951.* London: Oxford University Press.

Frank, D. 2001, ed. *Kwéyòl Dictionary.* Castries, St Lucia: SIL International.

Gardner-Chloros, P. 1995. "Code-Switching in Community, Regional and National Repertoiores: The Myth of the Discreteness of Linguistic Systems". In *One Speaker, Two Languages: Cross-Disciplinary Perspectives on Code-Switching,* ed. L. Milroy and P. Muysken, 68–89. New York: Cambridge University Press.

Grice, H. 1975. "Logic and Conversation". In *Syntax and Semantics 3: Speech Acts,* ed. P. Cole and J. Morgan, 41–58. New York: Academic Press.

Gumperz, J. 1972. "Sociolinguistics and Communication in Small Groups". In *Sociolinguistics,* ed. J.B. Holmes and J. Holmes, 203–24. Harmondsworth: Penguin.

———. 1982. *Discourse Strategies.* New York: Cambridge University Press.

Hymes, D. 1972. "Models of the Interaction of Language and Social Life". In

Directions in Sociolinguistics: The Ethnography of Communication, ed. J. Gumperz and D. Hymes, 35–71. Oxford: Blackwell.

———. 1974. *Foundations of Sociolinguistics: An Ethnographic Approach*. Philadelphia: University of Pennsylvania Press.

Isaac, M. 1986. "French Creole Interference in the Written English of Fifth Form Secondary School Students in St Lucia". MPhil thesis. University of the West Indies.

Kachru, B. 1978. "Toward Structuring Code Mixing: An Indian Perspective". *International Journal of the Sociology of Language*, no. 27: 46.

Krashen, S. D. 1996. *Under Attack: The Case Against Bilingual Education*. Culver City, California: Language Education Associates.

Le Page, R. 1998. "You Can Never Tell Where a Word Comes From: Language Contact in a Diffuse Setting". In *The Sociolinguistic Reader*, vol. 1, ed. P. Trudgill and J. Cheshire, 85–88. London: Arnold.

Milroy, L., and P. Muysken, eds. 1995. *One Speaker, Two Languages: Cross Disciplinary Perspectives on Code-Switching*. New York: Cambridge University Press.

Mondesir, J. *Dictionary of St Lucian Creole*. Ed. L. Carrington. Berlin: Mouton de Gruyter.

Myers-Scotton, C. 1995. "A Lexically Based Model of Code-Switching". In *One Speaker, Two Languages: Cross-Disciplinary Perspectives on Code-Switching*, ed. L. Milroy and P. Muysken, 233–56. New York: Cambridge University Press.

———. 1998. Introduction. *Codes and Consequences: Choosing Linguistic Varieties*, ed. C. Myers-Scotton. Oxford: Oxford University Press.

———. 2000. "Code-Switching as Indexical of Social Negations". In *The Bilingualism Reader*, ed. L. Wei, 137–65. London: Routledge.

Pennycook, A. 1994. *The Cultural Politics of English as an International Language*. Harlow, Essex: Longman.

Poplack, S. 1998. "Contrasting Patterns of Code Switching in Two Communities". In *The Sociolinguistic Reader*, vol. 1, ed. P. Trudgill and J. Cheshire, 44–65. London: Arnold.

Robertson, I. 1982. "Re-Defining the Post-Creole Continuum: Evidence from Berbice Dutch". Occasional Paper No. 17. St Augustine, Trinidad: Society for Caribbean Linguistics.

Romaine, S. 1989. *Bilingualism*. Oxford: Blackwell.

Saville-Troike, M. 1989. *The Ethnography of Communication: An Introduction*. Cambridge, Mass.: Blackwell.

Skiba, R. 1997. "Code Switching as a Countenance of Language Interference". *Internet TESL Journal* 3, no. 10.

Tabouret-Keller, A. 1995. "Conclusion: Code-Switching Research as a Theoretical Challenge". In *One Speaker, Two Languages: Cross Disciplinary Perspectives on Code-Switching,* ed. L. Milroy and P. Muysken, 344–55. New York: Cambridge University Press.

Thomason, S., and T. Kaufman. 1988. *Language Contact, Creolization and Genetic Linguistics.* Berkeley: University of California Press.

Trudgill, P. 1998. "Language Contact and Inherent Variability: The Absence of Hypercorrection in East Anglian Present-Tense Verb Forms. In *The Sociolinguistic Reader,* vol. 1, ed. P. Trudgill and J. Cheshire, 103–12. London: Arnold.

Wardaugh, R. 1992. *An Introduction to Sociolinguistics.* Cambridge, Mass.: Blackwell.

Weinreich, U. 1953. *Languages in Contact.* New York: Linguistic Circle of New York.

Winch, C., and J. Gingell. 1992. "Dialect Interference and Difficulties with Writing: An Investigation in St Lucian Primary Schools. A Report to the St Lucian Ministry of Education". Nene College, Northampton, UK.

Winford, D. 2003. *An Introduction to Contact Linguistics.* Oxford: Blackwell.

Chapter 11

GLOBALIZATION AND THE LANGUAGE OF RASTAFARI
Velma Pollard

RASTAFARI, A NEW WORLD twentieth-century socio-religious movement, speaking at first to the Jamaican poor, has in seventy years or so spread not only to the rest of the Caribbean but to North and South America, Europe, Africa, Asia, and the Pacific. Frank Jan van Dijk's article "Chanting Down Babylon Outernational" (1998, 179) gives a comprehensive and enlightening review of Rastafari communities outside of Jamaica. van Dijk identifies migration and travel as one route by which the philosophy spread but also identifies radio and television as means by which "the message of Jah people, cached in the powerful rhymes and pulsating rhythms of reggae, travels almost without restriction and sweeps 'Rastology' into even the remotest corners of the earth". Pollard (1994, 48) comments on the relationship between the spread of the Rasta philosophy and language and the spread of Reggae music, particularly through the lyrics "on the tongues of its more charismatic proponents". Neil Savishinsky (1994, 259), commenting on the "processes relating to the diffusion and globalization of culture", points to the effect of "low cost/highly sophisticated technologies, widespread transnational corporate expansion, global mediaization" on the spread of the philosophy of the "Jamaican Rastafari Movement". Rastafari, with its call for equal rights and justice, has easily attracted oppressed people everywhere, but it is reggae music that has taken the message far beyond the destinations which would have been possible had the messenger been the traveller or the migrant only.[1]

By the time reggae reached the airwaves of the world, the language of Rastafari had become an integral part of the culture. A code had emerged, custom-made to suit the demands of the philosophy, expressing, *inter alia*, the relationship between the oppressed and the oppressor, brethren and Babylon. Simpson, one of the earliest researchers into Jamaican religion and indeed into Rastafari, comments (1998, 219) that he did not, in the 1950s when he was researching, "encounter the distinctive form of 'Rasta Talk' based on the use of the self-reflective 'I' or 'I-an-I' that is now a widely noted aspect of Rasta culture". He mentions, however, the existence of the term "Babylon", which "was used to refer to the colonial structure". Simpson's comment supports the notion that Dread Talk, a language which evolved in a self-conscious way for a specific purpose, was not born at the same time as the philosophy and way of life that came to be known as Rastafari. Brother W (Pollard 1994, 3) says the code started with the desire of the Brethren to "step-up" with the language and to speak in a way that would not be easily decoded by Babylon. The latter objective got lost or was overtaken as the language became interesting to people outside of Rastafari. Certain processes, however, had been established and the code developed and expanded with the movement. The code has spread with Rastafari to places where neither English nor the English-related (Jamaican) Creole (JC) which spawned Dread Talk is spoken.

Language contact and its effects on the languages involved is an interesting and well-researched aspect of linguistics. The research focuses on how languages are altered in the interactive situation in different societies, noting for example which categories of word succumb most easily to change. In "Rastafarian Language in St Lucia and Barbados", Pollard (1994, 45–57) describes the talk of Rastafari adherents in Barbados, where English as well as a version of anglophone Creole are the languages of the society, and in St Lucia, where English shares the linguistic space with both francophone and anglophone Creoles. The essay tries to answer the question of how the language of Rastafari is transformed as it interfaces with languages outside of Jamaica.

This chapter looks at the language of Rastafari as it serves the needs of populations with different linguistic heritages. It does not comment on how the language is used in the interface between itself and languages not necessarily related to English. It examines the body of words available to speakers of such languages who wish to understand, perhaps eventually to use, the words Rastafarians use. To this end, it comments on two dictionaries offered to the global village through the Internet, using the categories established earlier to comment on previous lists. One may regard the dictionaries as consisting of words the Web page creators see as the minimum necessary for an interested reader to have access to lyrics of songs and other pronouncements from within the Rasta community. Far more comprehensive than either of these lists is *Rastafari and Reggae: A Dictionary and Sourcebook* by Rebekah Mulvaney. Included in this book is a ninety-five-page dictionary of words "selected for their direct relationship to Rastafari and reggae and/or for their historical value in offering a broader context from which to better understand these related subject matters" (1990, x). This dictionary includes, *inter alia*, the names of people associated with reggae music. The Web page is preferred for consideration here because it more truly represents the global village: it is immediately accessible all over the world in a way books cannot be. The term these online dictionaries use for Dread Talk is "Rasta Patois".

Rasta Patois Dictionary?

Dread Talk is an adjustment of the lexicon and, to a lesser extent, to the grammar of Patwa (Patois/Jamaican Creole), reflecting the philosophical and religious stance of the Rastafari community, whose members see themselves as oppressed by society (Babylon, the system/shistim). So indeed this version of Jamaican Creole (JC) might justifiably be labelled Rasta Patois. A dictionary of this language might be expected to have words used by the population that speaks Patois as Rastas speak it. The two dictionaries discussed in this chapter are the *Rasta Patois Dictionary*, referred to as D1, and the *Rasta Patois-Russian Dictionary*, referred to as D2. The compilers have used the same thirteen sources, consisting of books, handouts, notes from records and personal information. D2 has an additional three sources. That the sources are numbered identically, with D2 adding another three, suggests that D2 is largely derived from D1.

The dictionaries under discussion both go beyond the expected dictionary function by providing detail on the grammatical functions of some forms. So, for example, there is an entry "a go" in both, described in D1 (p. 2) as "aux w/v 'going to do' as in 'me a go tell him'" and in D2 (p. 1) as "going to do", with the same exemplifying sentence. Both regard the construction as indicating future action. Neither mentions the fact that "a+verb" expresses the continuous aspect in JC so that "me a go home" translates to English "I am/was going home".

The dictionaries include idiomatic utterances with glosses,[2] as in "coo pan, look upon" (D1, 6; D2, 3), "everything cook and curry" (D1, 10; D2, 5), glossed in the former as "all is well taken care of", and "mash it up" (D1, 16, D2, 10), glossed in D1 as "a huge success". The last example illustrates a slight inaccuracy. An imperative sentence is represented, in translation, by a noun phrase. A more accurate translation would be "Do very well!" "We mash it up" would translate "Our act was a huge success".

The vocabulary lists offered in the dictionaries include words which were part of JC long before Rastafari emerged in the 1930s. Some of these words came into the language unchanged from African parent languages. "Bafan", for example, is a form with both adjectival and nominal functions and comes hardly altered from Twi, one of the languages of Ghana. In both lists it is erroneously presented as two words, "bafan" and "bafang", the one identified as noun, the other adjective.

The meanings, however, are accurate. "Bafan", listed as a noun (D1, 3), is the same as in the *Dictionary of Jamaican English* (DJE): "a child who did not learn to walk the first 2–7 years". "Bafang", listed as an adjective meaning "clumsy, awkward", is similar to the DJE's additional meaning: "A useless, clumsy person"(1980, 20). This chapter is concerned less with such words than with those which are identifiably part of the lexicon of Rastafari, those which have been adjusted in one way or other to signal the Rasta point of view or have been created where this has been considered necessary.

van Dijk (1998, 194) observes that "the dissemination of rastafarian ideas and belief to Europe, the Caribbean and the Pacific gave rise to an extremely heterogeneous counterculture". What he sees as constant, however, are the "social, political and cultural ideas associated with the movement". Hepner (1998, 210), also commenting on heterogeneity within a more limited geographical area, notes that the one theme that remains unchanged whether the brethren speak in Jamaica or North America is the "militant rejection of Babylon". The language of Rasta–Dread Talk is used to articulate common sentiments. Hutton and Murrell (1998, 50), restating a point made by Nettleford three decades earlier, comment that the Rastas "In their self-affirmation . . . have gone beyond the use of African names and linguistic adaptation to actual language creation. That is, they have created a language with its own vocabulary, much of which was never encountered before in Jamaica."

WORD-MAKING

All living languages are dynamic. Accordingly, the language used by Rastafari is constantly evolving within identifiable categories. There are four categories resulting from four processes of word formation. A theory informs each process. The process itself, however, once understood, can be applied without a knowledge of the theory. Let us examine first the process generating the I-words (Category III); this is the category most commonly recognized as Rasta words. Behind the strength and importance of these words is the power of the sound /ai/ "I". This is the same sound heard in /aiman/ "I-man", /aianai/ "I-an-I", /diai/ the-"I, all of which represent first and second person pronouns, both singular and plural, and in /ai/"eye", the organ of sight. A pun on "eye" recognizes "fari" (far-eye) in the third and fourth syllables of Rastafari as the "far-seeing eye" so important in Rasta philosophy. Words receive a certain elevation by being brought into this category which has proved easy to manipulate. Schoolboys in the 1970s, for example, anxious to identify with Rasta before they could understand the philosophy, could manipulate this category the way their grandparents manipulated "Pig-Latin/Gypsy" in elementary schools of yesteryear.[3] This ease of manipulation perhaps accounts for the fact that the lists include a relatively small number of these words. Any such list can be extended by simply replacing the initial syllable of a given noun with "I" (so for example "apple" would become "I-ple"). There are some words that begin with the sound associated with the letter "y" rather than "I", such as "yude/food" (Pollard 1994, 37). D2 (p. 16) would include "yod/trod" "yound/sound" and "yunder/thunder" in such a list.[4]

Sound is paramount in Dread Talk. "Wordsound" is a seminal concept.

Consistency is also highly valued. Category II consists of English words adjusted to relate sound to meaning. The direction "up", which is usually positive, is required to be consistent in indicating a positive direction. The word "oppress" cannot be allowed its English meaning: the pronunciation of the first syllable indicates upward movement, contradicting the downward movement of the second syllable. So the often-quoted "DOWNpress" replaces OPpress(UPress). Similarly OVERstand replaces UNDERstand.

Certain English words are considered negative by Rastas. Wherever they occur the meaning is negative. "Blind" is one such word. It is in opposition to "see", which is particularly positive because of its relationship to the organ of sight. So "cigarette", which is a negative item, becomes "blindjarete" (Pollard 1994, 6) Equally negative words are "hate" and "dead". These have to be replaced with positive words. So DEADline becomes LIFEline and DEADicate (dedicate) becomes LIVIcate. In order to manipulate this process adequately, however, the speaker needs to be aware of certain pronunciations common in Jamaica, particularly the addition of the "H" before vowels in a random list of words or syllables and its omission in an equally random list. Barbadian Rastas, hearing Jamaicans pronounce "Ital" with an initial "H" – "hightal" – to describe clean, Rasta-approved food, invented the opposite "lotal" to describe unclean food (Pollard 1994, 50), thus introducing a Barbadian Rasta item which would not be generated in Jamaica, where people who say "hightal" automatically write "ital". D1 and D2 both include "Apprecilove" which is what "appreciate" becomes when the negative "hate" in "apreciHATE" is replaced with the positive "love". D2 includes "arguMANT" which replaces "argument" since the form "men", meaning "homosexual" in Dread Talk, must always be avoided in a movement that views homosexuality negatively within a Jamaica that is distinctly homophobic. The avoidance of the term "men" does not become problematic since the Creole plural *man+dem* is an available substitute.

Another category of word represented in the lists is Category I, where known English items are given new meanings. Some of the most important words in the Dread Talk vocabulary fall within this category. "Babylon" has already been mentioned as the term for the establishment and is a term recognized by Simpson as having existed from the earliest days of the movement. "Dread" soon came to mean a person with (dread) locks, a Rasta man, as opposed to "baaled/bald-headed" – a clean-shaven and therefore non-Rasta man. Additional meanings have come to include possible meanings of the word in English. The following are offered in D1 (p. 9), where the word is given as both noun and adjective:

1. a person with dreadlocks
2. a serious idea or thing
3. dangerous situation or person
4. the "dreadful power of the holy"
5. experientially "awesome, fearful confrontation of a people with a primordial but historically denied racial selfhood"

Another word in that category is "red", which is not only a colour but a modifier meaning "very high on herb" (D1, 20). "Herb" is marijuana, sacred to the Rastas as the herb of the sacrament. This plant itself is referred to by a multiplicity of names, one of the more popular being "Collie weed". This term is rendered "Kali/Cooly" in D2 (p. 9). The second spelling here should be avoided since it might lead to the unlikely pronunciation "coolie", which, in Jamaica, is a derogatory label for a person of East Indian ancestry. There is also "Lambsbread" (D1, 16), which refers to a particularly high quality of marijuana ("Lamb's Bread" in D2, 10), "Sinsemilla; sensie", glossed (D1, 22) as "popular, potent, seedless, unpollinated, female strain of marijuana" (see also D2, 14). Another Category I word is "Chalice", the pipe for smoking marijuana. This might be considered a natural transfer from the Chalice, the cup of the Eucharist in the Christian church. Other names for it – "cutchie (D1, 8; D2, 4) chillum, chalewa" (D2, 3; D1, 5) – all fall within Category IV: "New Items".

The category "New Items" refers to words created by Rasta. "Spliff", the term used for the herb when it is rolled (prepared like a cigarette), falls within this category. (D2, 15; D1, 23) Some others are "Deaders", for meat and its by-products (D1, 8; D2, 4); and "Elizabitch" (D2, 5), which expresses a particular attitude to Queen Elizabeth, the reigning monarch of Great Britain (a person much hated by Jamaican Rastas, second only to the Pope of Rome). "Livity" and "upful" are treated as synonyms in D2, though the former is a noun and the latter an adjective glossed as "positive; encouraging" in D1 (p. 25) and "Niaman: Rasta man" (D1, 17).

PROCESS AND THEORY

I mentioned earlier the existence of a theory or rationale behind word-making. An example of what happens when the process is used without an understanding of the rationale is the unlikely entry "Niamen" in D2 (p. 11). For reasons explained above, the term "men" is stigmatized. It would be sacrilege to attach it to a word which is an alternative for Rasta man. An American pronunciation of the word "niaman" might have caused the confusion here. Another unlikely creation is "Lovepreciate", which appears in D2, p. 10. Perhaps a "new Rasta" tried to make a word without an understanding of the rationale – eliminating negative sounds. "Aprecilove" is legitimate, "Lovepreciate" is not. This is easily tested by pronouncing it LOVEpreciHATE and noting the inherent contradiction.

WORD-MAKING REVISITED OR DISCOURSE ON ORIGINS

With the spread of reggae lyrics and therefore the language of Rastafari, interest in the theories behind the formation of words has grown and thinkers both inside and outside the movement have applied various levels of logic to the emergence of the different categories of word. Predictably, Category III, the "I-words" – the most distinctive feature of the code – has received the most attention. Here are some recent comments on that feature.

Hepner (1998, 211) quotes Brother Judah, a New York Rasta man and member of the Twelve Tribes of Israel, a "house" (denomination) within the Rastafarian movement, who explains the use of the pronominal "I-an-I" in this way: "we refer to one another [other Rastas] as 'I-an-I' – we don't make no one a second person. We don't say 'I and him' or 'us'. We just say 'I-an-I' because every person is a first person."

Edmonds (1998, 33) reasons as follows: "Since 'I' in Rastafarian thought signifies the divine principle that is in all humanity, 'I-an-I' is an expression of the oneness between two (or more) persons and between the speaker and God (whether Selassie or the god principle that rules in all creation)."

On the preference of the subject pronoun "I" in both subject and object positions where JC uses "me", Edmonds says: "Rastas use 'I-an-I' (as subject even when the sentence calls for an object) to indicate that all people are active, creative agents and not passive objects."

Mulvaney (1990, 39) gives a slightly different explanation for the same phenomenon: "Rastas believe 'me' connotes subservience or objectification of the human individual whereas 'I' is thought to emphasize the subjective and individual character of a person."

Defining "I and I" Mulvaney writes: "Both singular and plural pronoun in Rasta language. As singular, the speaker chooses I and I to signify the ever presence of Jah. As plural, the choice of I an I signifies the existence of a spirituality and metaphysically intimate relationship among the speaker, other individuals present or spoken of, and Jah."

McFarlane's discourse (1998, 107) on the "Epistemological Significance of 'I-an-I'" describes the form as the "self-reflexive use of the subject pronoun" and sees the "I" words as "the means by which Rastas make all informed utterances related to their principles, cultic practices, and self affirmation". He reaffirms the link identified by earlier researchers, including Yawney, for example (Pollard 1994, 21), between the "I" words and the "I" in "Jah Selassie I, previously known as Ras Tafari" and both to 'the word made flesh' of early Christian theology" and to the early Rastas (punning) reconfiguration of the title as Rasta-for-I. In McFarlane's discourse the "I" that ends Rastafari is the first principle of Rasta life "which reverses the order of things to make the last first and the first last" (1998, 108).

Notably absent from any of these descriptions is the connection between the eye, the organ of sight, and the first person pronoun as well as the effect of that convergence of sound on the power behind the "I" words. This was a point emphasized in the earlier research. Perhaps this omission is a warning that something is changing. What is added to the discourse and what gets lost is unpredictable. It could be that as the research moves further and further away from Jamaica, the locale of the beginnings of the movement and the home of some of the oldest interviewees, emphases change. What is clear is that interest in the culture and so in the language of a movement which speaks to oppressed black people and eventually to the oppressed of all races, is not waning. And perhaps the language has the greatest likelihood of becoming entrenched in new communities, since language is one outlet for defiance which the oppressor is unlikely to succeed in frustrating.

This chapter has commented on word lists offered by the global media as

Rasta Patois dictionaries. It does not say anything about the code in its interaction with the languages with which it comes in contact. It would be interesting to note, for example, which words are accepted unchanged into these languages and which are translated. Questions like the acceptance/rejection of the power of word-sound need to be examined in conjunction with the question of the heterogeneity of the culture outside of Jamaica. Dread Talk in the French and Spanish Caribbean and in Latin America immediately offers itself for prospective study. In the 1970s the Rastafari culture spread to Cuba, Jamaica's nearest neighbour, taken there both by travellers and by reggae music. Furé Davis (1999) spoke about Cuban youth and the influence of reggae, hip-hop and other imported lifestyles which, he says, are quickly adapted to the new context. With regard to expression among the youth, he indicated that certain adjustments have had to be made in a situation where, for example, Rastas are using Spanish to discuss an imported topic with a foreign vocabulary. He commented that the process was yielding "something new and different" and used the term *transculturación*.

Indeed *transculturación* is an excellent term to describe the feature to which this chapter drew attention at the beginning – the spread of the culture of Rastafari to all continents and its influence in the new lands. The variation inherent in such a spread (the heterogeneity of which van Dijk and Hepner write) are part of what Furé Davis describes as "something new and different". This is a phrase reminiscent of "something torn and new", which Edward Brathwaite, writing three decades earlier (1969, 113), used to describe the rhythms of the steel pan, a metaphor for the new Caribbean man:

now waking
. . . making
with their
rhythms some-
thing torn
and new

Perhaps a new Rasta man or several versions of such a man is emerging.[5] Perhaps several versions of the code will emerge to express the new realities.

Acknowledgements

A version of this chapter appears as chapter 6 in the revised edition of *Dread Talk*, published jointly by Canoe Press and McGill–Queen's University Press 2000.

Notes

1. See also Chevannes (1995, 269), where reference is made to Peter Lee's 1991 tribute to Bob Marley in which the love for Marley's music is seen as "the common bond linking a blues guitarist in Mississippi, a black South African soldier serving in Namibia, a young accordion player in a South African township, and a group of Australians, New Zealanders, and Scotsmen in London."
2. Glosses in D2 are mostly in Russian. Comments here are restricted to those which are also given in English.
3. For a discussion on Gypsy, see Aceto 1995.
4. I have some difficulty recognizing these, especially "yod", since "trod" is a particularly well used item in the Rasta vocabulary.
5. Jan de Cosmo, in a recent presentation, described the Rastafarian community in Bahia, Brazil, and pointed to variations on the Rastafari theology as it interacts with fundamentalist Christian beliefs. See also Neil Savishinsky on Rastafari in the Pacific and South Africa.

References

Aceto, M. 1995. "Variation in a Secret Creole Language of Panama". *Language in Society* 24: 537–60.

Brathwaite, E. 1969. *Islands*. London: Oxford University Press.

Chevannes, B. 1995. *Rastafari: Roots and Ideology*. Kinston, Jamaica: The Press, University of the West Indies.

Cassidy, F., and R. Le Page. 1980. *Dictionary of Jamaican English*, Cambridge: Cambridge University Press.

De Cosmo, J. 1999. "A New Christianity for the Modern World: Rastafari Fundamentalism in Salvador, Bahia, Brazil". Paper presented at the twenty-fourth Annual Conference of the Caribbean Studies Association, Panama City.

Edmonds, E. 1998. "Dread 'I' In-a-Babylon: Ideological Resistance and Cultural Revitalization" In *Chanting Down Babylon,* ed. N. Murrell and A. McFarlane, 23–35. Philadelphia: Temple University Press.

Furé Davis, S. 1999. Paper presented at the Twenty-Fourth Annual Conference of the Caribbean Studies Association, Panama City.

Hepner, R. 1998. "Chanting Down Babylon in the Belly of the Beast: The Rastafarian Movement in the Metropolitan United States". In *Chanting Down Babylon,* ed. N. Murrell and A. McFarlane, 199–216. Philadelphia: Temple University Press.

Hutton, C., and N. Murrell. 1998. "Rastas' Psychology of Blackness". In *Chanting Down Babylon,* ed. N. Murrell and A. McFarlane. Philadelphia: Temple University Press.

McFarlane, A. 1998. "The Epistemological Significance of 'I-an-I' as a Response to Quashie and Anancyism in Jamaican Culture". In *Chanting Down Babylon,* ed. N. Murrell and A. McFarlane. Philadelphia: Temple University Press.

Mulvaney, R. 1990. *Rastafari and Reggae: A Dictionary and Sourcebook.* New York: Greenwood Press.

Pollard, V. 1994. *Dread Talk: The Language of Rastafari.* Kingston: Canoe Press.

Rasta Patois-Russian Dictionary. http://niceup.com/patois.txt

Rasta Patois-Russian Dictionary. http://www.zhurnal.ru/music/rasta/patois.html.

Savishinsky, N. 1994. "Traditional Popular Culture and the Global Spread of the Jamaican Rastafari Movement". *New West Indian Guide* 68, nos. 3 and 4.

———. 1998. *"African Dimensions of the Jamaican Rastafari Movement".* In *Chanting Down Babylon,* ed. N. Murrell and A. McFarlane. Philadelphia: Temple University Press.

Simpson, G.E. 1998. "Personal Reflections on Rastafari in West Kingston in the Early 1950s". In *Chanting Down Babylon,* ed. N. Murrell and A. McFarlane. Philadelphia: Temple University Press.

van Dijk, F. 1998. "Chanting Down Babylon Outernational: The Rise of Rastafari in Europe, the Caribbean, and the Pacific". In *Chanting Down Babylon,* ed. N. Murrell and A. McFarlane. Philadelphia: Temple University Press.

CONTRIBUTORS

Hazel Simmons-McDonald is Professor of Applied Linguistics and Dean of the Faculty of Humanities and Education, University of the West Indies, Cave Hill, Barbados. She served as head of the Department of Linguistics from 1995–1996 and as head of the amalgamated Department of Language, Linguistics and Literature from 1996 to 1999. She is co-chair of the university's Cultural Studies Initative, with responsibility for the Cave Hill campus. Her research focuses on language acquisition, literacy, bilingualism and the use of vernacular in education in Creole contexts. She has published several papers on a range of topics in these areas.

Ian Robertson is Senior Lecturer in Linguistics and Education and Dean of the Faculty of Humanities and Education, University of the West Indies, St Augustine, Trinidad and Tobago. He specializes in Berbice Dutch but is also interested in Creole linguistics, language education and sociolinguistics. He has published widely in these areas.

Dennis Craig was a highly qualified applied linguist who conducted research and published extensively on education and Creole linguistics. He taught at the University of the West Indies, Mona, Jamaica, from 1964 to 1988, and from there he went back to Guyana, his native land, where he served as vice chancellor of the University of Guyana from 1991 to 1995. He published his last and very successful book on the teaching of English to Creole-influenced vernacular speakers in 1999. Dennis submitted his chapter to this volume just a few months before his death.

Hubert Devonish is Professor of Linguistics, University of the West Indies, Mona, Jamaica. He served as head of the department from 1987 to 1992 and 1996 to 2002. Among his publications are *Language and Liberation* (1986), *Talking in Tones* (1989), *Talking Rhythm, Stressing Tone* (2002) and numerous articles in scholarly journals and in collected works. His areas of special interest and research include sociolinguistics, language policy, phonology and the history of Caribbean Creole languages. He is the coordinator of the Jamaican Language Unit, a unit set up to carry out research and public education on the issue of language rights for speakers of the Jamaican language.

Martha Isaac is Lecturer in Sociolinguistics, University of the West Indies, Cave Hill, Barbados. Her research interests are language, literacy and education in bilingual contexts, especially the Caribbean. She has a special interest in curriculum issues, Creole linguistics, narrative inquiry and other ethnographic methods of research.

Winford James holds the PhD in Linguistics from the University of the West Indies, St Augustine, Trinidad and Tobago. He lectures in the teaching of English and associated courses in the Faculty of Humanities and Education. One of his chief research interests is the scientific description of Creole speech, especially the Creole speech of his native Tobago. He is co-author (with Valerie Youssef) of *The Languages of Tobago: Genesis, Structure, and Perspectives* (2002).

Barbara Lalla is Professor of Language and Literature, Department of Liberal Arts, University of the West Indies, St Augustine, Trinidad and Tobago, and co-chair of the university's Cultural Studies Initiative, with responsibility for the St Augustine campus. Her publications include *Language in Exile: Three Hundred Years of Jamaican Creole* (1990) and *Voices in Exile: Jamaican Texts of the Eighteenth and Nineteenth Centuries* (1989), co-authored/co-edited with Jean D'Costa; *Defining Jamaican Fiction: Marronage and the Discourse of Survival* (1996); *English for Academic Purposes* (1997); numerous articles on language history and literary discourse in the postcolonial Caribbean; and a historical novel, *Arch of Fire* (1998).

Velma Pollard is retired Senior Lecturer in Language Education, Department of Educational Studies, Faculty of Arts and Education, University of the West Indies, Mona, Jamaica. Her major research intersts have been Creole languages of the anglophone Caribbean, the language of Caribbean literature and Caribbean women's writing. Articles in these areas appear in local and international journals. She is the author of *From Jamaican Creole to Standard English: A Handbook for Teachers* (1994) and *Dread Talk: The Language of Rastafari* (1994, 2000).

Kathryn Shields-Brodber is Senior Lecturer and Head of the Department of Language, Linguistics and Philosophy, University of the West Indies, Mona, Jamaica. Her published papers focus on discourse in Jamaica, especially in the mass media, and include the analysis of turn-taking, variation in English, code-switching and -mixing, the language-gender interface, and the politeness phenomena. She is currently researching verbal interaction in the Caribbean mass media and in Jamaican law courts.

Donald Winford is Professor of Linguistics at Ohio State University, where he has been teaching since 1988. His areas of specialization include Creole linguistics, sociolinguistic theory and methodology, variation theory, contact linguistics, and applied linguistics, particularly the educational applications of sociolinguistic research in Creole communities and the teaching of English as a second or foreign language. He is the author of *Predication in Caribbean English Creoles* (1993) and *An Introduction to Contact Linguistics* (2003). He has published widely in journals and anthologies and has edited or co-edited several volumes.

Valerie Youssef is Senior Lecturer in Linguistics, University of the West Indies, St Augustine, Trinidad and Tobago. She teaches and researches language acquisition, sociolinguistics and descriptive linguistics. She is co-author (with Winford James) of *The Languages of Tobago: Genesis, Structure, and Perspectives* (2002) and (with Paula Morgan) of *Writing Rage: Unmasking Violence through Caribbean Discourse* (2006). She is particularly interested in all aspects of socially relevant linguistics, seeking through her research to throw light on social discourse practices which disempower groups and individuals, and to use the work to support egalitarian development in a range of areas.

www.ingramcontent.com/pod-product-compliance
Lightning Source LLC
Chambersburg PA
CBHW021823300426
44114CB00009BA/294